PROPERTY OF
BEEBE LIBRARY
345 MAIN STREET
WAKEFIELD, MA

X-MEN BY JONATHAN HICKMAN VOL. 2. Contains material originally published in magazine form as X-MEN (2019) #7-11. Second printing 2021. ISBN 978-1-302-91982-5. Published by MARVEL WORLDWIDE, INC., a subsidiary of MARVEL ENTERTAINMENT, LLC. OFFICE OF PUBLICATION: 1290 Avenue of the Americas, New York, NY 10104. © 2020 MARVEL No similarity between any of the names, characters, persons, and/or institutions in this magazine with those of any living or dead person or institution is intended, and any such similarity which may exist is purely coincidental. **Printed in Canada.** KEVIN FEIGE, Chief Creative Officer; DAN BUCKLEY, President, Marvel Entertainment; JOE QUESADA, EVP & Creative Director; DAVID BOGART, Associate Publisher & SVP of Talent Affairs; TOM BREVOORT, VP, Executive Editor; NICK LOWE, Executive Editor, VP of Content, Digital Publishing; DAVID GABRIEL, VP of Print & Digital Publishing; JEFF YOUNGQUIST, VP of Production & Special Projects; ALEX MORALES, Director of Publishing Operations; DAN EDINGTON, Managing Editor; RICKEY PURDIN, Director of Talent Relations; JENNIFER GRÜNWALD, Senior Editor, Special Projects; SUSAN CRESPI, Production Manager; STAN LEE, Chairman Emeritus. For information regarding advertising in Marvel Comics or on Marvel.com, please contact Vit DeBellis, Custom Solutions & Integrated Advertising Manager, at vdebellis@marvel.com. For Marvel subscription inquiries, please call 888-511-5480. **Manufactured between 7/23/2021 and 8/24/2021 by SOLISCO PRINTERS, SCOTT, QC, CANADA.**

10 9 8 7 6 5 4 3 2

Vol. 2

Writer: Jonathan Hickman
Artists: Leinil Francis Yu (#7, #9-12)
                                           & Mahmud Asrar (#8)
Color Artist: Sunny Gho
Letterer: VC's Clayton Cowles

Cover Art: Leinil Francis Yu &
                                           Sunny Gho

Head of X: Jonathan Hickman
Design: Tom Muller
Assistant Editor: Annalise Bissa
Editor: Jordan D. White

X-Men created by   Stan Lee
                                           & Jack Kirby

Collection Editor: Jennifer Grünwald
Assistant Editor: Daniel Kirchhoffer
Assistant Managing Editor: Maia Loy
Assistant Managing Editor: Lisa Montalbano
VP Production & Special Projects: Jeff Youngquist
SVP Print, Sales & Marketing: David Gabriel
Editor in Chief: C.B. Cebulski

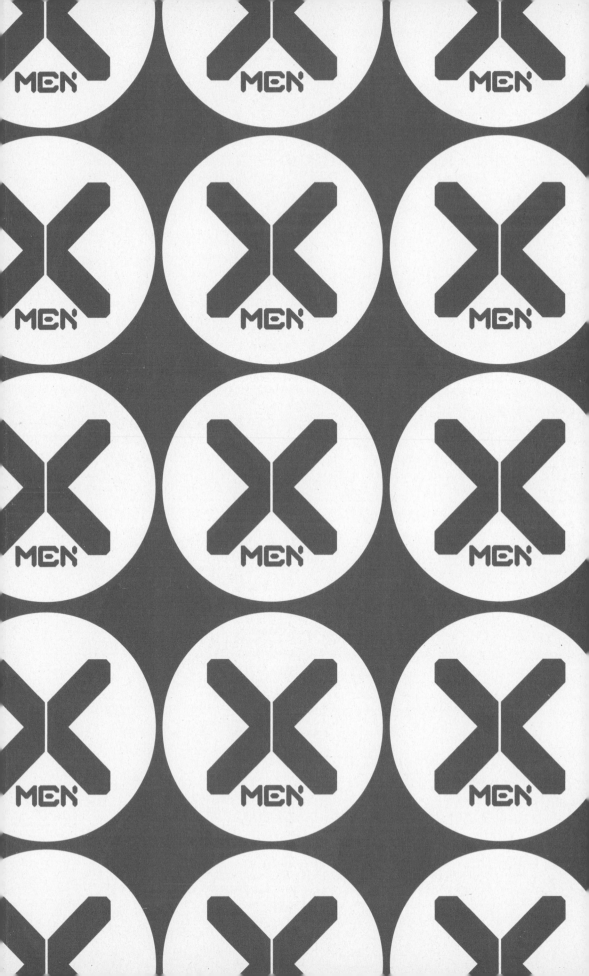

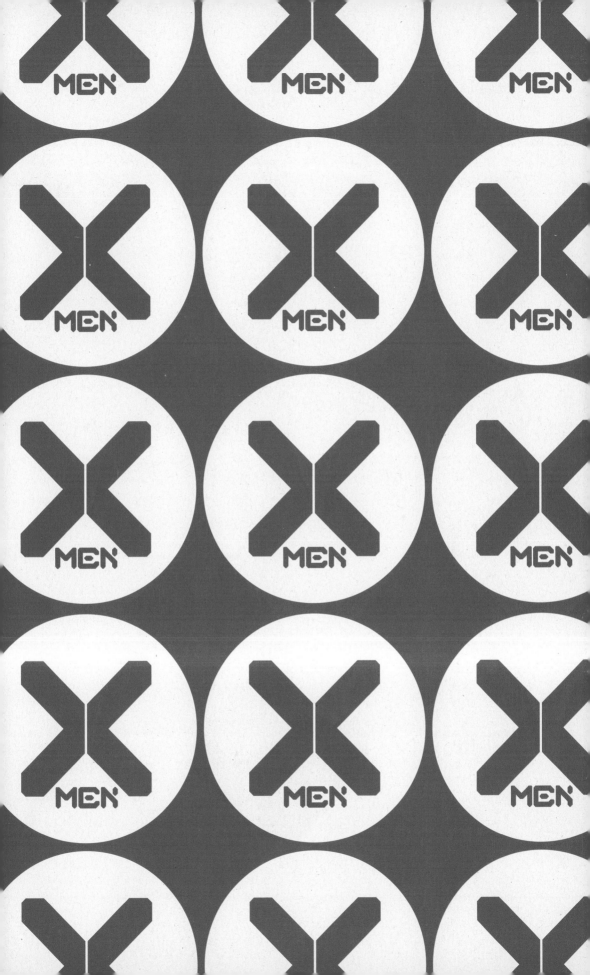

[dawn_of_x]

[kra_]
[koa_]

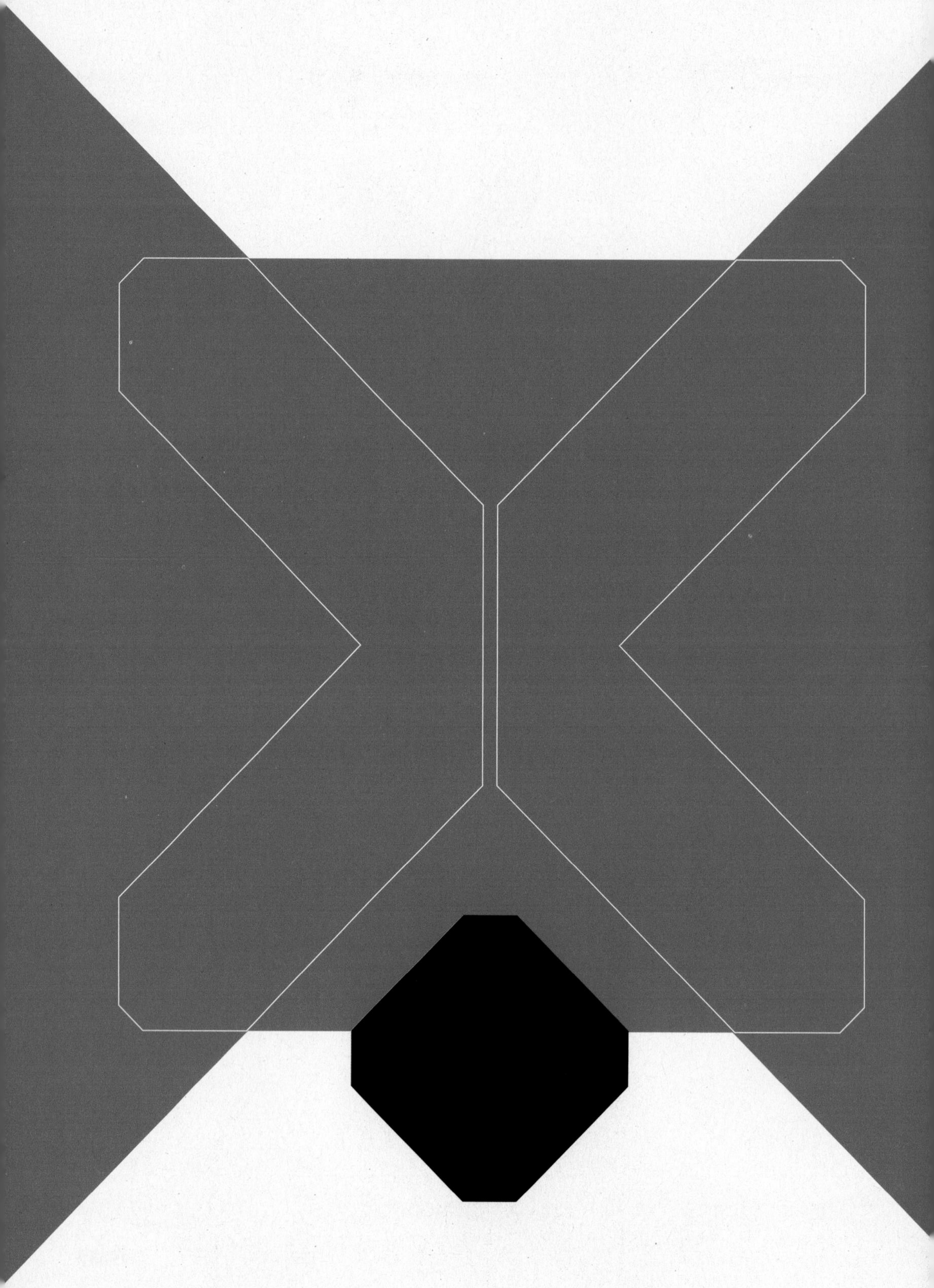

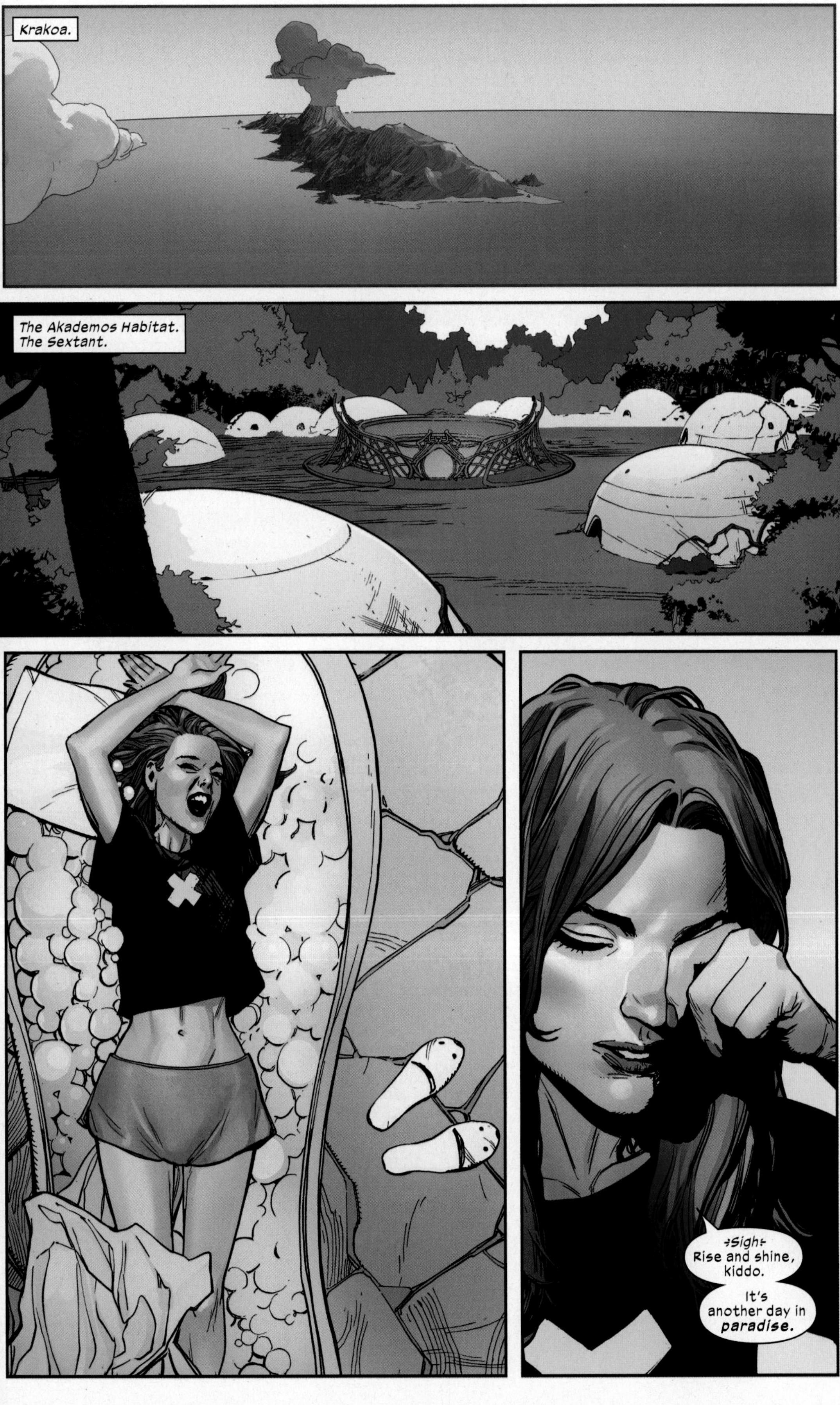
Krakoa.
The Akademos Habitat.
The Sextant.
⁓Sigh⁓
Rise and shine, kiddo.
It's another day in paradise.

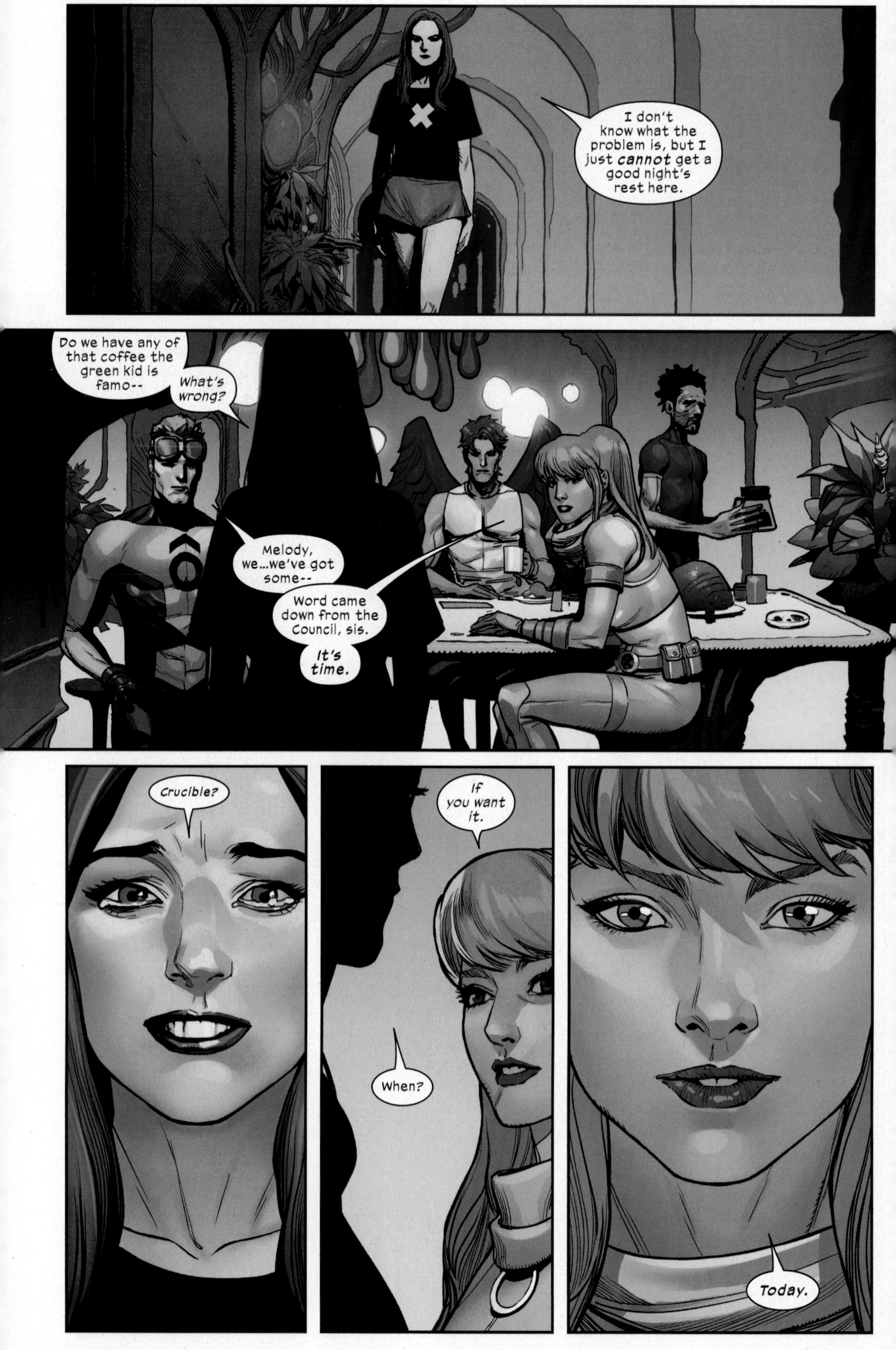
I don't know what the problem is, but I just *cannot* get a good night's rest here.
Do we have any of that coffee the green kid is famo--
What's wrong?
Melody, we...we've got some--
Word came down from the Council, sis.
It's time.
Crucible?
If you want it.
When?
Today.

[kra_[0.7]
[koa_[0.7]

[kra_[0.X]
[koa_[0.X]

FAITH

By combining their mutant powers, the Five have given the X-MEN -- and the Krakoan people -- the miraculous opportunity to be reborn after death. But nothing so incredible comes without a cost...

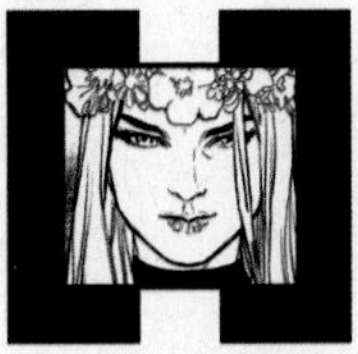
Melody Guthrie

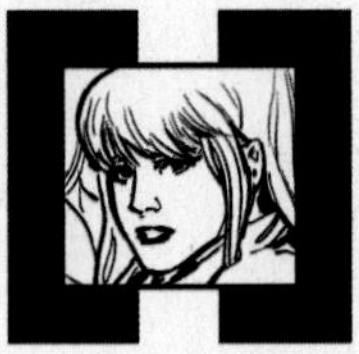
Paige Guthrie

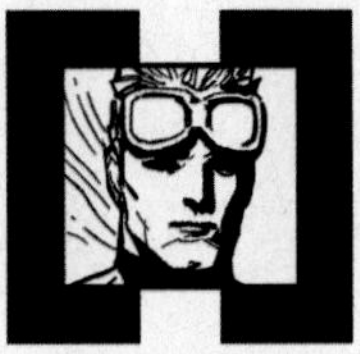
Sam Guthrie

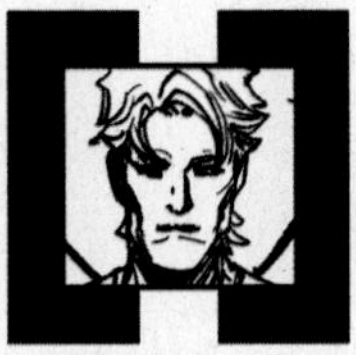
Joshua Guthrie

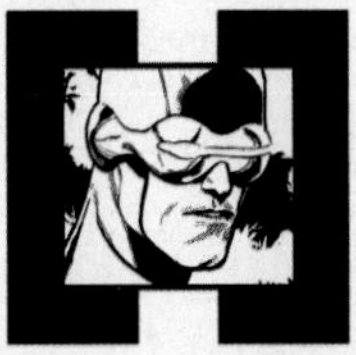
Cyclops

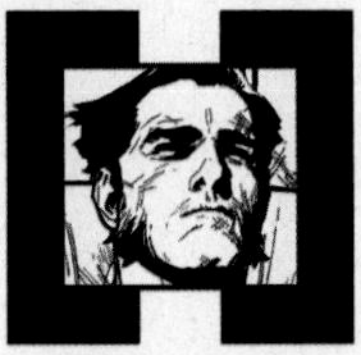
Wolverine

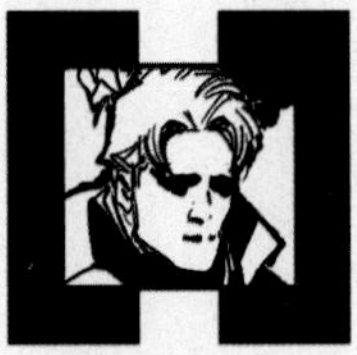
Cypher

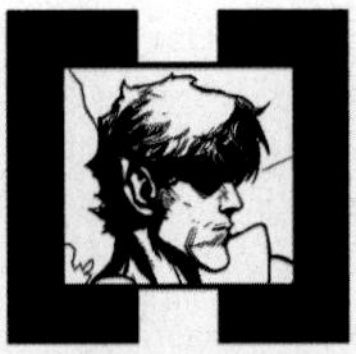
Nightcrawler

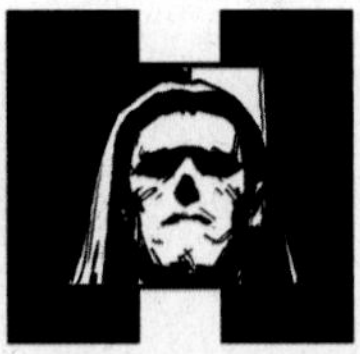
Exodus

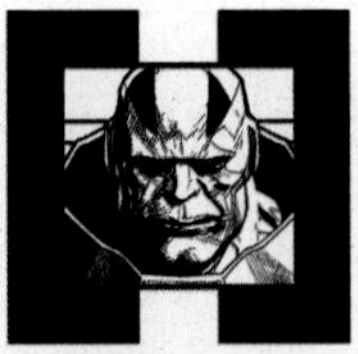
Apocalypse

[kra_[0.7]...]
[koa_[0.7]...]

[A._New_World]

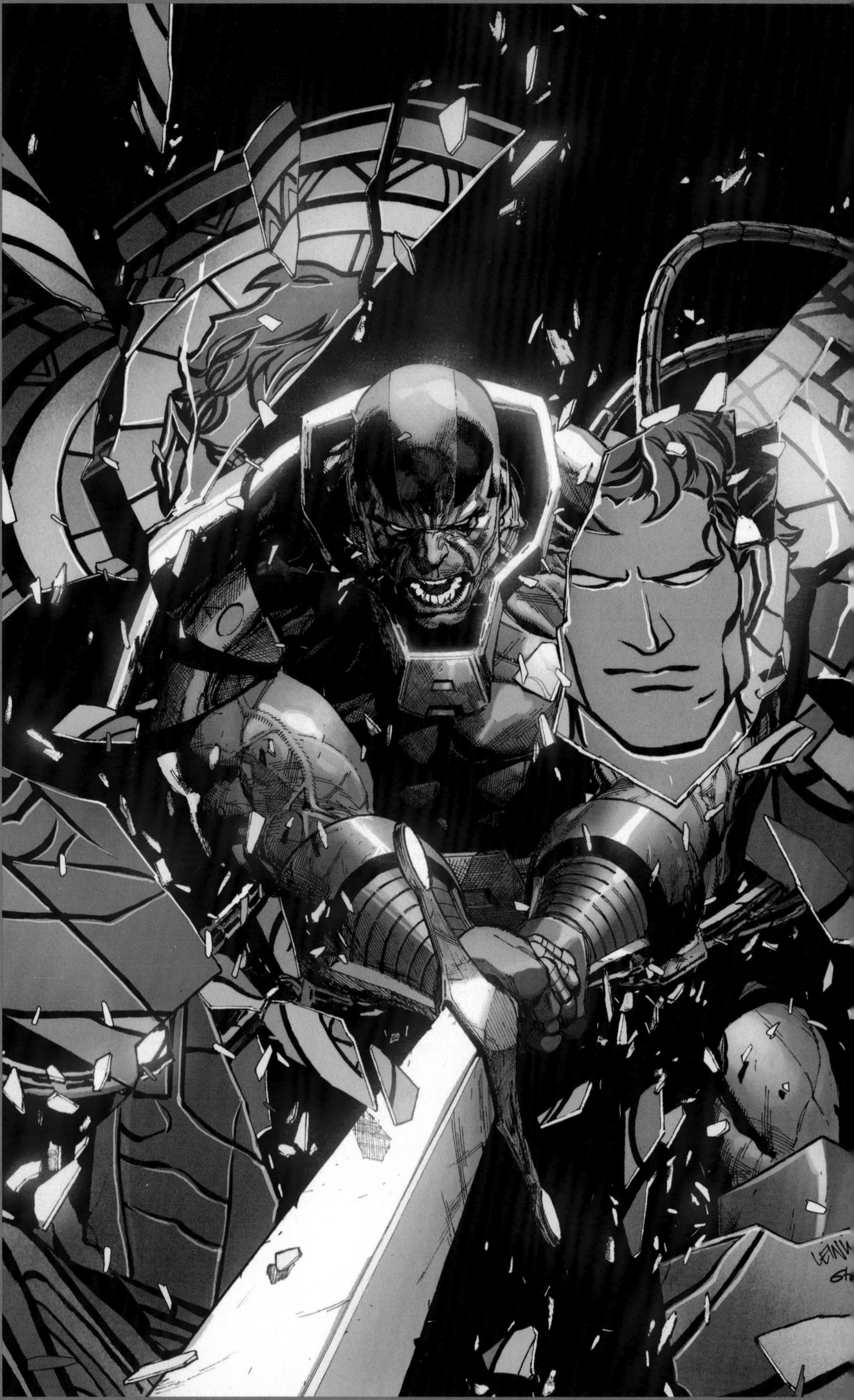

Lifedeath

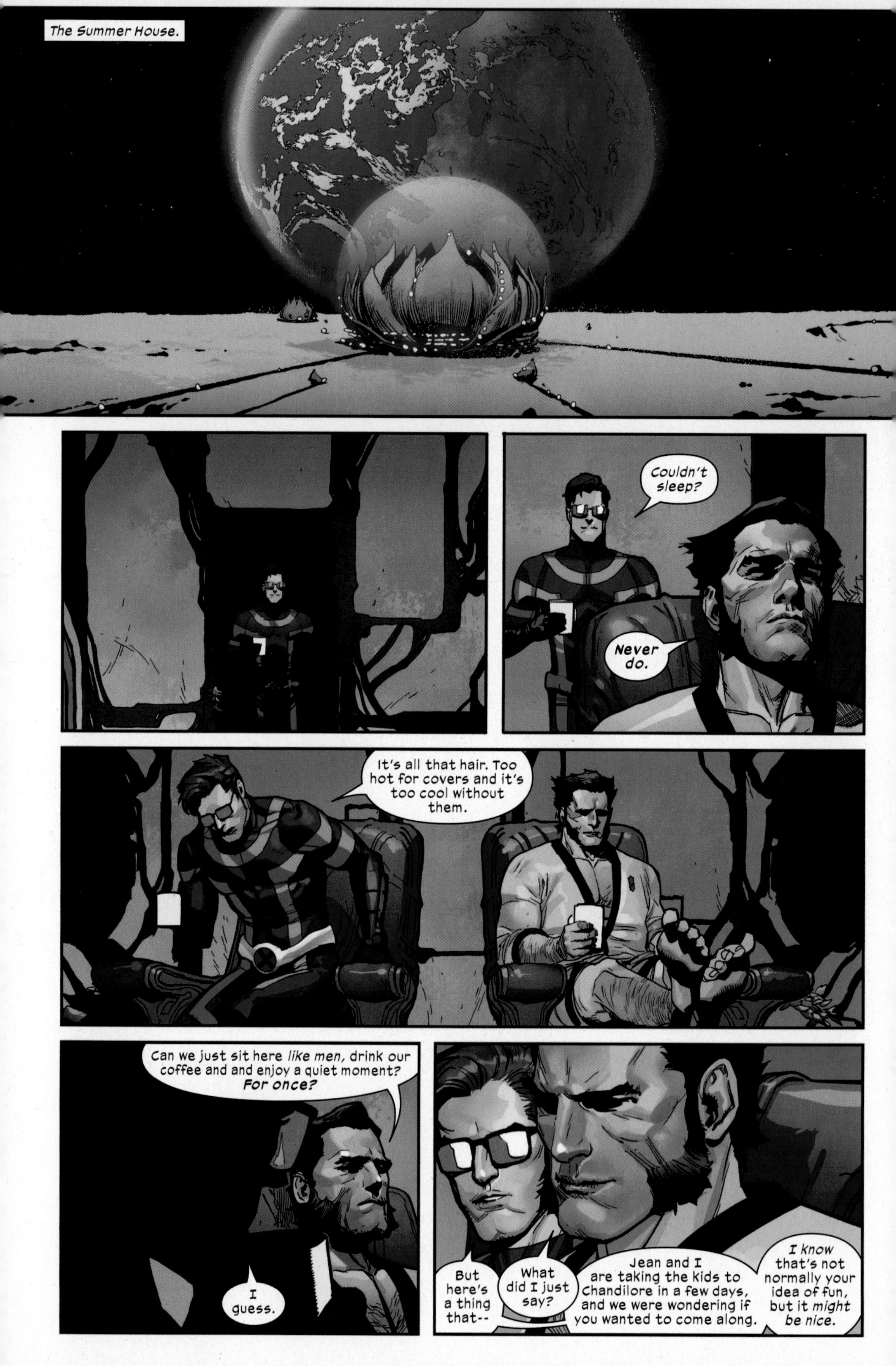
The Summer House.
Couldn't sleep?
Never do.
It's all that hair. Too hot for covers and it's too cool without them.
Can we just sit here *like men,* drink our coffee and and enjoy a quiet moment? **For once?**
I guess.
But here's a thing that--
What did I just say?
Jean and I are taking the kids to Chandilore in a few days, and we were wondering if you wanted to come along.
I know that's not normally your idea of fun, but it *might be nice.*

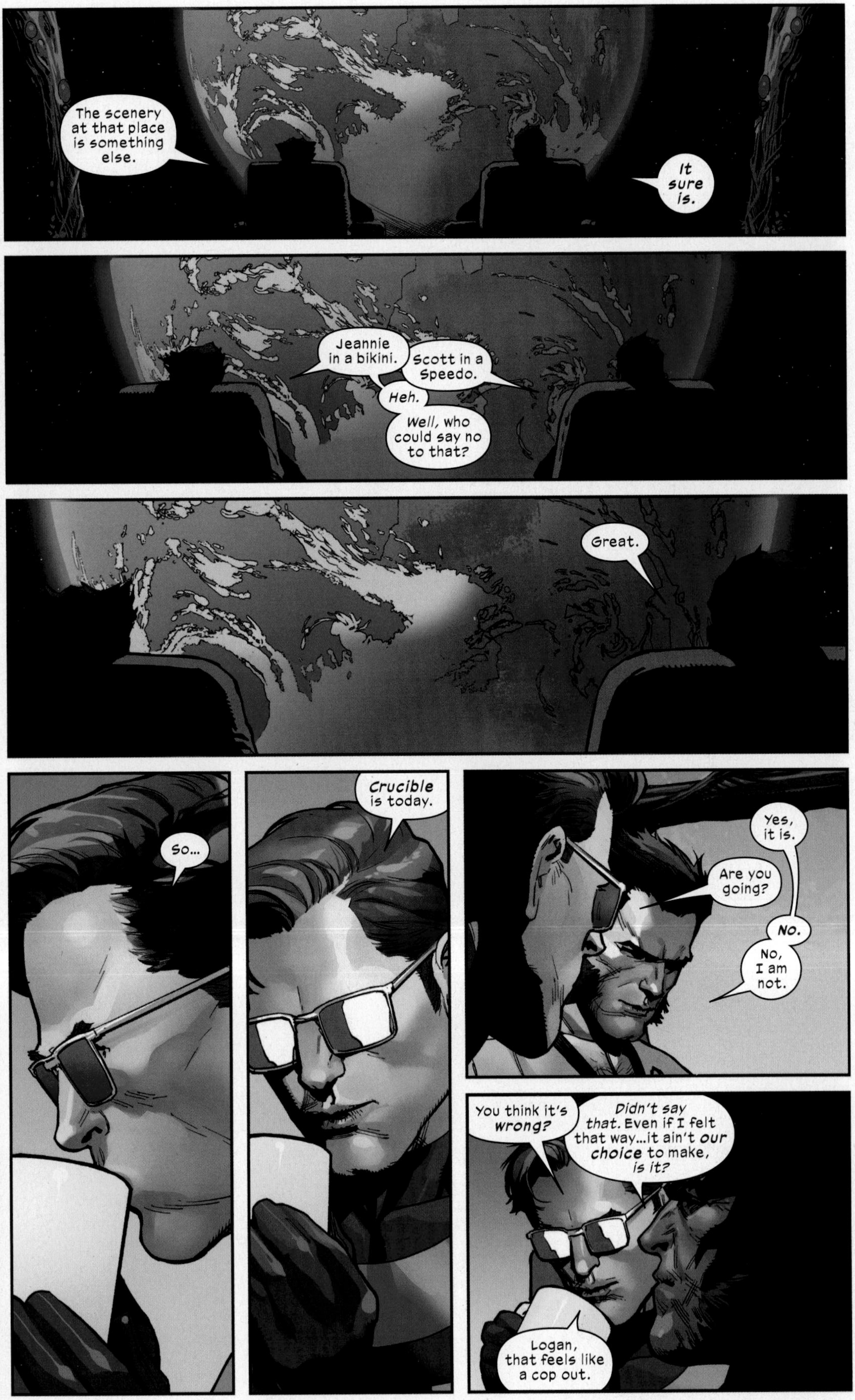
The scenery at that place is something else.
It sure is.
Jeannie in a bikini.
Scott in a Speedo.
Heh.
Well, who could say no to that?
Great.
So...
Crucible is today.
Yes, it is.
Are you going?
No.
No, I am not.
You think it's wrong?
Didn't say that. Even if I felt that way...it ain't our choice to make, is it?
Logan, that feels like a cop out.

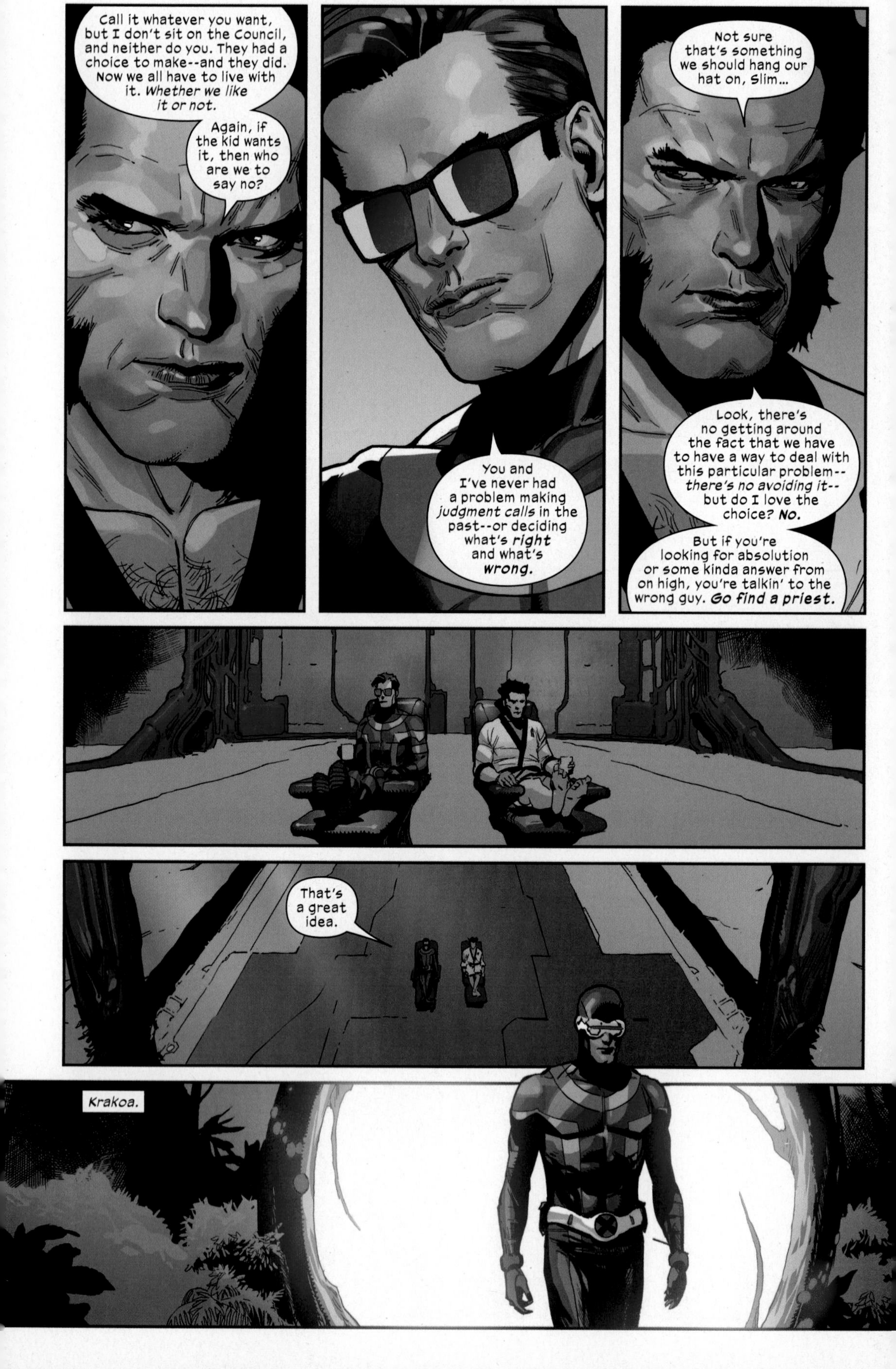

Call it whatever you want, but I don't sit on the Council, and neither do you. They had a choice to make--and they did. Now we all have to live with it. *Whether we like it or not.*
Again, if the kid wants it, then who are we to say no?
You and I've never had a problem making *judgment calls* in the past--or deciding what's *right* and what's ***wrong.***
Not sure that's something we should hang our hat on, Slim...
Look, there's no getting around the fact that we have to have a way to deal with this particular problem-- *there's no avoiding it--* but do I love the choice? ***No.***
But if you're looking for absolution or some kinda answer from on high, you're talkin' to the wrong guy. ***Go find a priest.***
That's a great idea.
Krakoa.

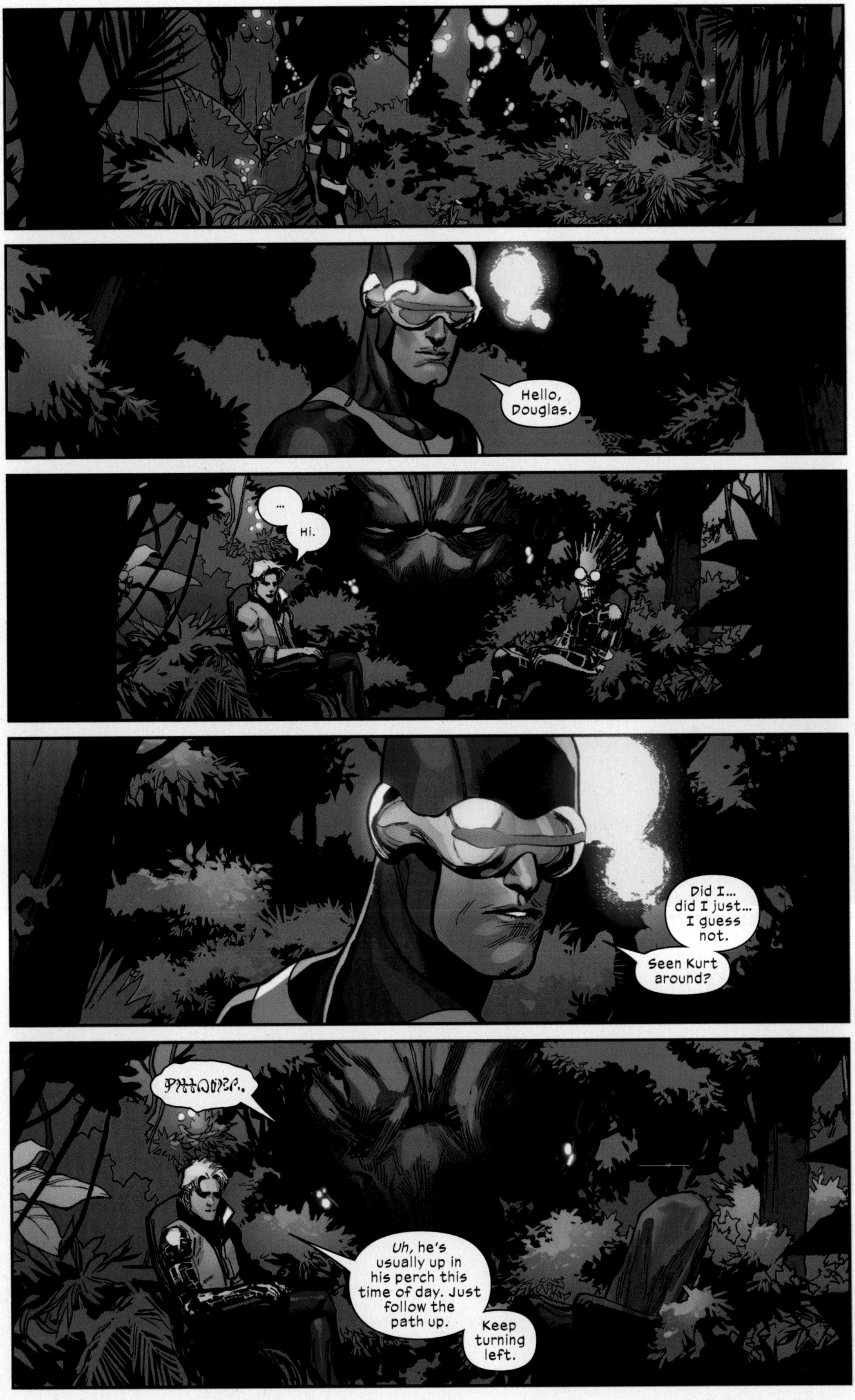
Hello, Douglas.
...
Hi.
Did I... did I just... I guess not.
Seen Kurt around?
Uh, he's usually up in his perch this time of day. Just follow the path up.
Keep turning left.

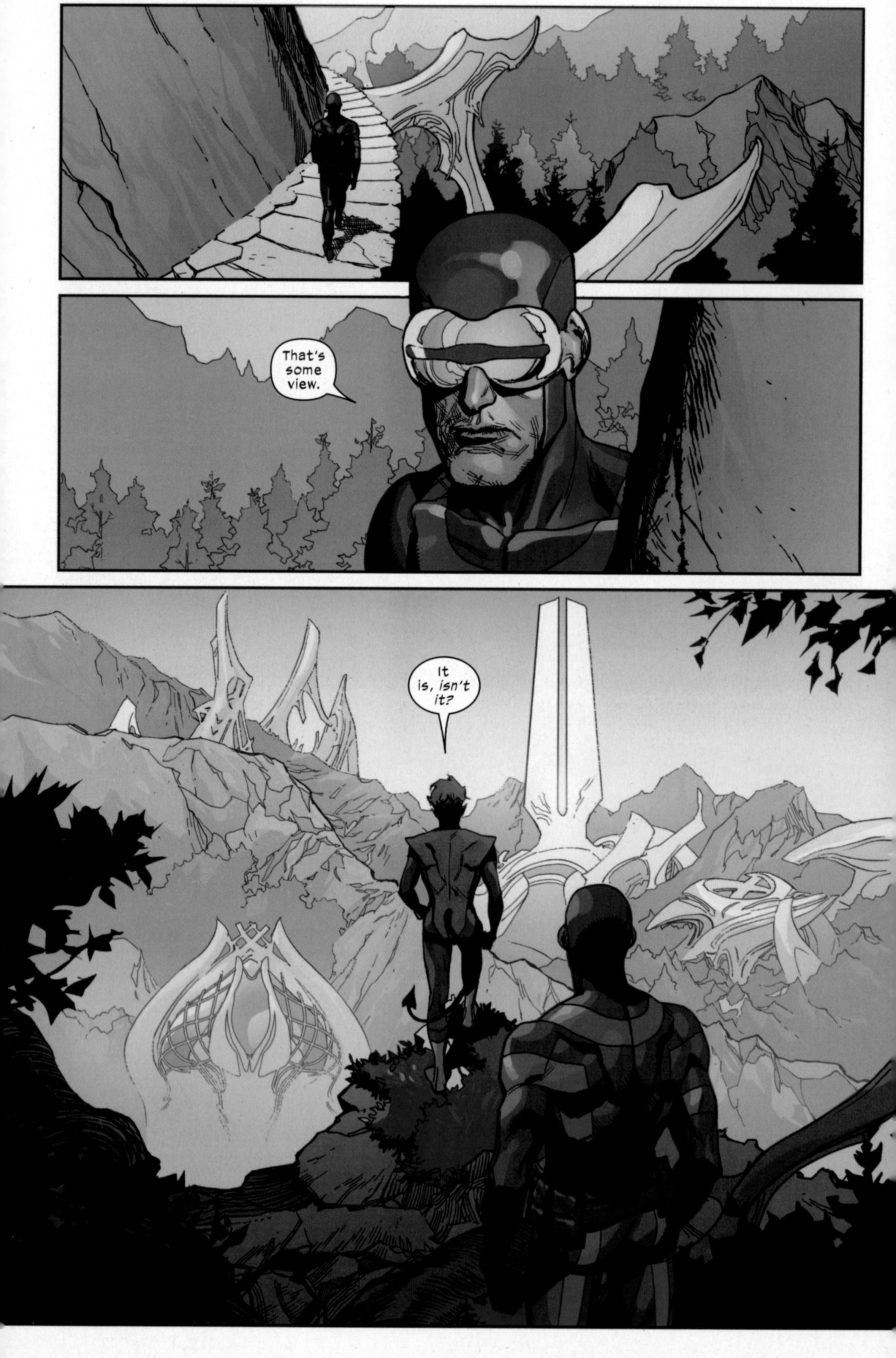
That's some view.
It is, isn't it?

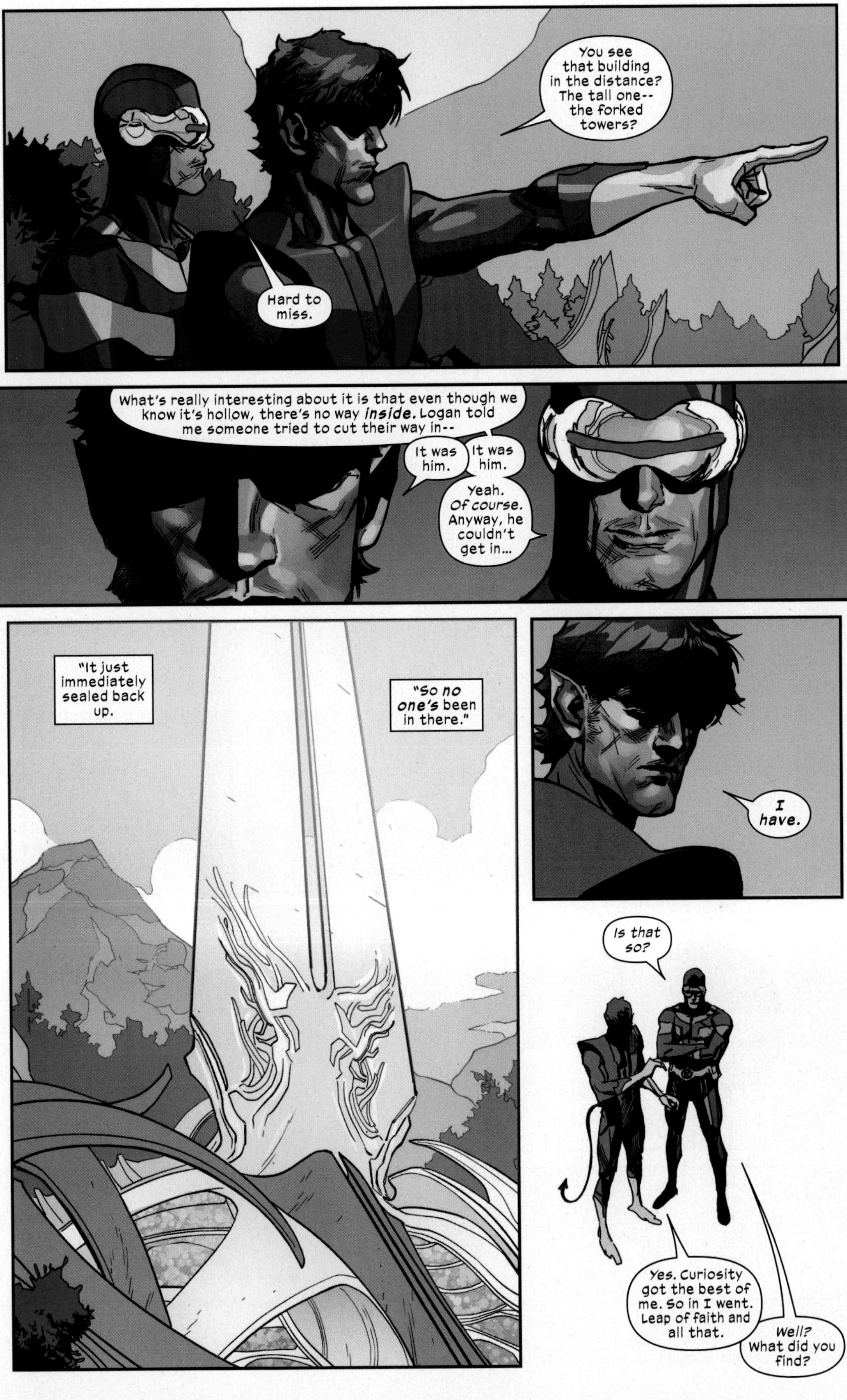

You see that building in the distance? The tall one-- the forked towers?
Hard to miss.
What's really interesting about it is that even though we know it's hollow, there's no way *inside.* Logan told me someone tried to cut their way in--
It was him.
It was him.
Yeah. *Of course.* Anyway, he couldn't get in...
"It just immediately sealed back up.
"So *no one's* been in there."
I have.
Is that so?
Yes. Curiosity got the best of me. So in I went. Leap of faith and all that.
Well? What did you find?

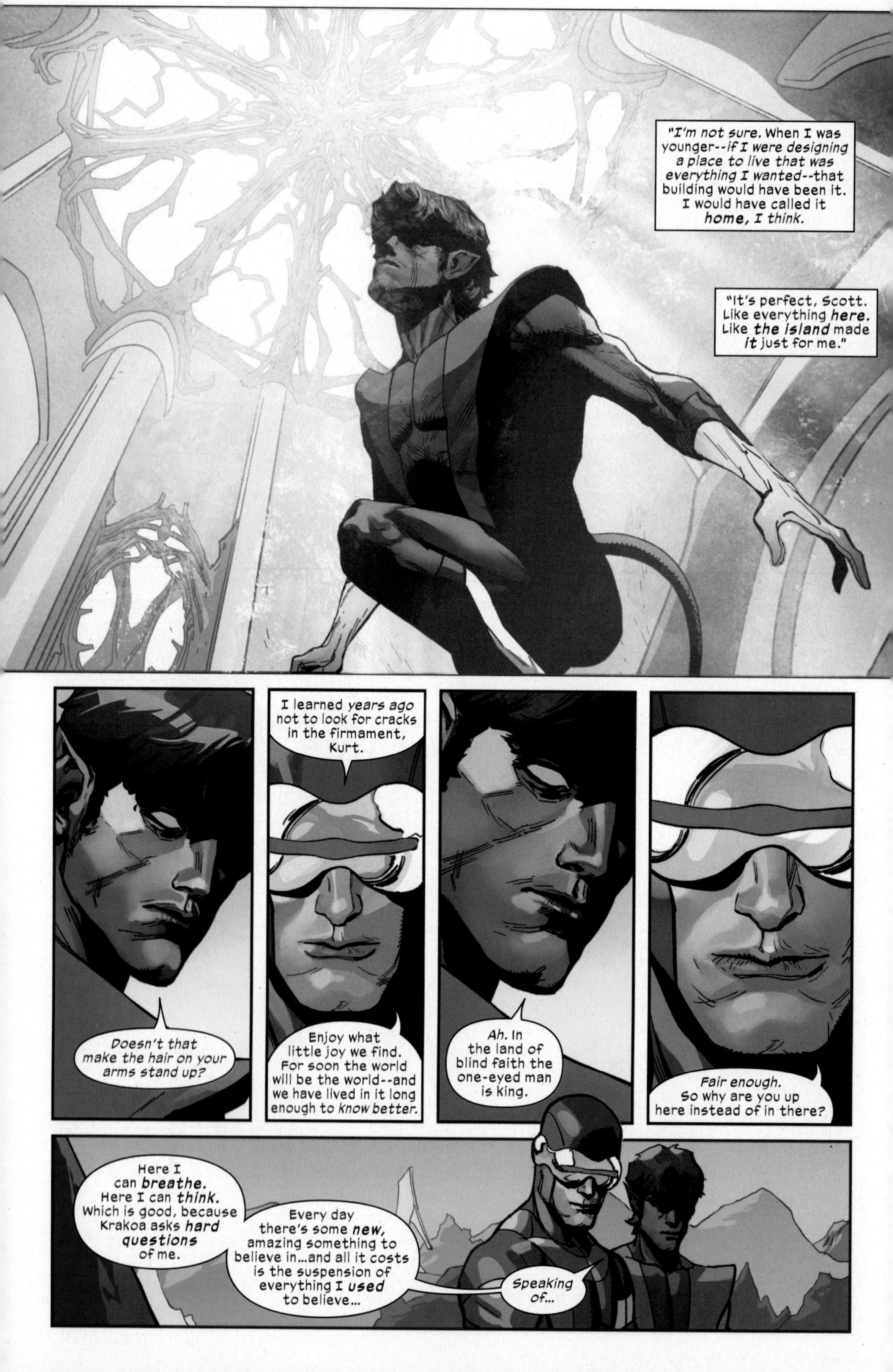
"I'm not sure. When I was younger--if I were designing a place to live that was everything I wanted--that building would have been it. I would have called it home, I think.
"It's perfect, Scott. Like everything here. Like the island made it just for me."
Doesn't that make the hair on your arms stand up?
I learned years ago not to look for cracks in the firmament, Kurt.
Enjoy what little joy we find. For soon the world will be the world--and we have lived in it long enough to know better.
Ah. In the land of blind faith the one-eyed man is king.
Fair enough. So why are you up here instead of in there?
Here I can breathe. Here I can think. Which is good, because Krakoa asks hard questions of me.
Every day there's some new, amazing something to believe in...and all it costs is the suspension of everything I used to believe...
Speaking of...

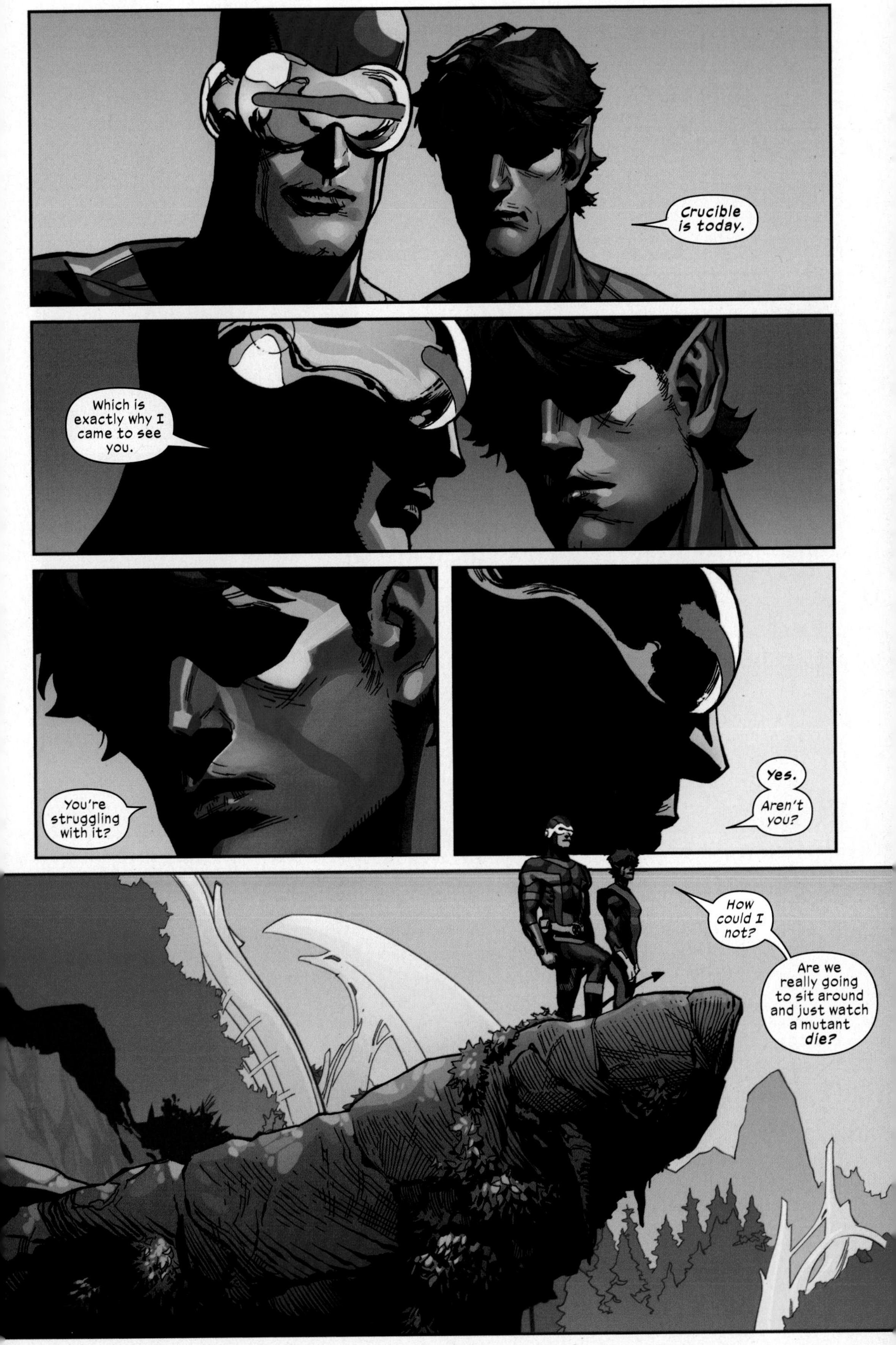
Crucible is today.
Which is exactly why I came to see you.
You're struggling with it?
Yes.
Aren't you?
How could I not?
Are we really going to sit around and just watch a mutant *die?*

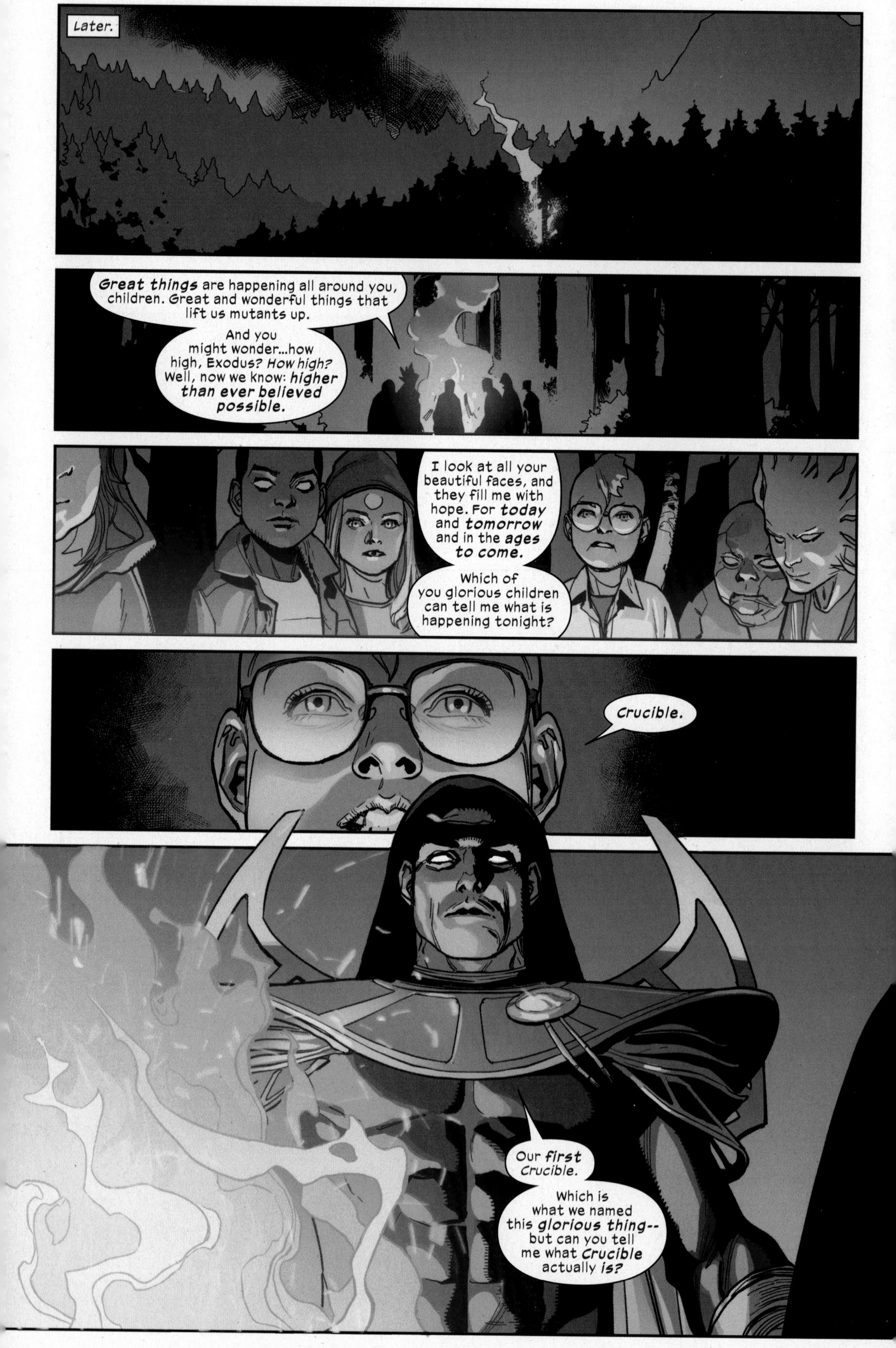
Later.
Great things are happening all around you, children. Great and wonderful things that lift us mutants up.
And you might wonder...how high, Exodus? How high? Well, now we know: higher than ever believed possible.
I look at all your beautiful faces, and they fill me with hope. For today and tomorrow and in the ages to come.
Which of you glorious children can tell me what is happening tonight?
Crucible.
Our first Crucible.
Which is what we named this glorious thing-- but can you tell me what Crucible actually is?

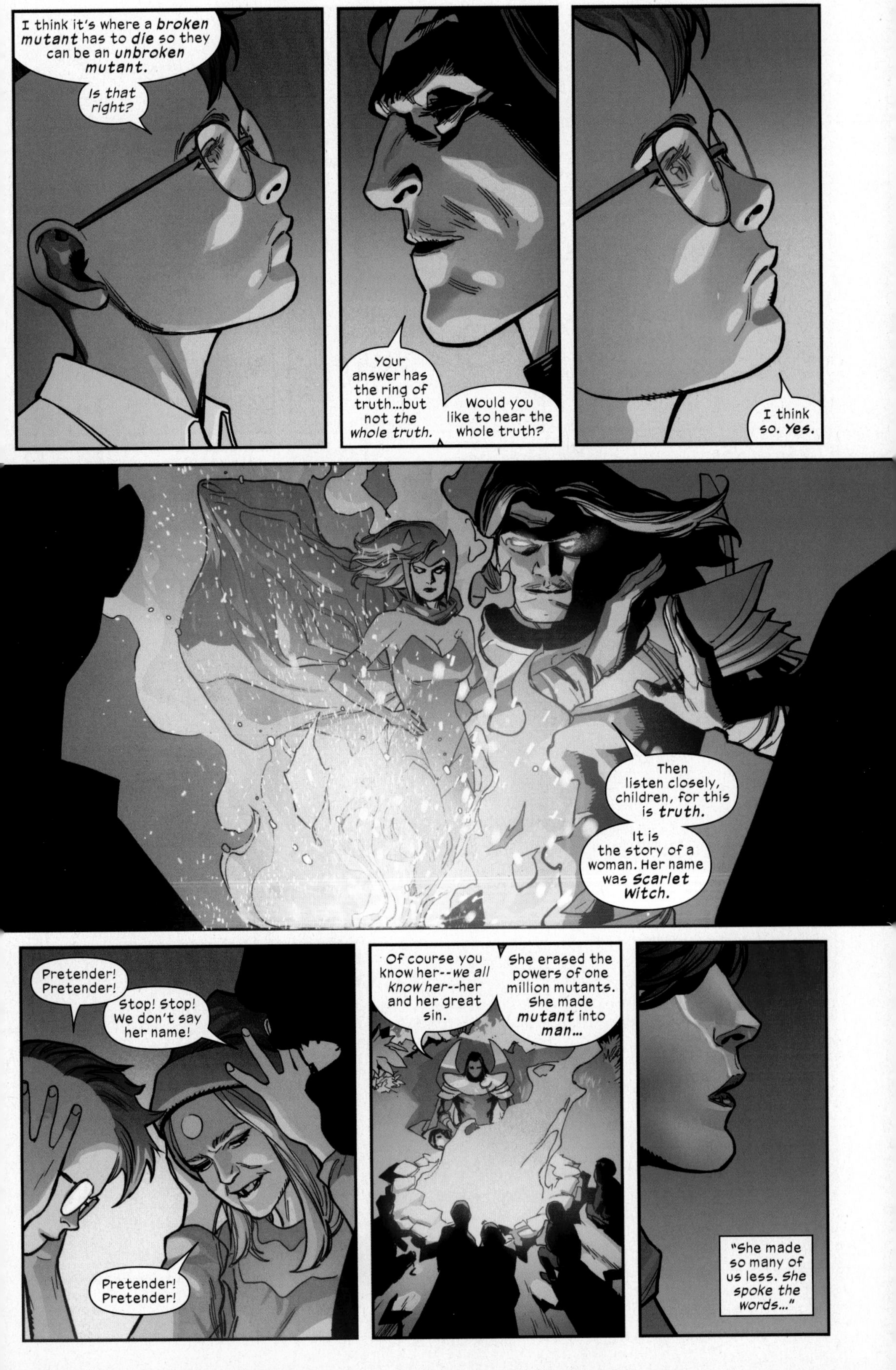
I think it's where a broken mutant has to die so they can be an unbroken mutant.
Is that right?
Your answer has the ring of truth...but not the whole truth.
Would you like to hear the whole truth?
I think so. Yes.
Then listen closely, children, for this is truth.
It is the story of a woman. Her name was Scarlet Witch.
Pretender! Pretender!
Stop! Stop! We don't say her name!
Pretender! Pretender!
Of course you know her--we all know her--her and her great sin.
She erased the powers of one million mutants. She made mutant into man...
"She made so many of us less. She spoke the words..."

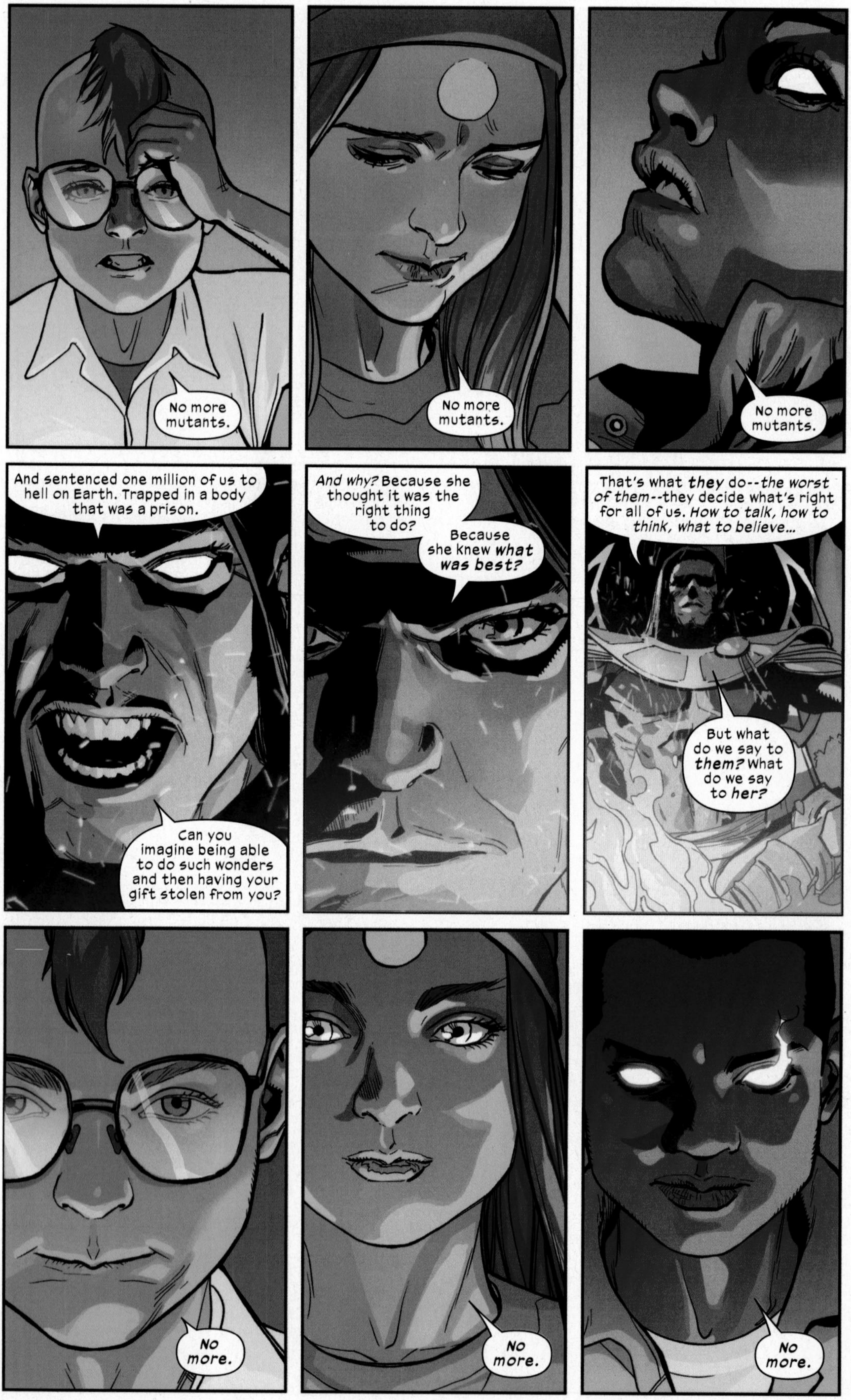
No more mutants.
No more mutants.
No more mutants.
And sentenced one million of us to hell on Earth. Trapped in a body that was a prison.
Can you imagine being able to do such wonders and then having your gift stolen from you?
And why? Because she thought it was the right thing to do?
Because she knew ***what was best?***
That's what ***they*** do--*the worst of them*--they decide what's right for all of us. *How to talk, how to think, what to believe...*
But what do we say to ***them?*** What do we say to ***her?***
No more.
No more.
No more.

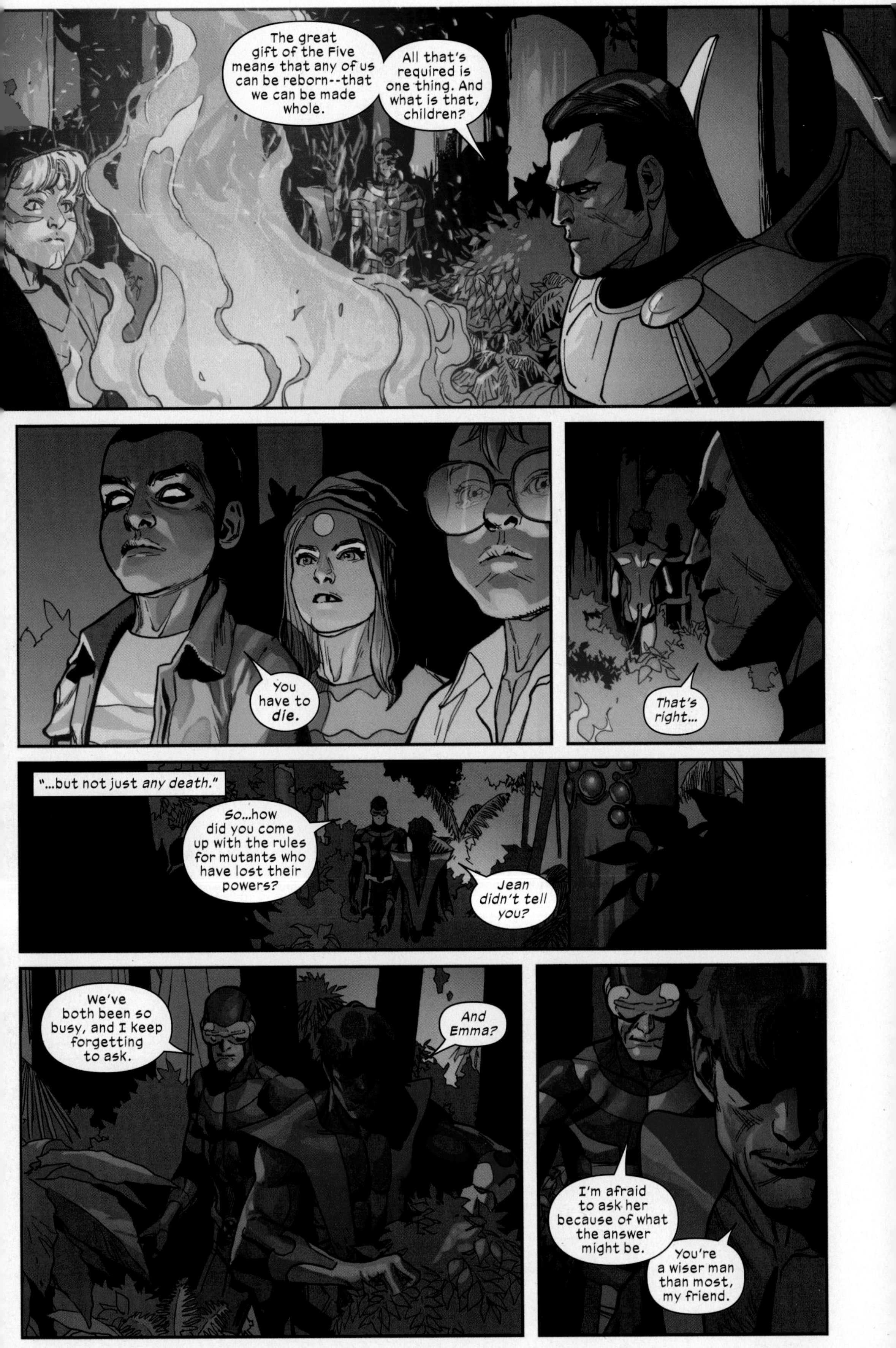

The great gift of the Five means that any of us can be reborn--that we can be made whole.
All that's required is one thing. And what is that, children?
You have to *die*.
That's right...
"...but not just *any death*."
So...how did you come up with the rules for mutants who have lost their powers?
Jean didn't tell you?
We've both been so busy, and I keep forgetting to ask.
And Emma?
I'm afraid to ask her because of what the answer might be.
You're a wiser man than most, my friend.

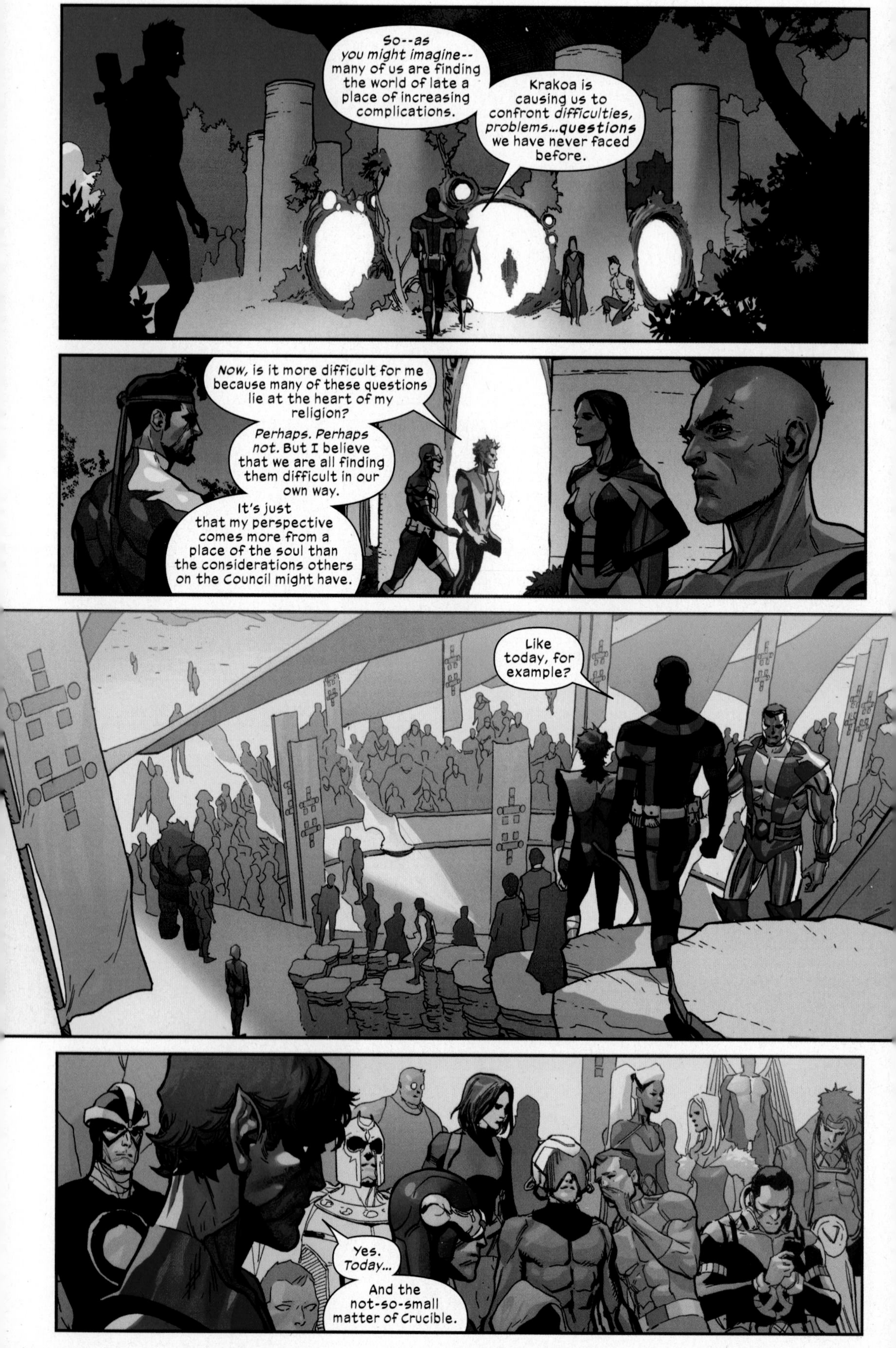
So--as you might imagine--many of us are finding the world of late a place of increasing complications.
Krakoa is causing us to confront difficulties, problems...questions we have never faced before.
Now, is it more difficult for me because many of these questions lie at the heart of my religion?
Perhaps. Perhaps not. But I believe that we are all finding them difficult in our own way.
It's just that my perspective comes more from a place of the soul than the considerations others on the Council might have.
Like today, for example?
Yes. Today...
And the not-so-small matter of Crucible.

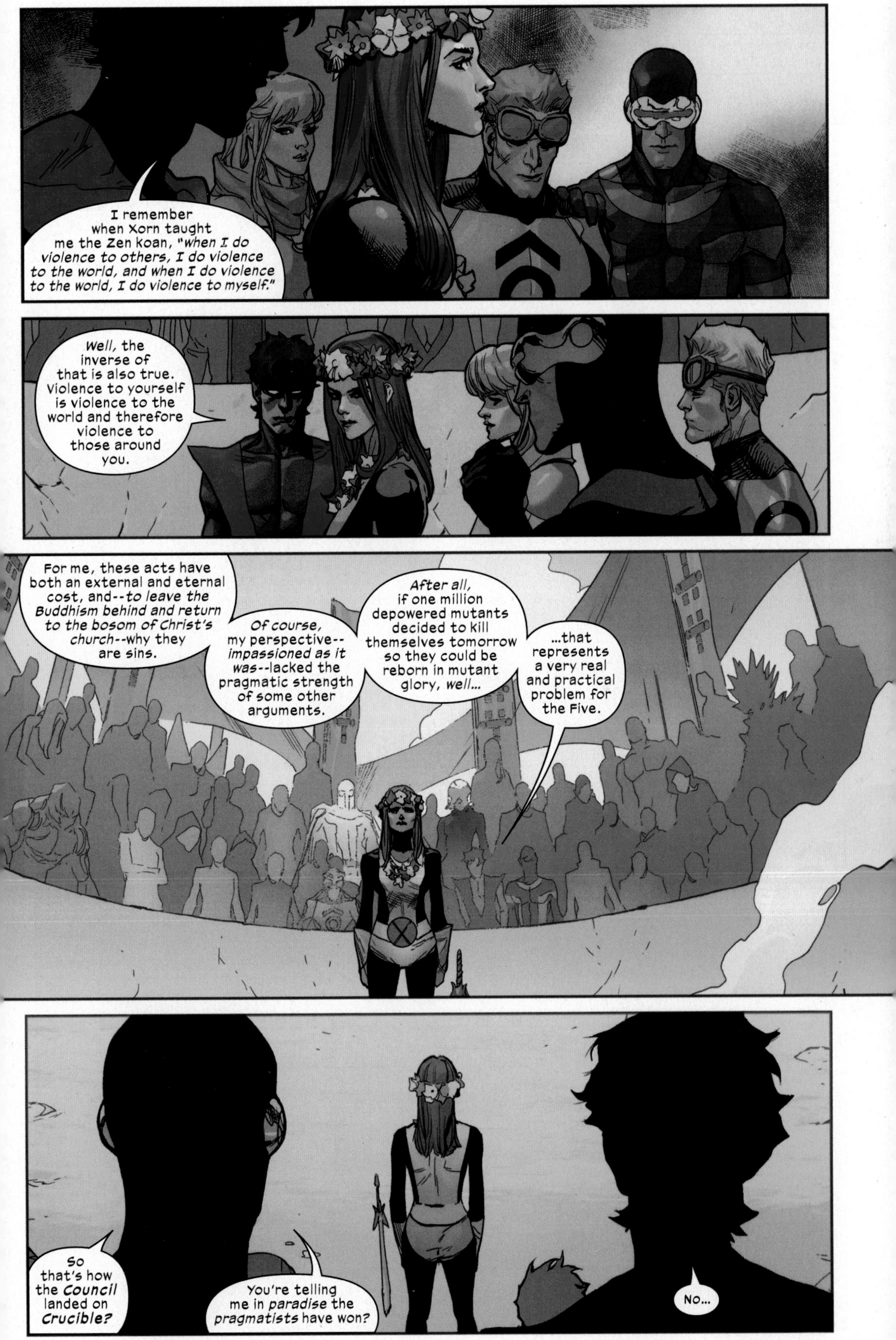

I remember when Xorn taught me the Zen koan, "when I do violence to others, I do violence to the world, and when I do violence to the world, I do violence to myself."
Well, the inverse of that is also true. Violence to yourself is violence to the world and therefore violence to those around you.
For me, these acts have both an external and eternal cost, and--to leave the Buddhism behind and return to the bosom of Christ's church--why they are sins.
Of course, my perspective--impassioned as it was--lacked the pragmatic strength of some other arguments.
After all, if one million depowered mutants decided to kill themselves tomorrow so they could be reborn in mutant glory, well...
...that represents a very real and practical problem for the Five.
So that's how the Council landed on Crucible?
You're telling me in paradise the pragmatists have won?
No...

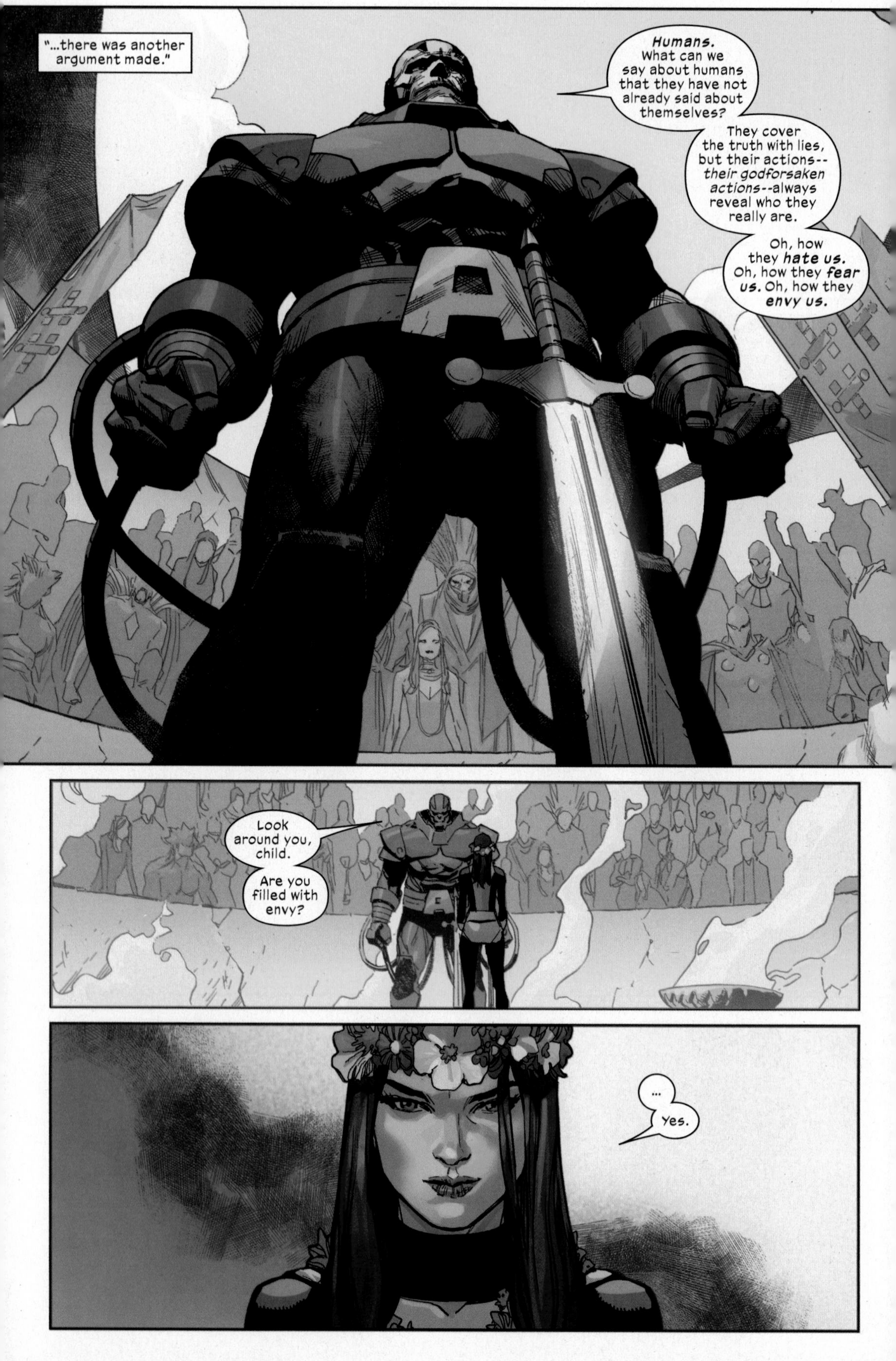
"...there was another argument made."
Humans. What can we say about humans that they have not already said about themselves?
They cover the truth with lies, but their actions-- *their godforsaken actions*--always reveal who they really are.
Oh, how they ***hate us.*** Oh, how they ***fear us.*** Oh, how they ***envy us.***
Look around you, child.
Are you filled with envy?
...
Yes.

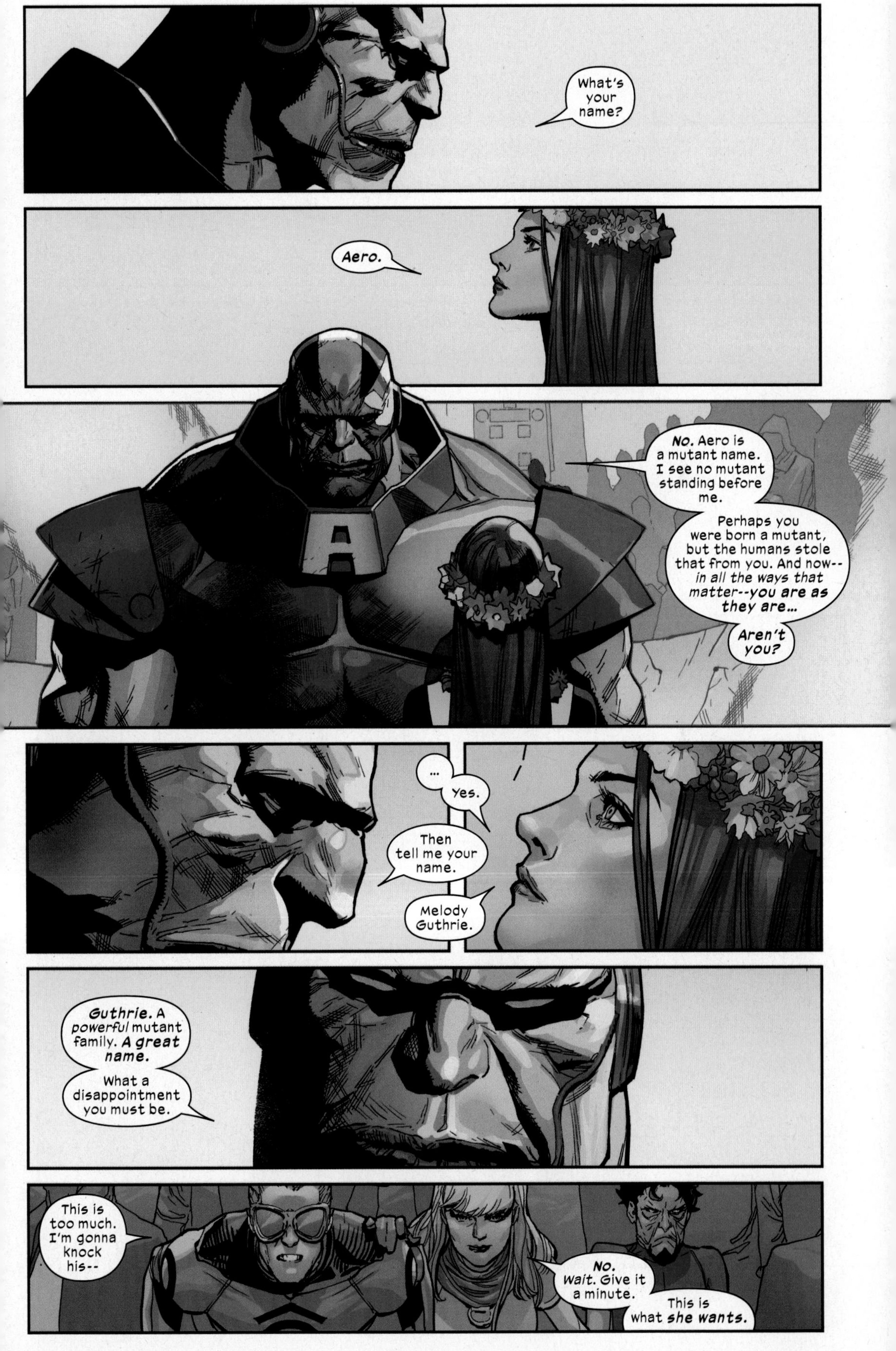
What's your name?
Aero.
No. Aero is a mutant name. I see no mutant standing before me.
Perhaps you were born a mutant, but the humans stole that from you. And now--in all the ways that matter--you are as they are...
Aren't you?
...
Yes.
Then tell me your name.
Melody Guthrie.
Guthrie. A powerful mutant family. A great name.
What a disappointment you must be.
This is too much. I'm gonna knock his--
No. Wait. Give it a minute.
This is what she wants.

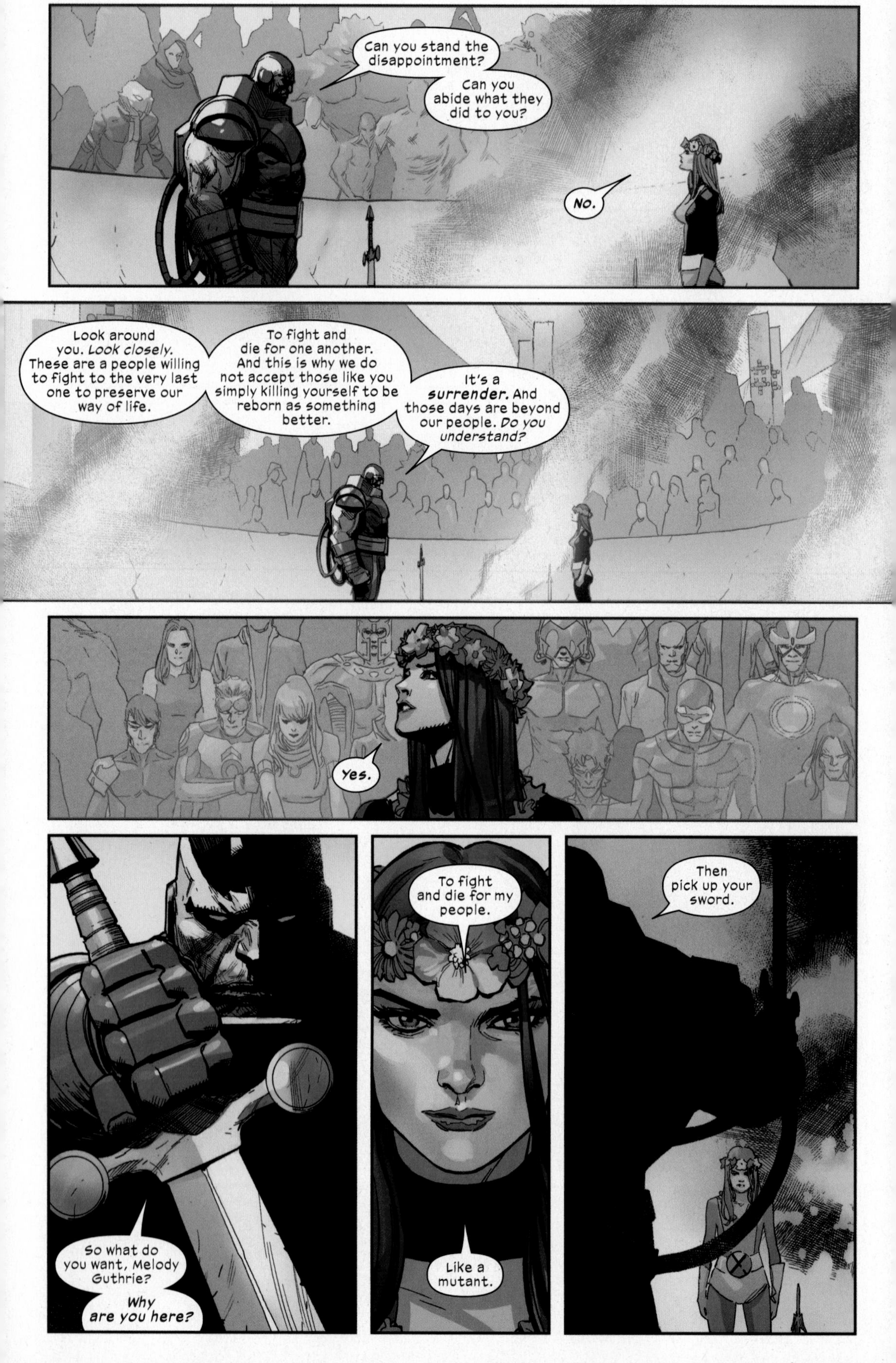

Can you stand the disappointment?
Can you abide what they did to you?
No.
Look around you. Look closely. These are a people willing to fight to the very last one to preserve our way of life.
To fight and die for one another. And this is why we do not accept those like you simply killing yourself to be reborn as something better.
It's a surrender. And those days are beyond our people. Do you understand?
Yes.
So what do you want, Melody Guthrie?
Why are you here?
To fight and die for my people.
Like a mutant.
Then pick up your sword.

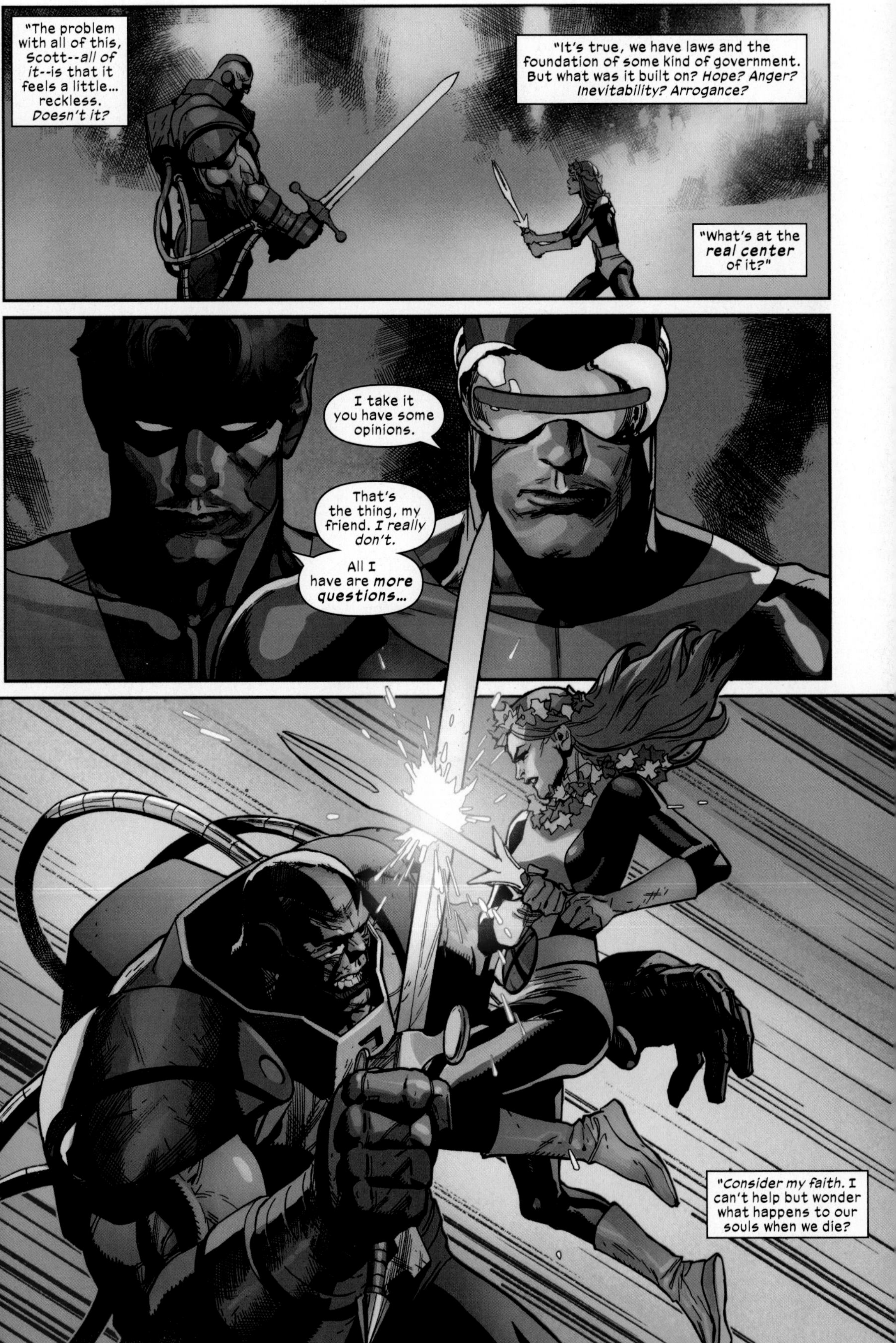
"The problem with all of this, Scott--all of it--is that it feels a little... reckless. Doesn't it?
"It's true, we have laws and the foundation of some kind of government. But what was it built on? Hope? Anger? Inevitability? Arrogance?
"What's at the real center of it?"
I take it you have some opinions.
That's the thing, my friend. I really don't.
All I have are more questions...
"Consider my faith. I can't help but wonder what happens to our souls when we die?

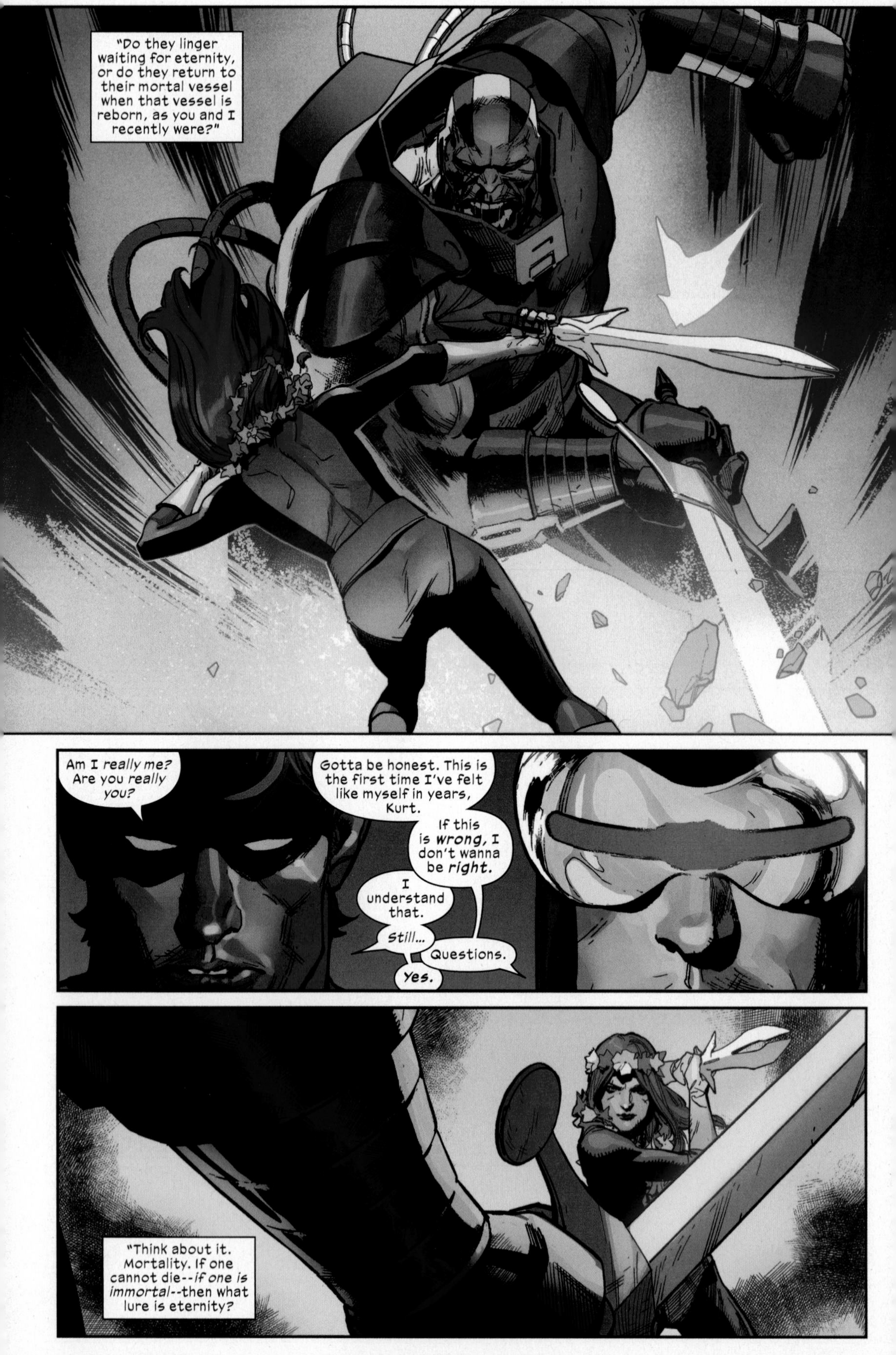
"Do they linger waiting for eternity, or do they return to their mortal vessel when that vessel is reborn, as you and I recently were?"
Am I *really me?* Are you *really you?*
Gotta be honest. This is the first time I've felt like myself in years, Kurt.
If this is *wrong,* I don't wanna be *right.*
I understand that.
Still...
Questions.
Yes.
"Think about it. Mortality. If one cannot die--*if one is immortal*--then what lure is eternity?

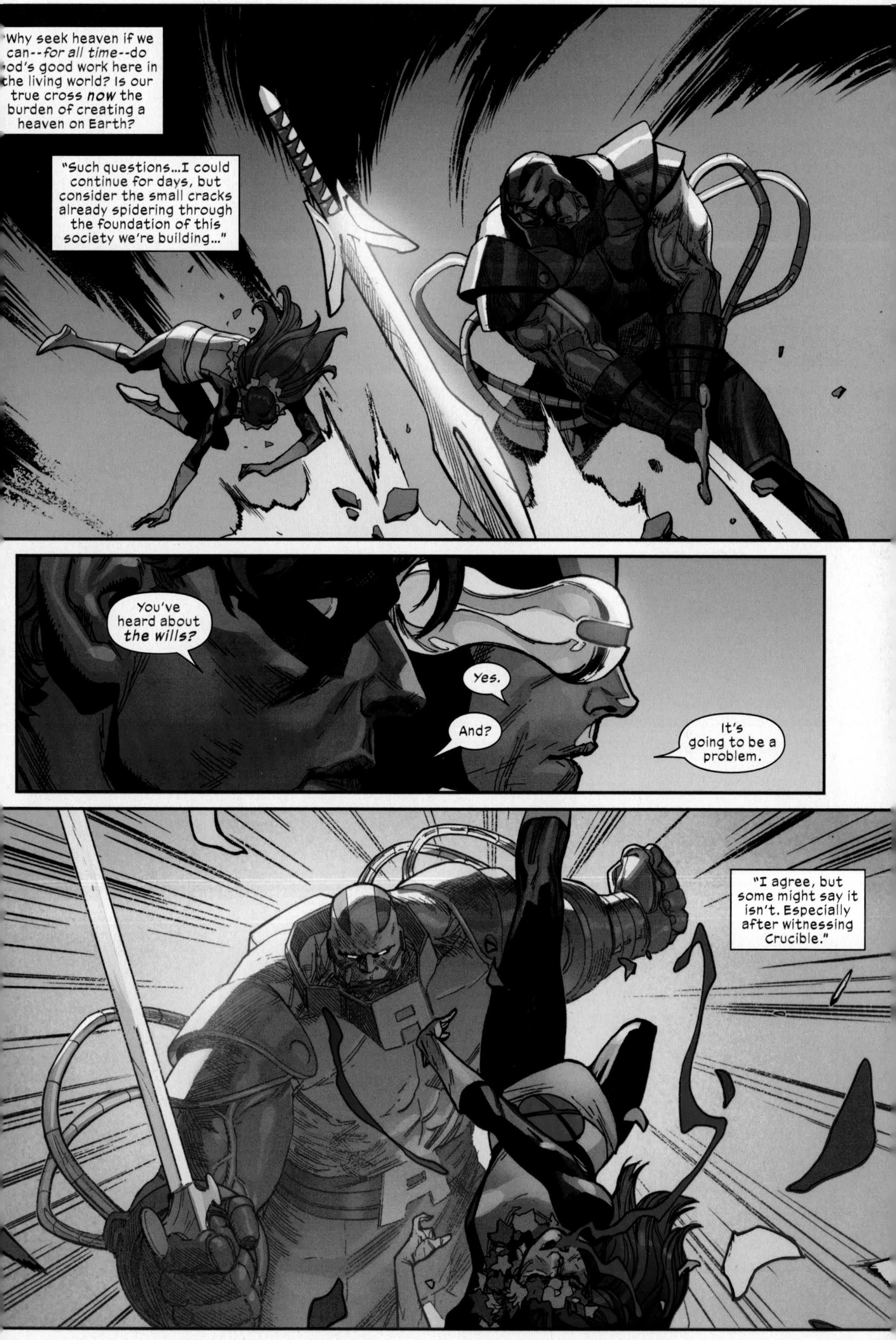

Why seek heaven if we can--*for all time*--do od's good work here in the living world? Is our true cross *now* the burden of creating a heaven on Earth?
"Such questions...I could continue for days, but consider the small cracks already spidering through the foundation of this society we're building..."
You've heard about *the wills?*
Yes.
And?
It's going to be a problem.
"I agree, but some might say it isn't. Especially after witnessing Crucible."

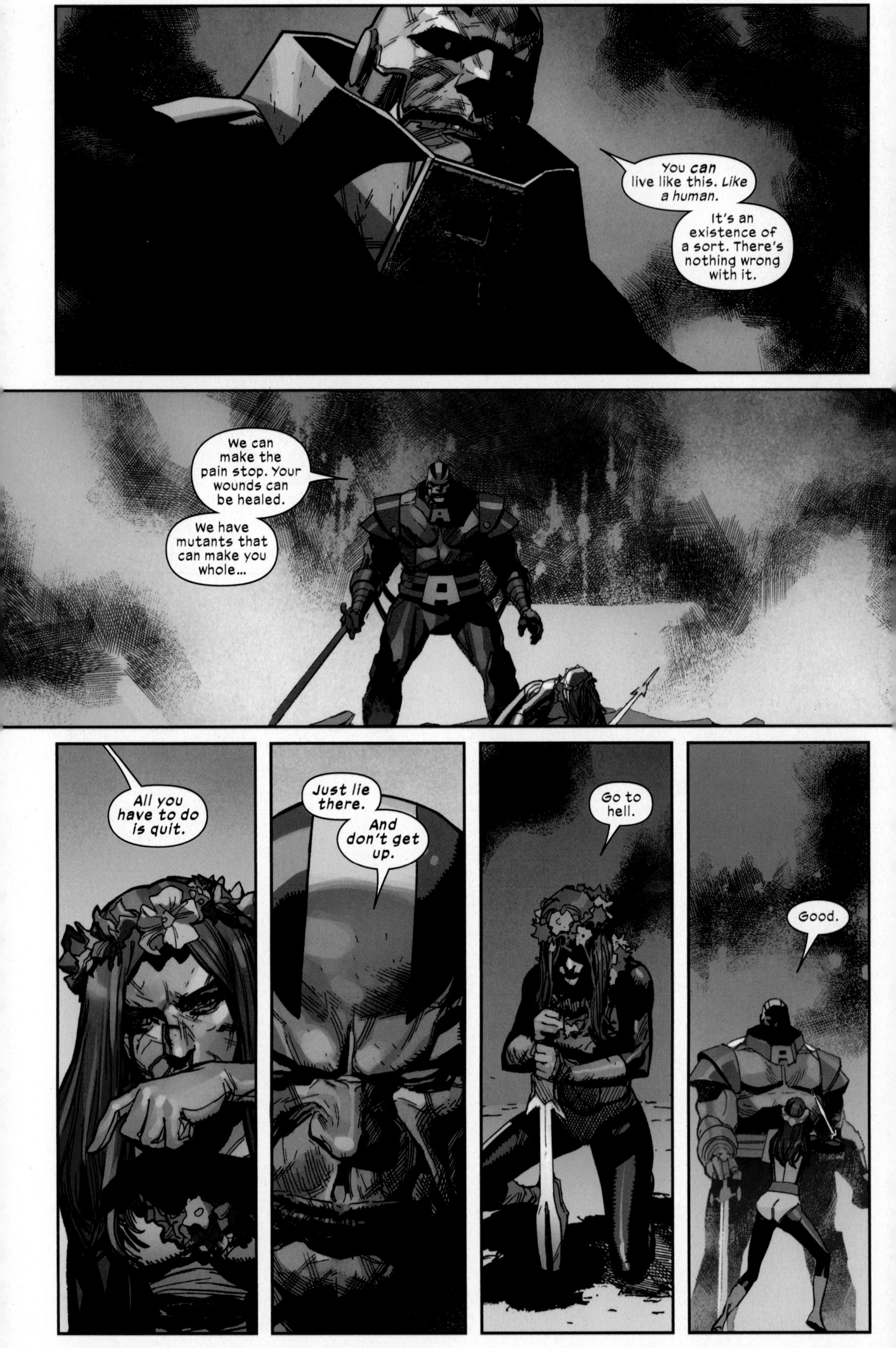
You *can* live like this. *Like a human.*
It's an existence of a sort. There's nothing wrong with it.
We can make the pain stop. Your wounds can be healed.
We have mutants that can make you whole...
All you have to do is quit.
Just lie there.
And don't get up.
Go to hell.
Good.

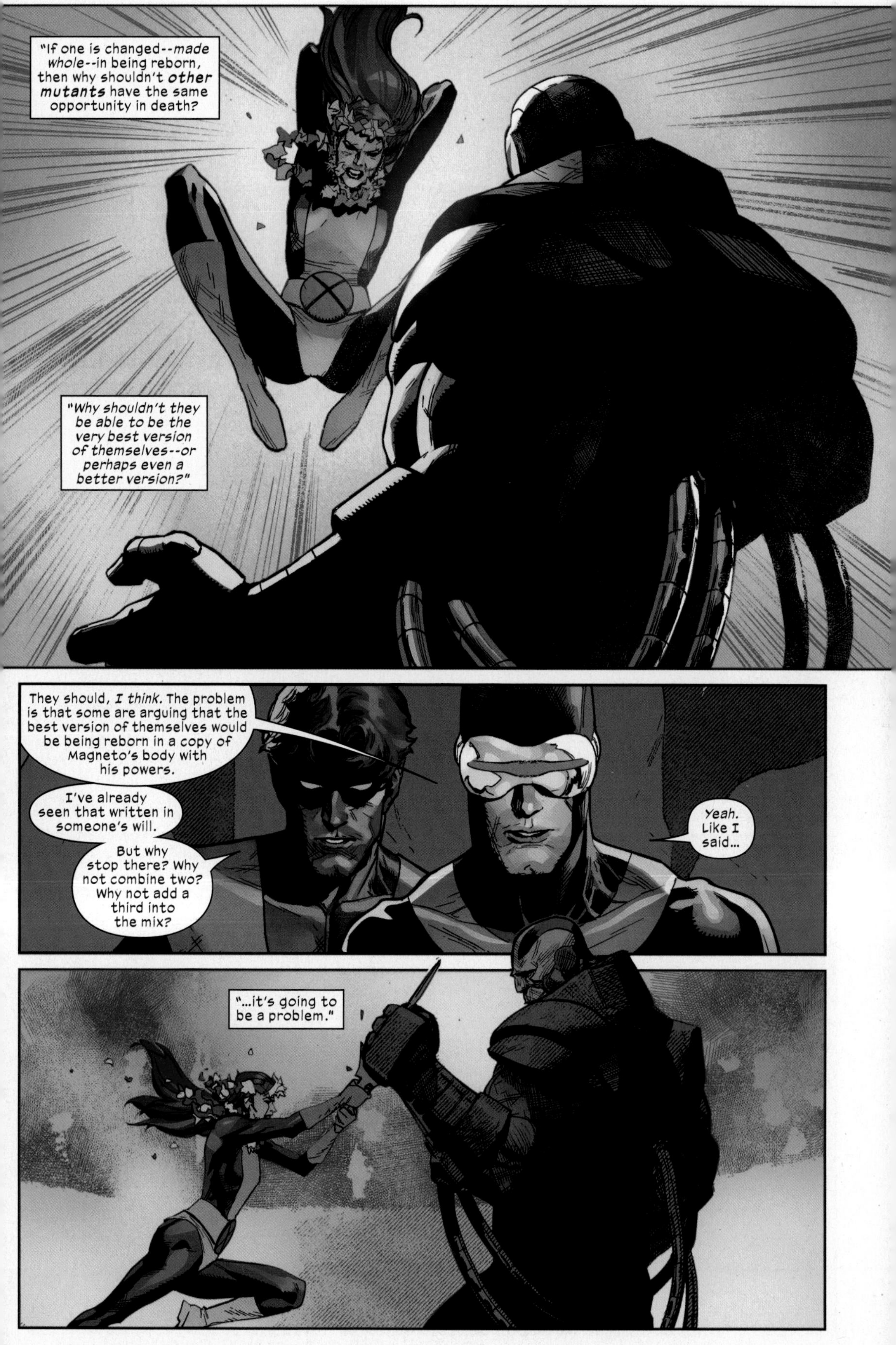

"If one is changed--*made whole*--in being reborn, then why shouldn't ***other mutants*** have the same opportunity in death?
"Why shouldn't they be able to be the very best version of themselves--or perhaps even a better version?"
They should, *I think.* The problem is that some are arguing that the best version of themselves would be being reborn in a copy of Magneto's body with his powers.
I've already seen that written in someone's will.
But why stop there? Why not combine two? Why not add a third into the mix?
Yeah. Like I said...
"...it's going to be a problem."

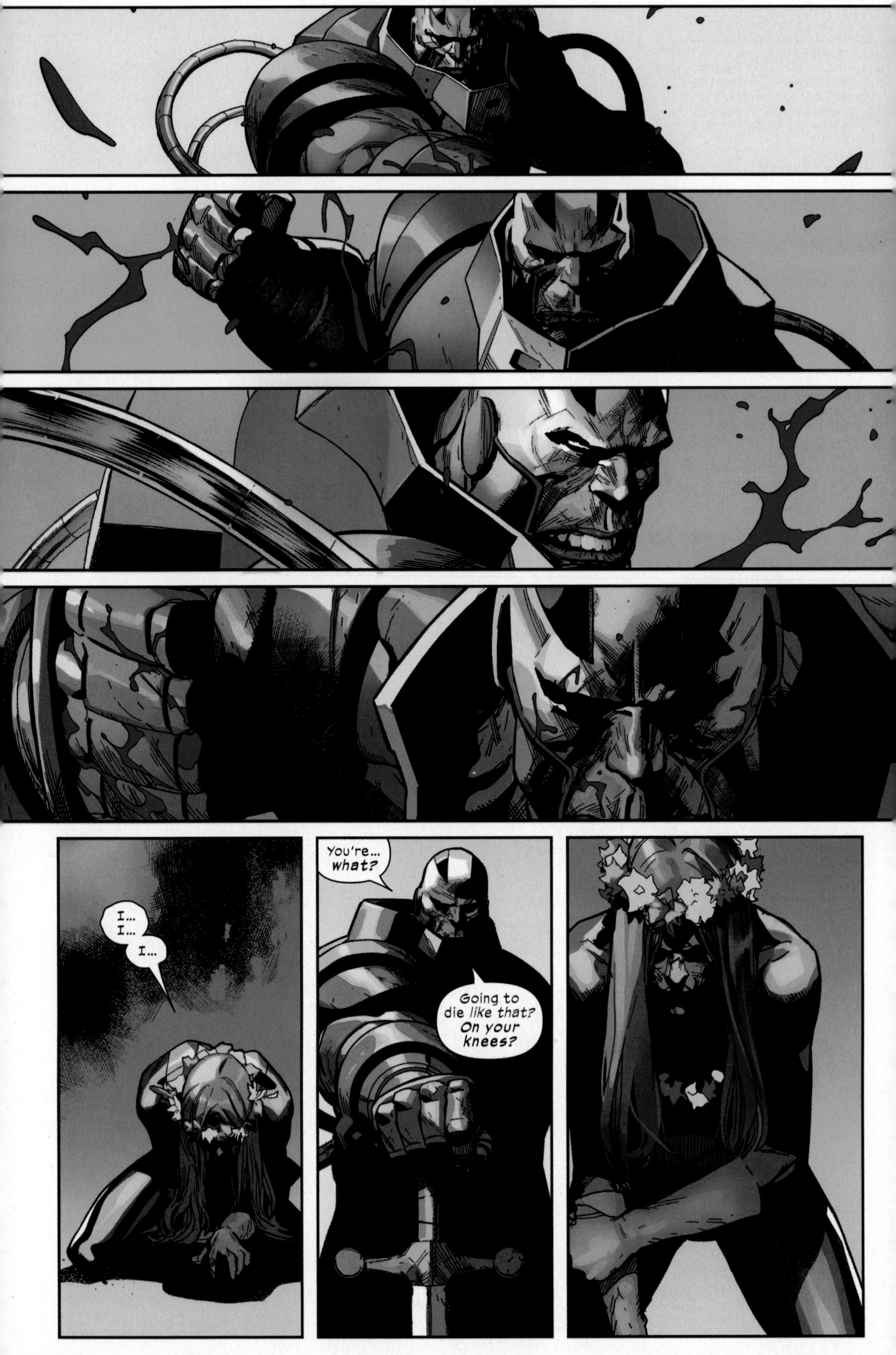
I... I... I...
You're... what?
Going to die like that? On your knees?

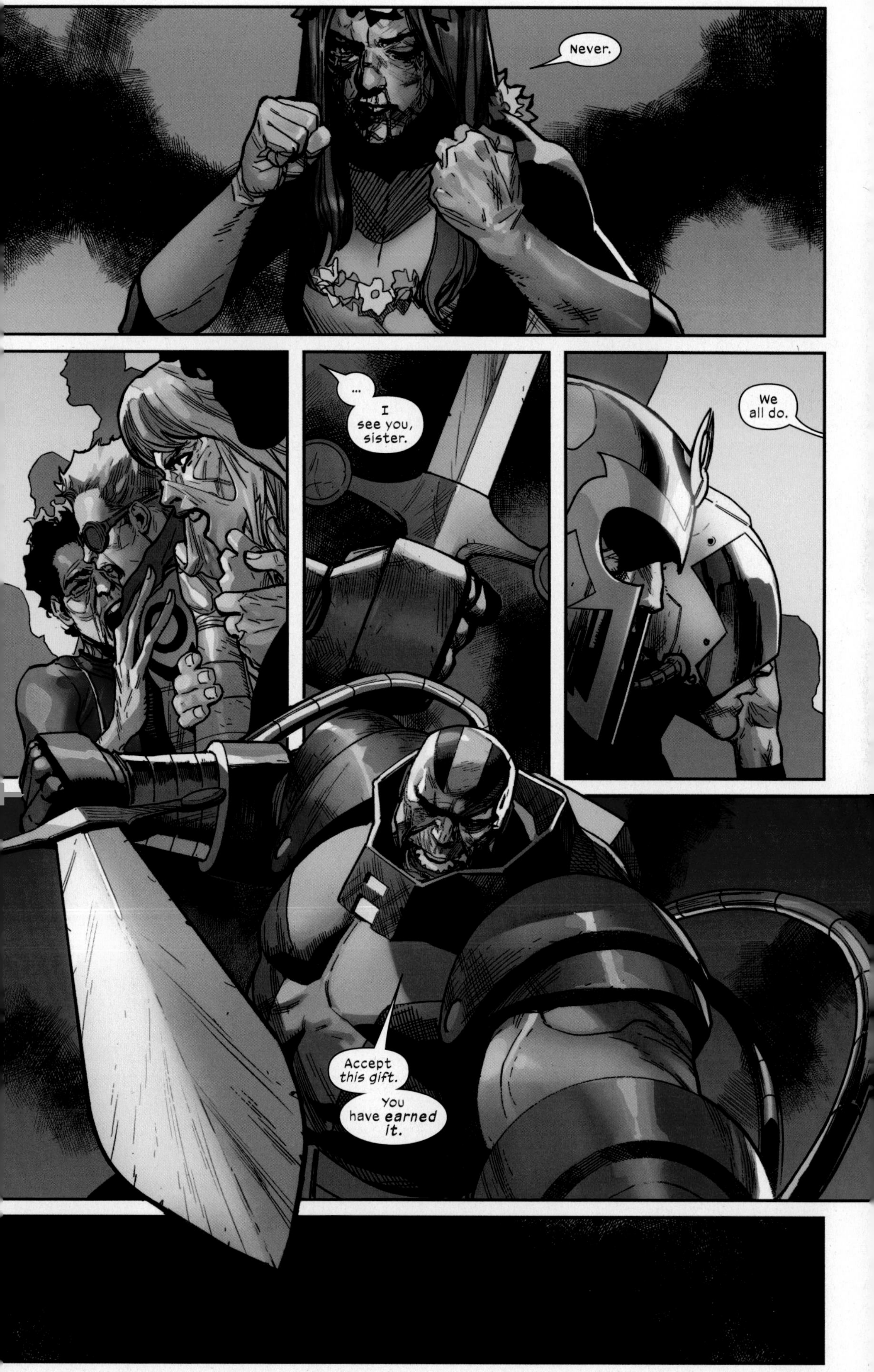
Never.
... I see you, sister.
We all do.
Accept this gift.
You have earned it.

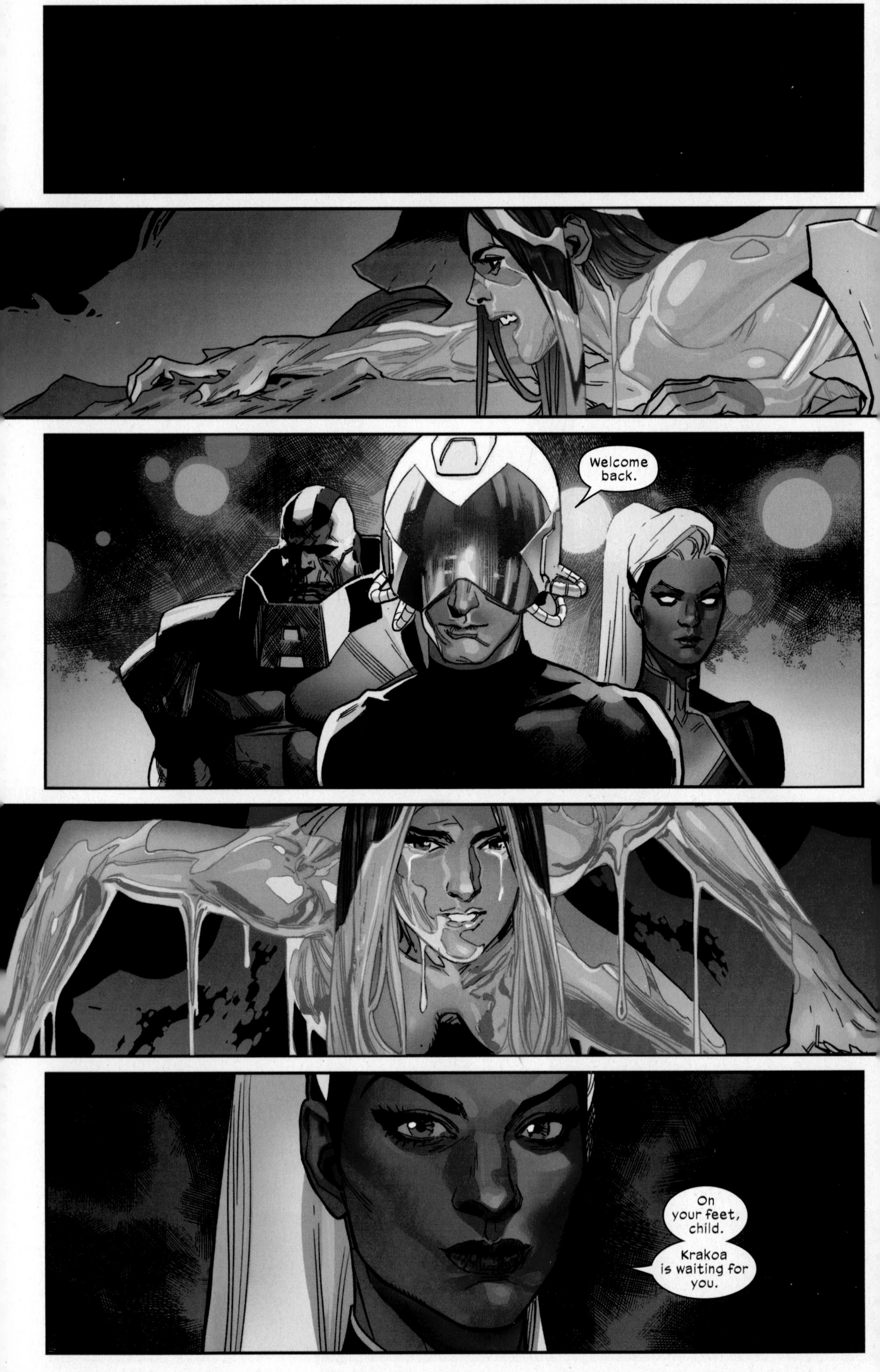
Welcome back.
On your feet, child.
Krakoa is waiting for you.

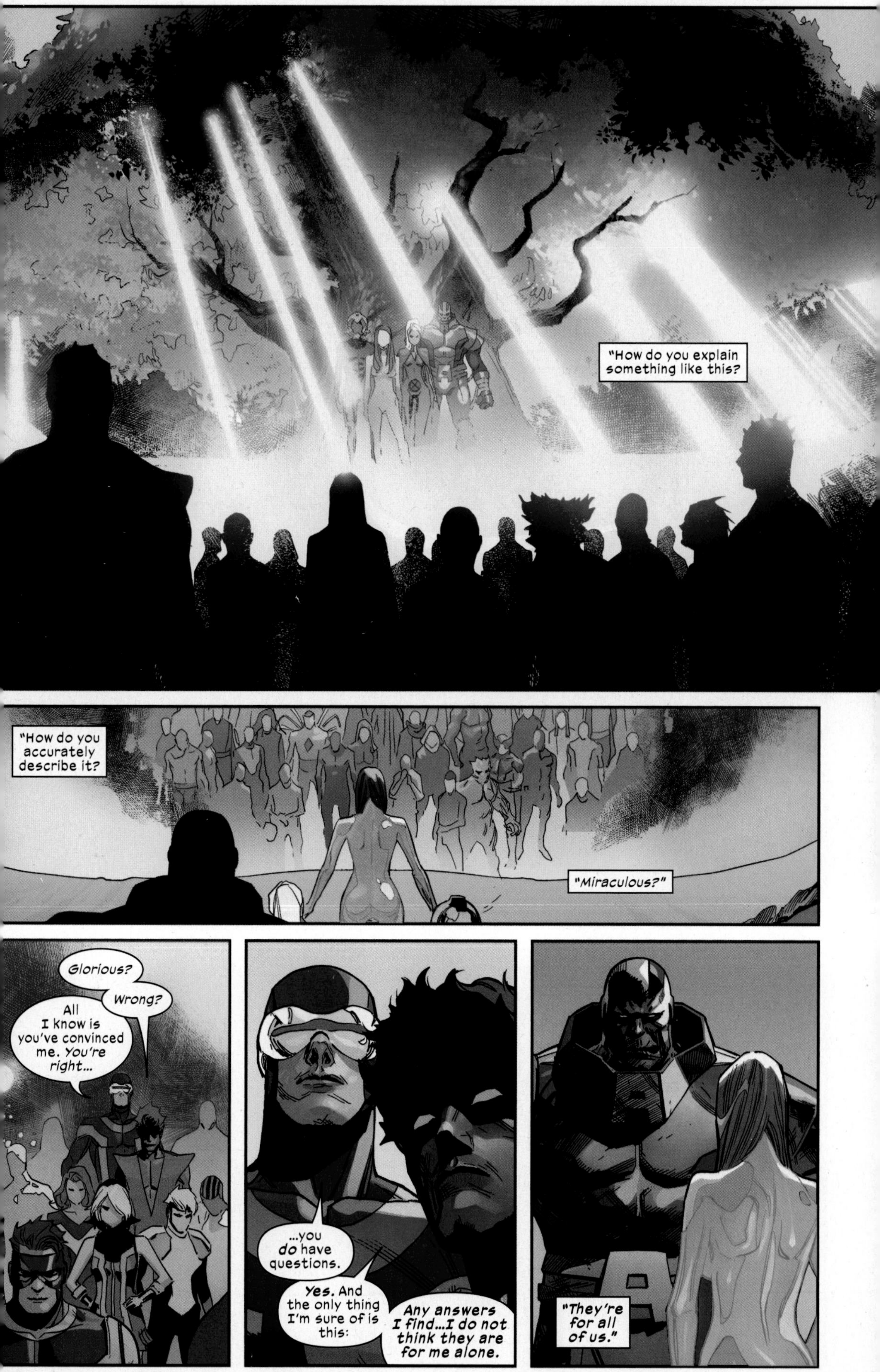

"How do you explain something like this?
"How do you accurately describe it?
"Miraculous?"
Glorious?
Wrong?
All I know is you've convinced me. *You're* right...
...you *do* have questions.
Yes. And the only thing I'm sure of is this:
Any answers I find...I do not think they are for me alone.
"They're for all of us."

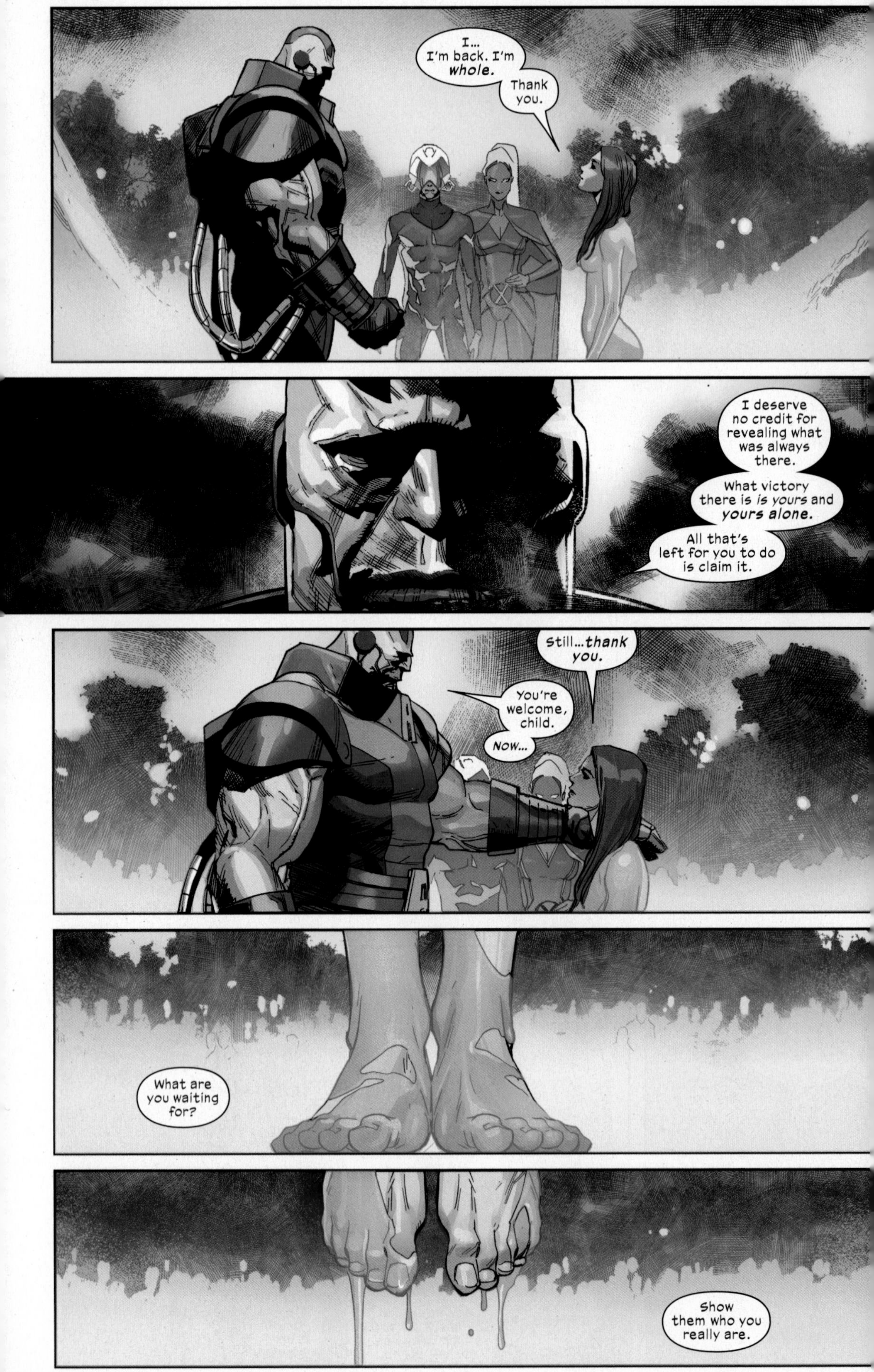
I... I'm back. I'm *whole.*
Thank you.
I deserve no credit for revealing what was always there.
What victory there is *is yours* and ***yours alone.***
All that's left for you to do is claim it.
Still...***thank you.***
You're welcome, child.
NOW...
What are you waiting for?
Show them who you really are.

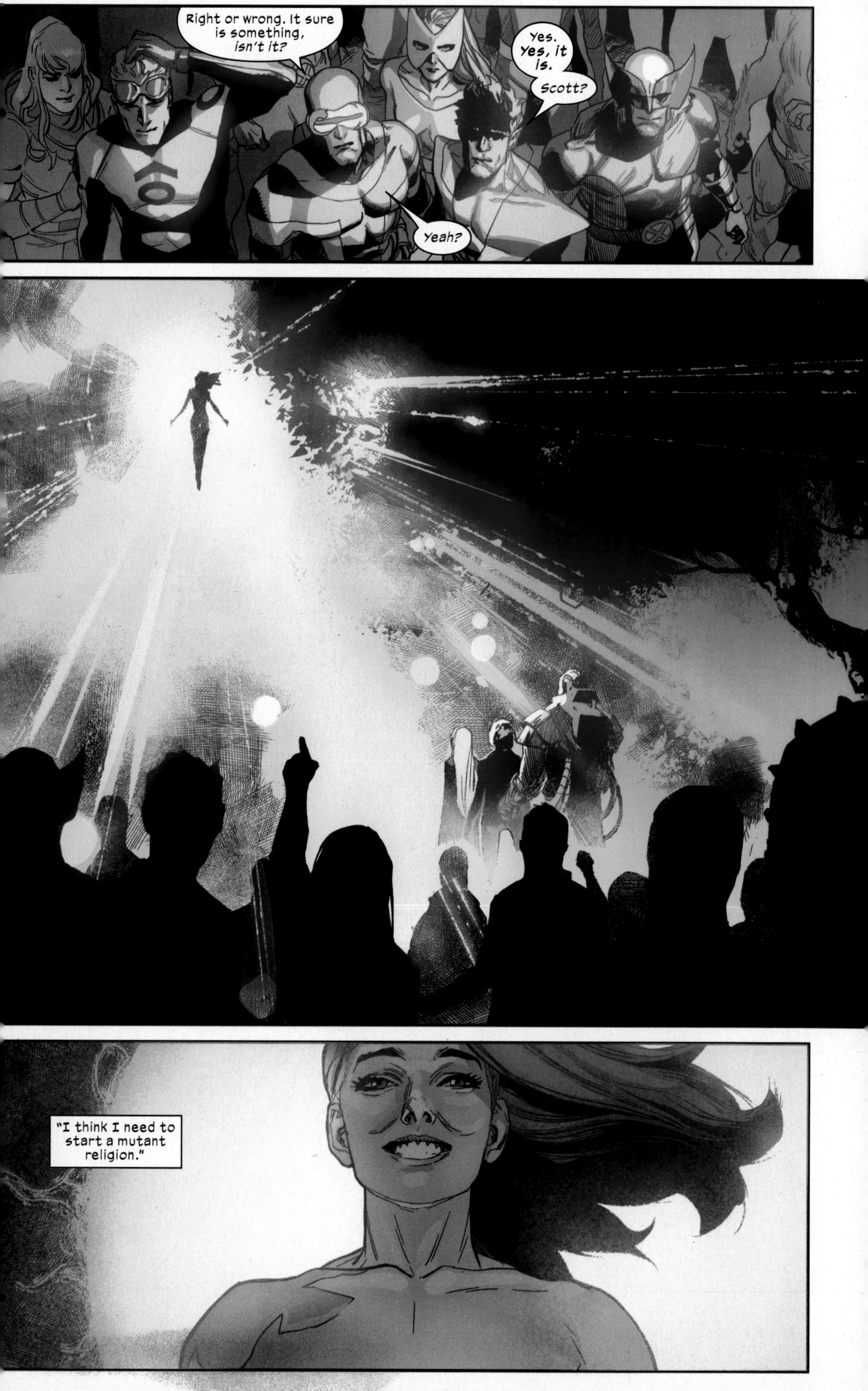
Right or wrong. It sure is something, isn't it?
Yes. Yes, it is.
Scott?
Yeah?
"I think I need to start a mutant religion."

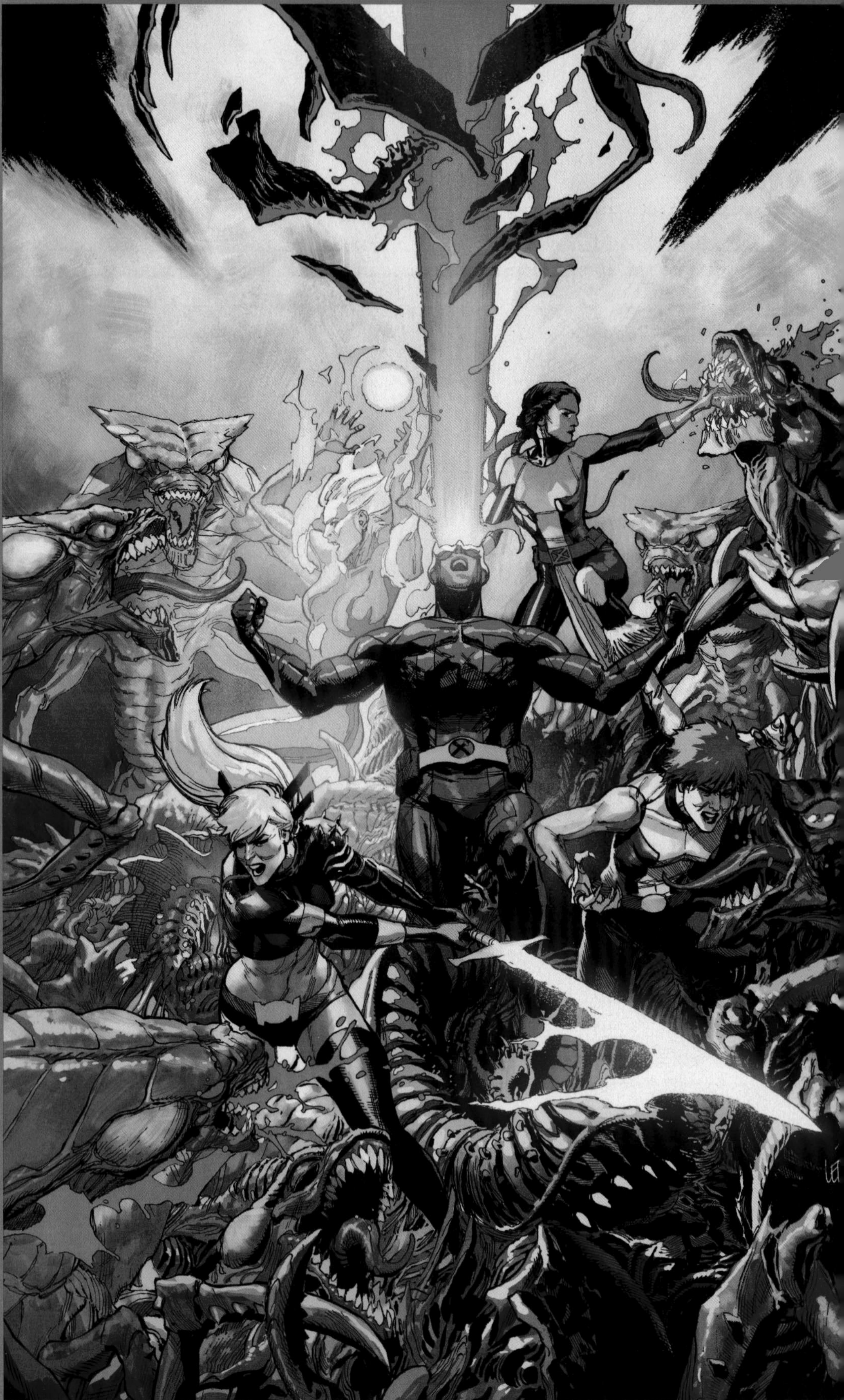

Swarm

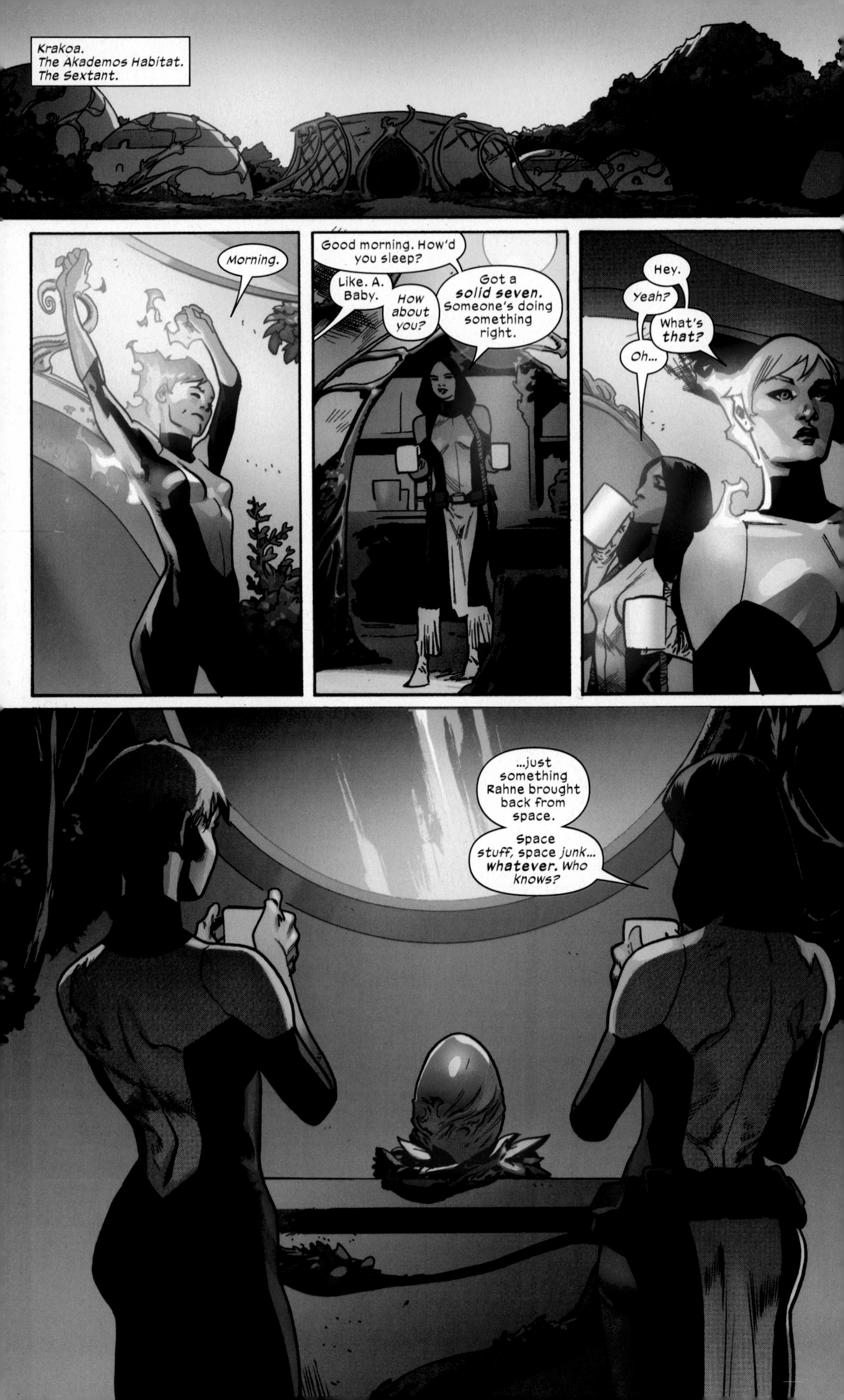
Krakoa.
The Akademos Habitat.
The Sextant.
Morning.
Good morning. How'd you sleep?
Like. A. Baby.
How about you?
Got a solid seven. Someone's doing something right.
Hey.
Yeah?
What's that?
Oh...
...just something Rahne brought back from space.
Space stuff, space junk... whatever. Who knows?

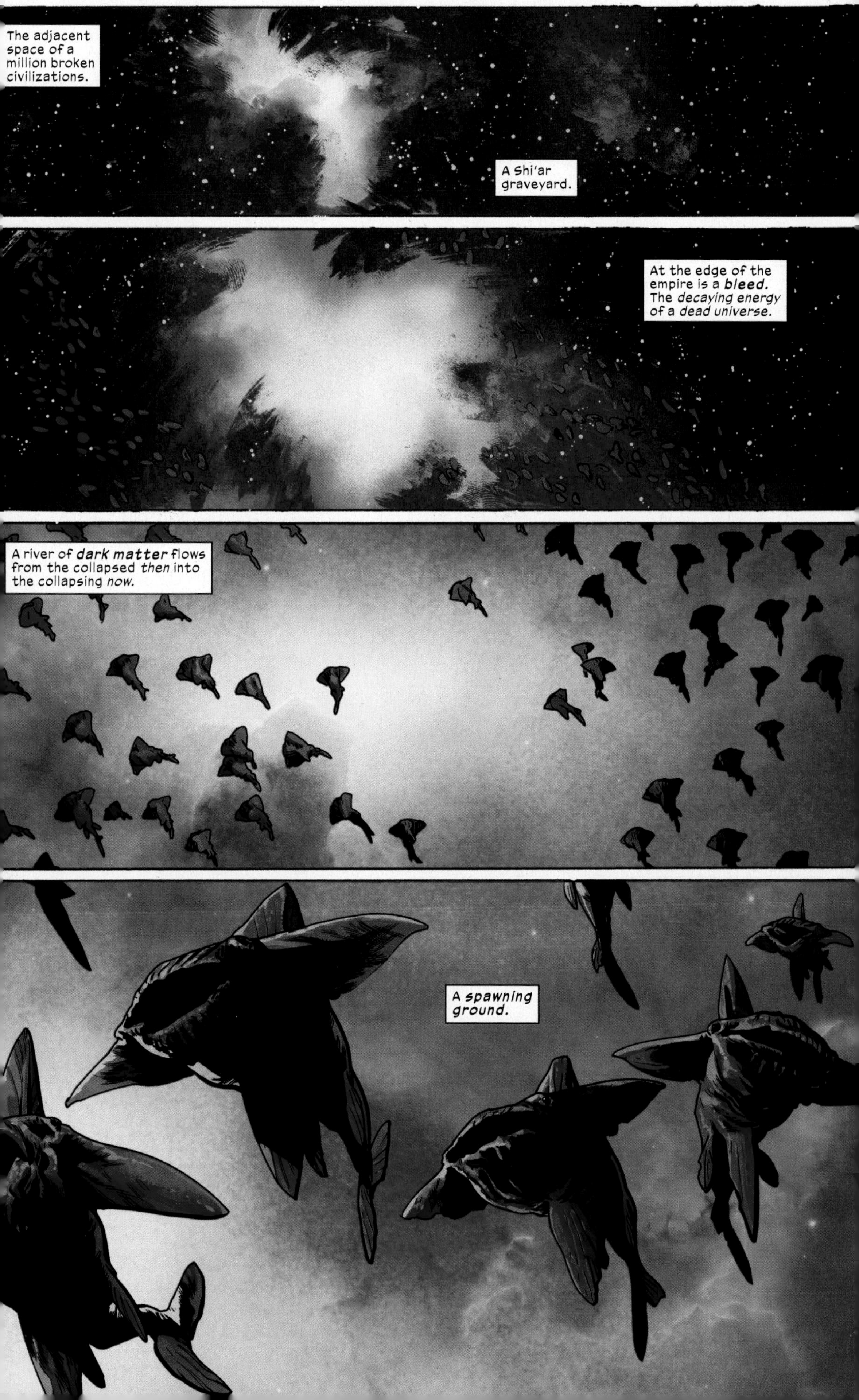
The adjacent space of a million broken civilizations.
A Shi'ar graveyard.
At the edge of the empire is a *bleed.* The *decaying energy* of a *dead universe.*
A river of *dark matter* flows from the collapsed *then* into the collapsing *now.*
A *spawning ground.*

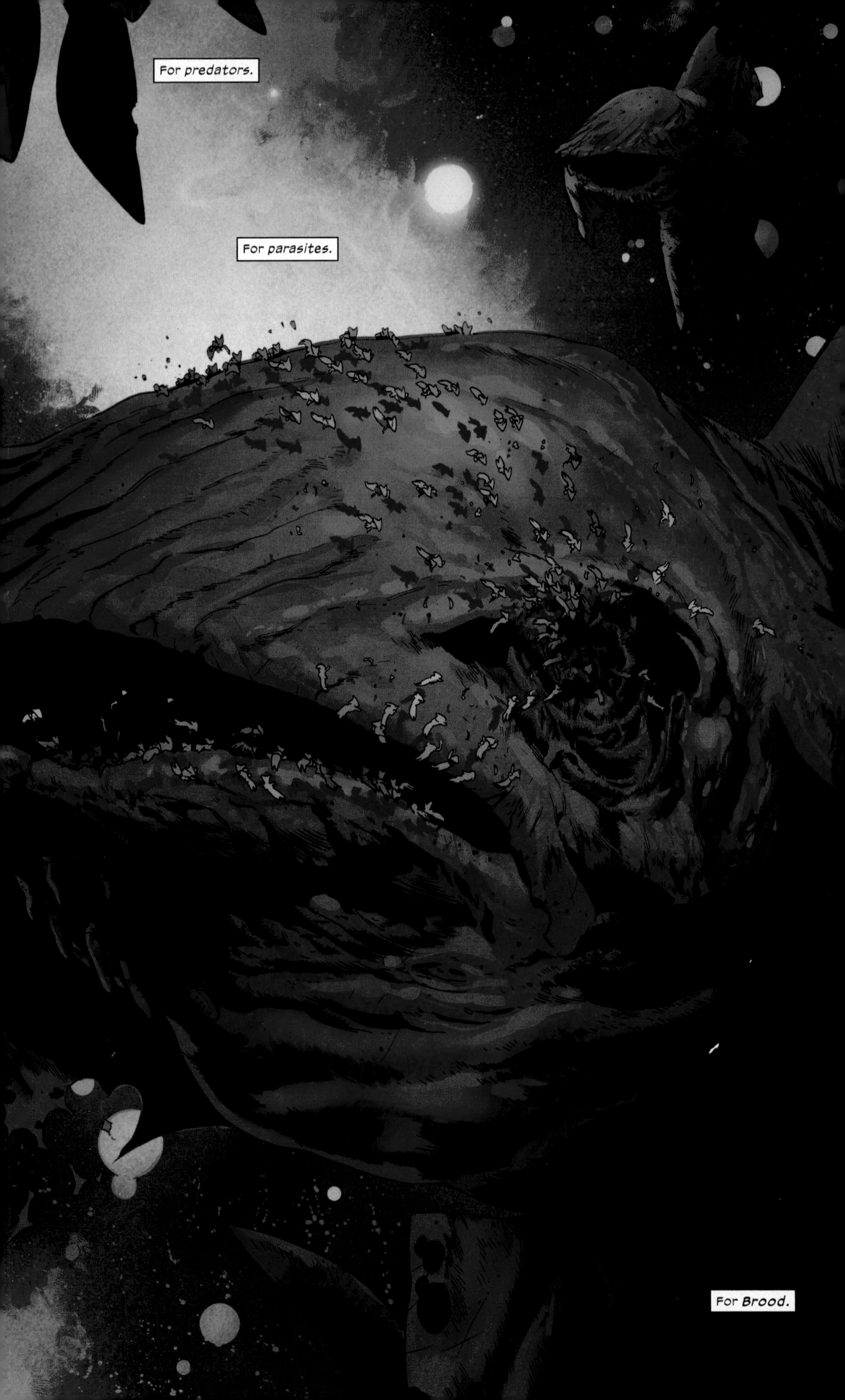
For predators.
For parasites.
For Brood.

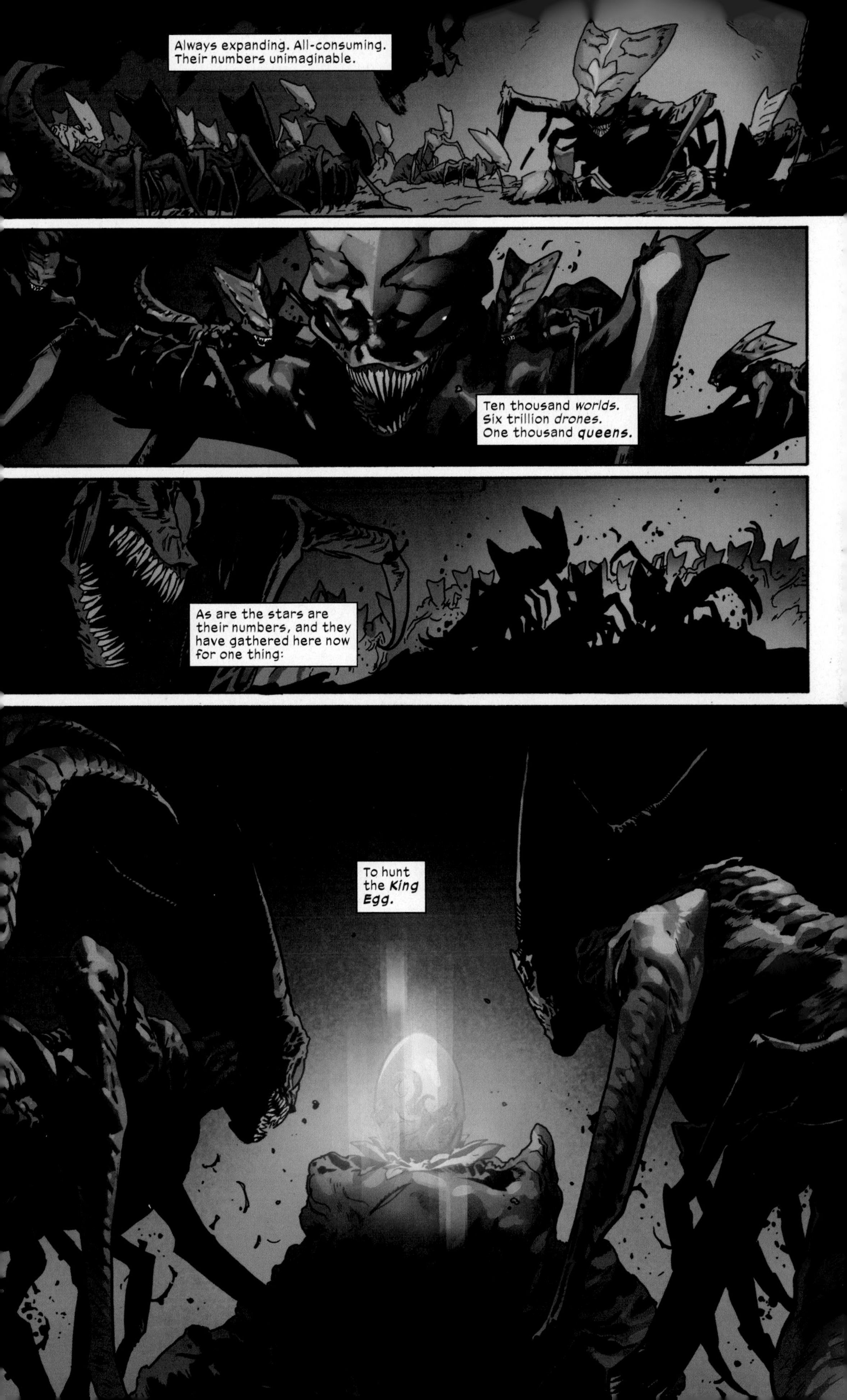
Always expanding. All-consuming. Their numbers unimaginable.
Ten thousand *worlds.* Six trillion *drones.* One thousand ***queens.***
As are the stars are their numbers, and they have gathered here now for one thing:
To hunt the ***King Egg.***

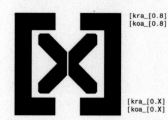

[kra_[0.8]
[koa_[0.8]

[kra_[0.X]
[koa_[0.X]

SOMETHING'S COMING

The New Mutants recently returned from
a mission in Shi'ar space... and they brought
more than memories back with them.

Wolfsbane

Mirage

Magma

Magik

Vulcan

Cyclops

Havok

Oya

Broo

Jean Grey

[kra_[0.8]...]
[koa_[0.8]...]

[A._New_World]

SHI'AR BATTLE RECORD

—

RE: THE FAULT

An after-action report of the events surrounding the War of Kings and the death of Lilandra Neramani.

[1]
GLADIATOR [Kallark]: Crowned Majestor of the empire after the death or exile of a Neramani heir. Former Superguardian and leader of the Imperial Guard.

—

[2]
BLACK BOLT [Blackagar Boltagon]: Killed at the conclusion of the war when a T-bomb detonated, ripping a hole in the fabric of space and time. This anomaly is known as the Fault, and nothing has ever escaped it.

—

[3]
VULCAN [Gabriel Summers]: Also killed at the conclusion of the war when the T-bomb detonated. VULCAN was also believed to have perished in the Fault.

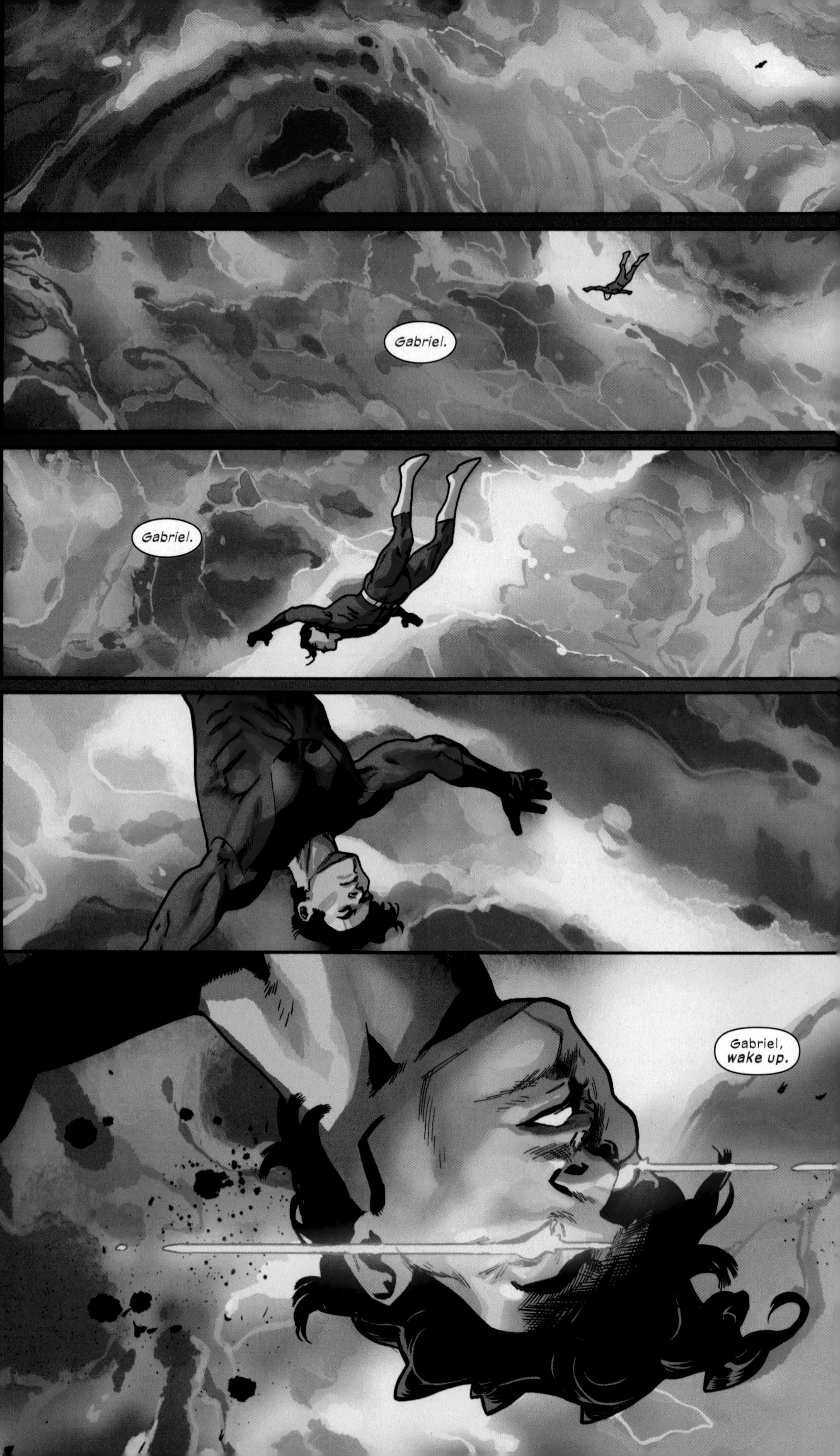
Gabriel.
Gabriel.
Gabriel,
wake up.

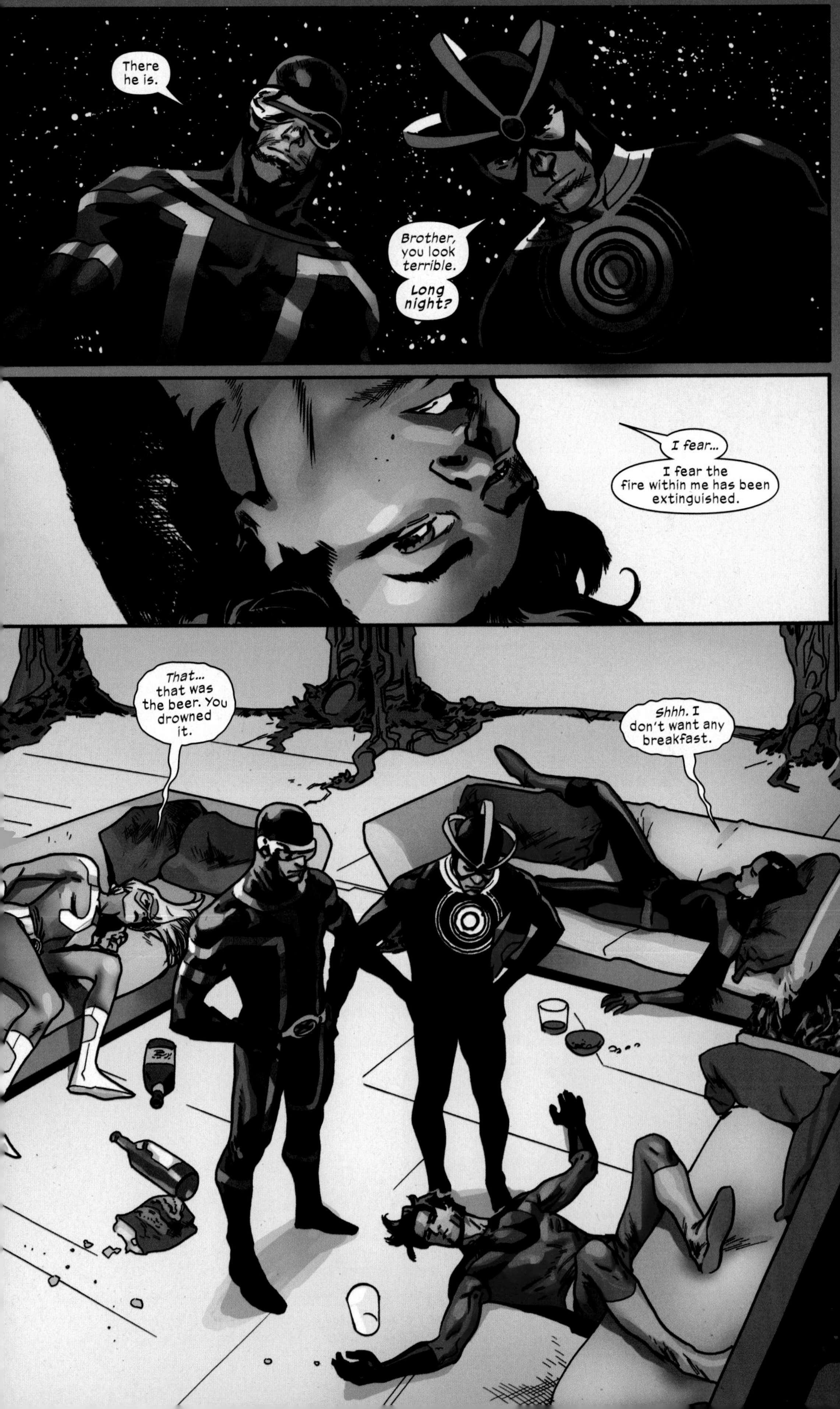
There he is.
Brother, you look terrible.
Long night?
I fear...
I fear the fire within me has been extinguished.
That... that was the beer. You drowned it.
Shhh. I don't want any breakfast.

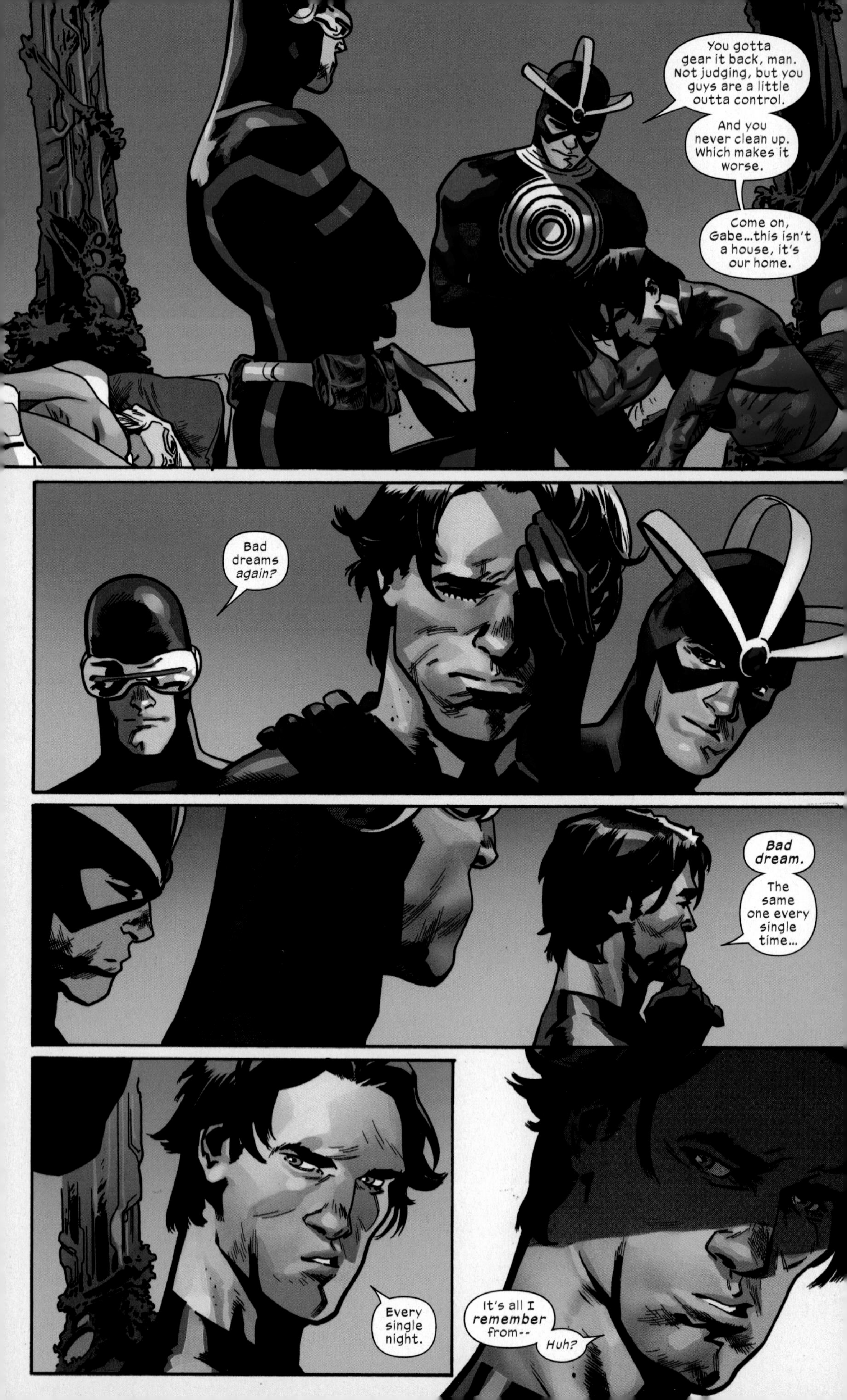
You gotta gear it back, man. Not judging, but you guys are a little outta control.
And you never clean up. Which makes it worse.
Come on, Gabe...this isn't a house, it's our home.
Bad dreams *again?*
Bad dream.
The same one every single time...
Every single night.
It's all I *remember* from--
Huh?

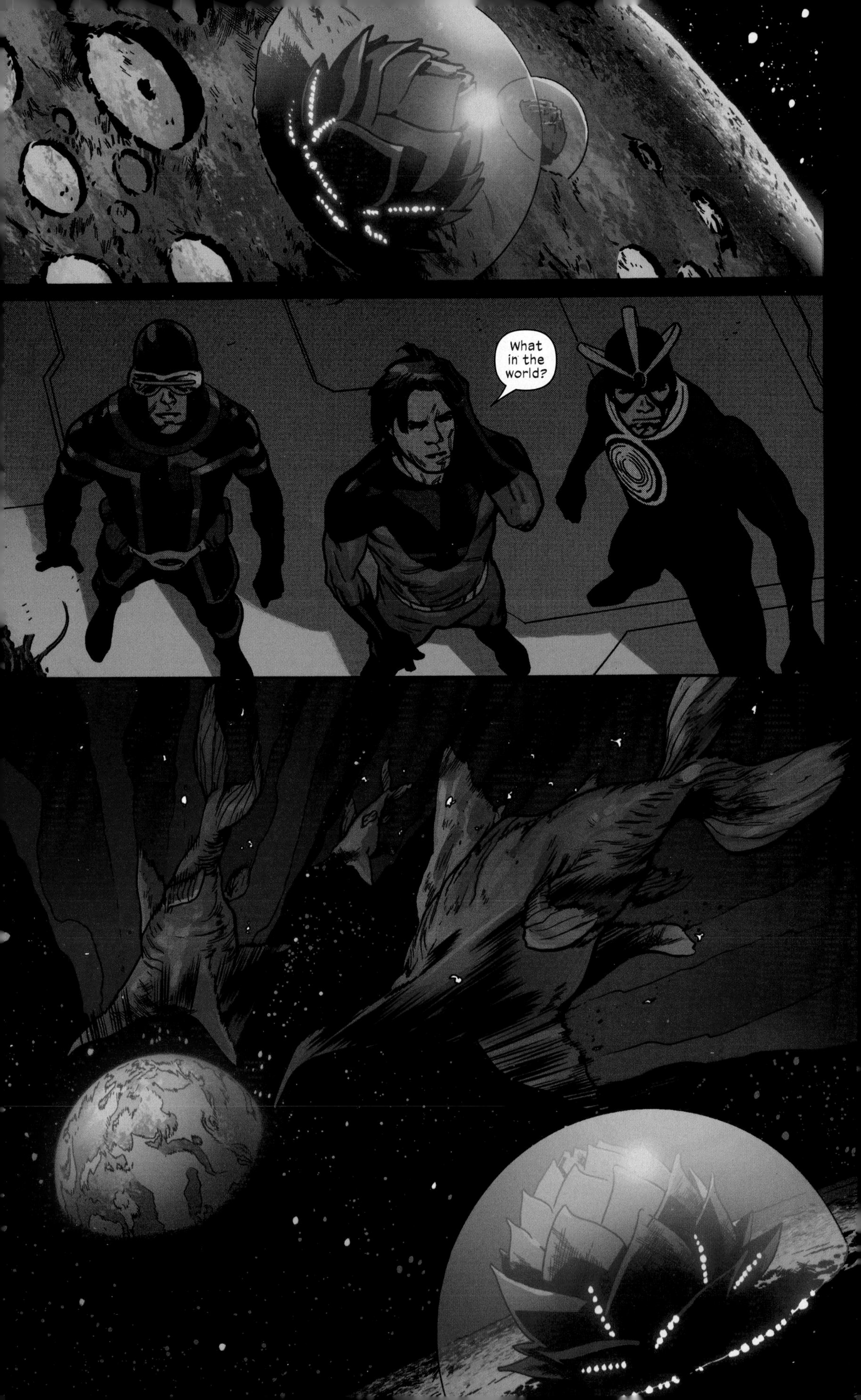
What in the world?

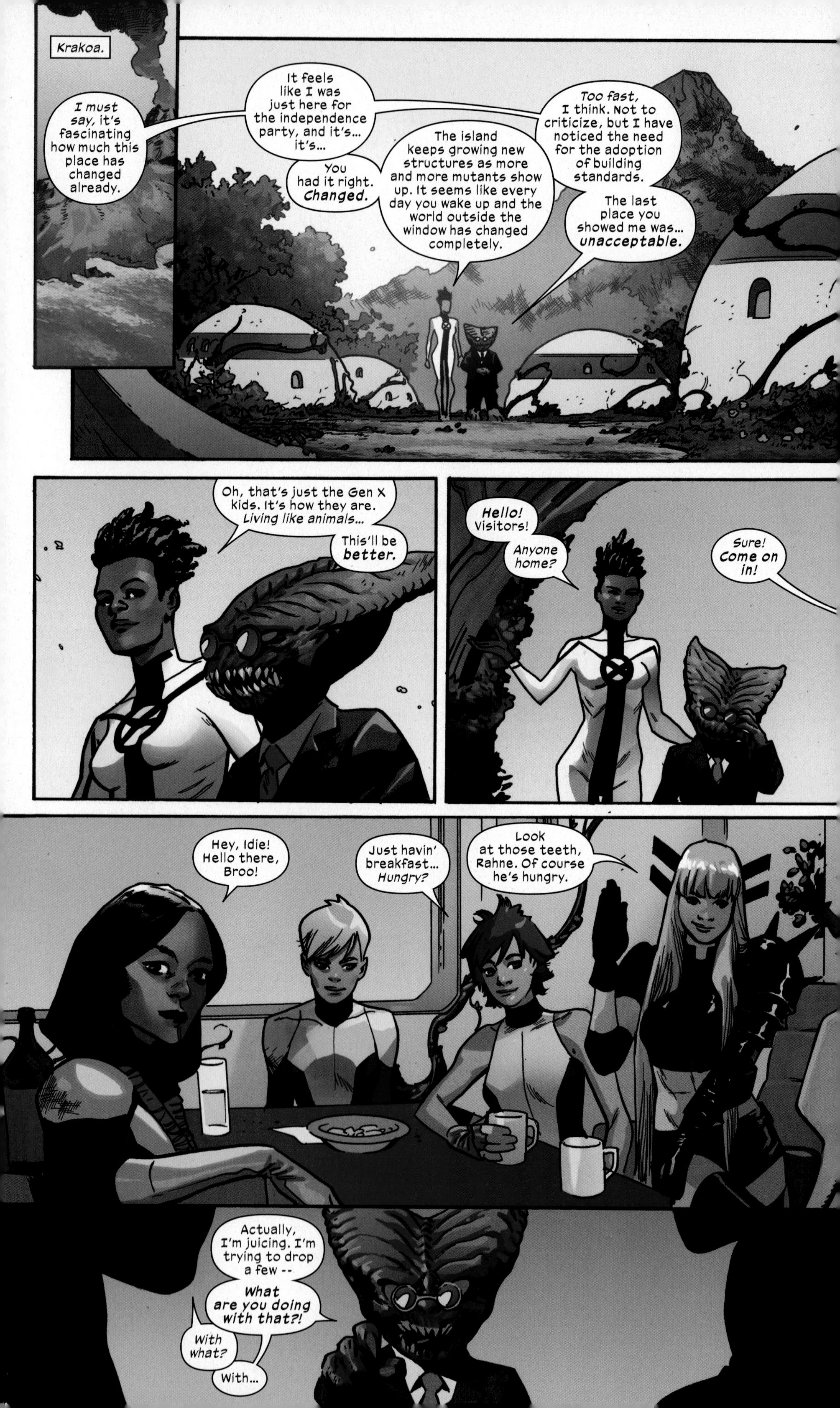

Krakoa.
I must say, it's fascinating how much this place has changed already.
It feels like I was just here for the independence party, and it's... it's...
You had it right. Changed.
The island keeps growing new structures as more and more mutants show up. It seems like every day you wake up and the world outside the window has changed completely.
Too fast, I think. Not to criticize, but I have noticed the need for the adoption of building standards.
The last place you showed me was... unacceptable.
Oh, that's just the Gen X kids. It's how they are. Living like animals...
This'll be better.
Hello! Visitors!
Anyone home?
Sure! Come on in!
Hey, Idie! Hello there, Broo!
Just havin' breakfast... Hungry?
Look at those teeth, Rahne. Of course he's hungry.
Actually, I'm juicing. I'm trying to drop a few --
What are you doing with that?!
With what?
With...

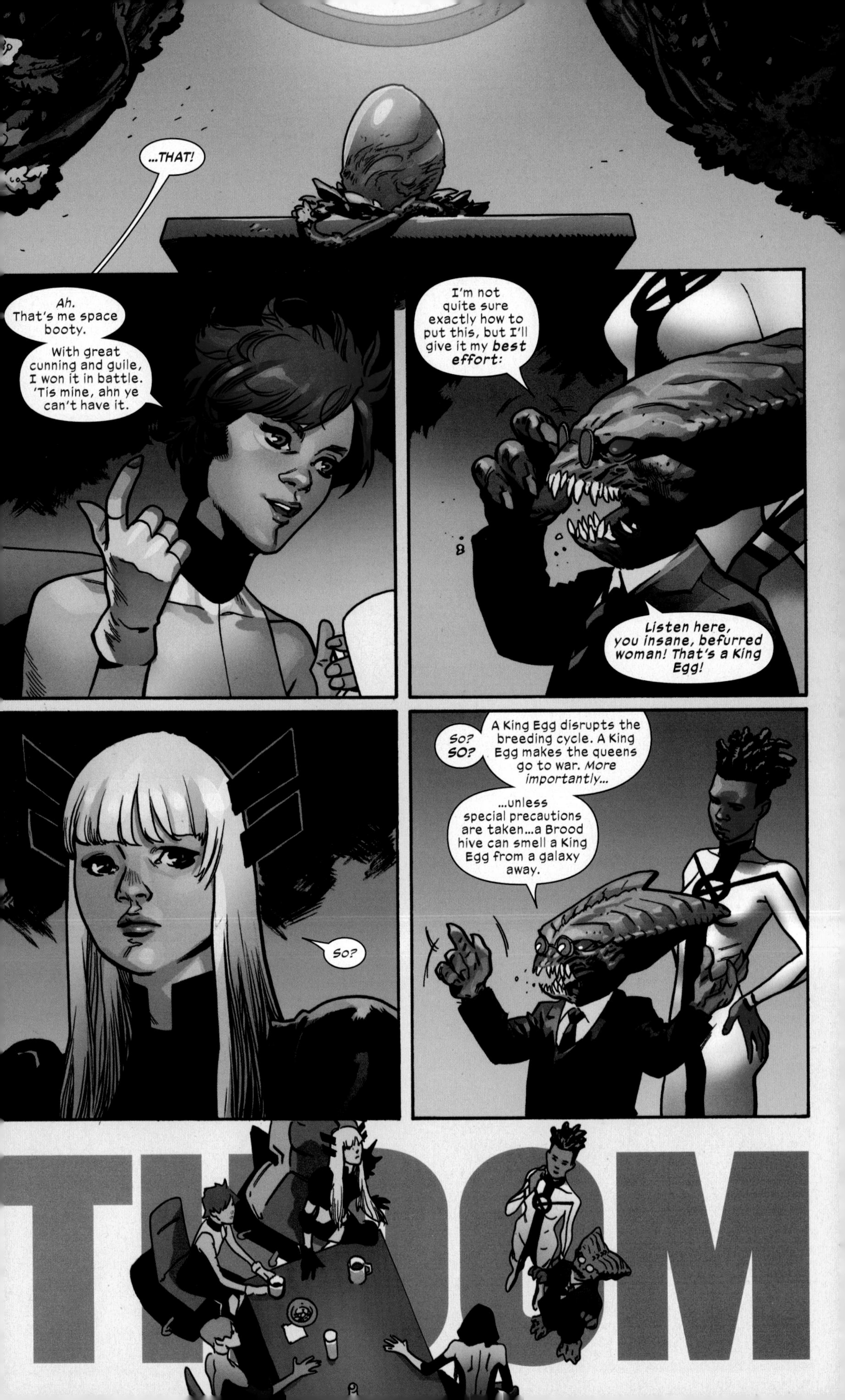
...THAT!
Ah. That's me space booty.
With great cunning and guile, I won it in battle. 'Tis mine, ahn ye can't have it.
I'm not quite sure exactly how to put this, but I'll give it my best effort:
Listen here, you insane, befurred woman! That's a King Egg!
So?
So? SO?
A King Egg disrupts the breeding cycle. A King Egg makes the queens go to war. More importantly...
...unless special precautions are taken...a Brood hive can smell a King Egg from a galaxy away.
THOOM

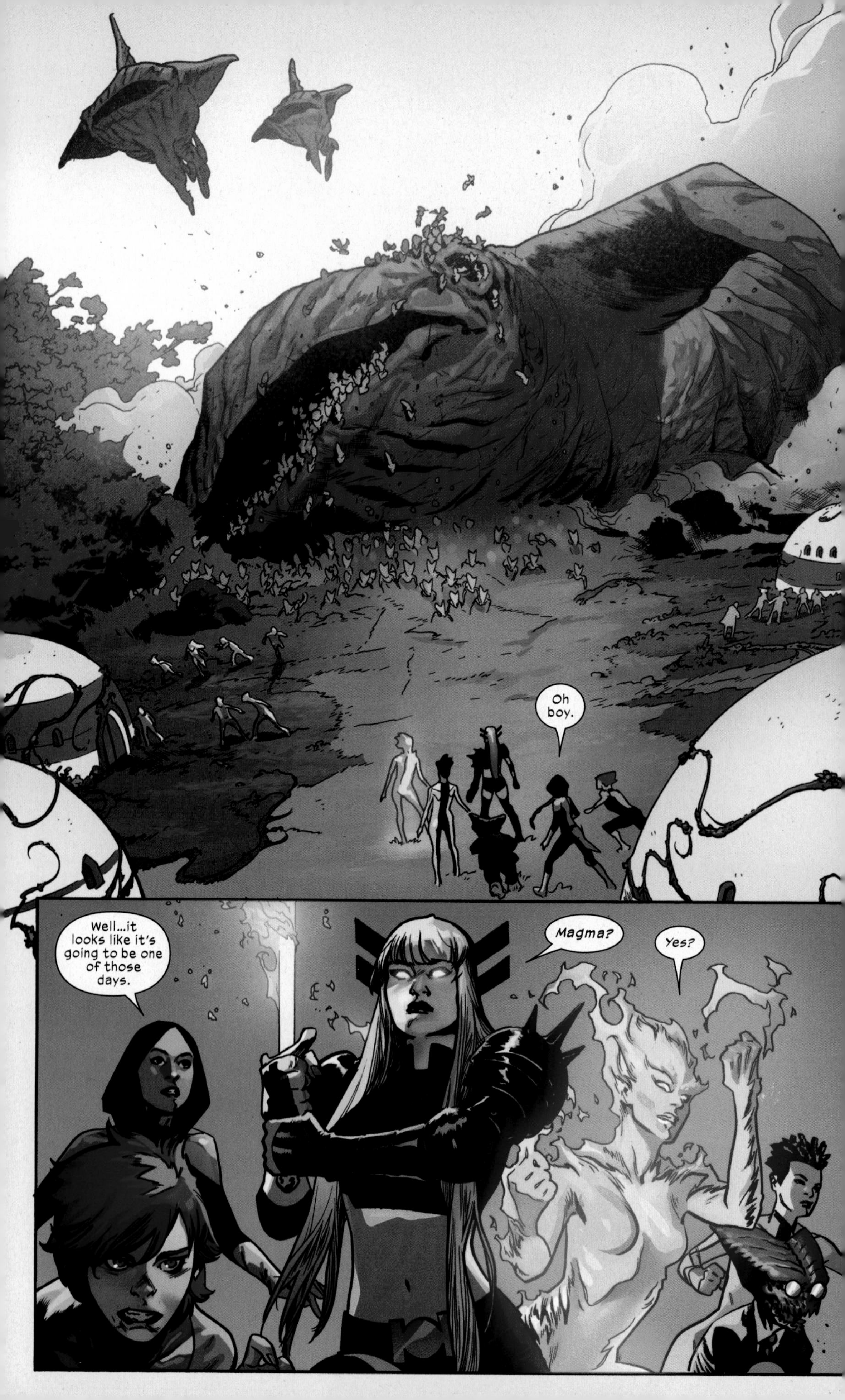
Oh boy.
Well...it looks like it's going to be one of those days.
Magma?
Yes?

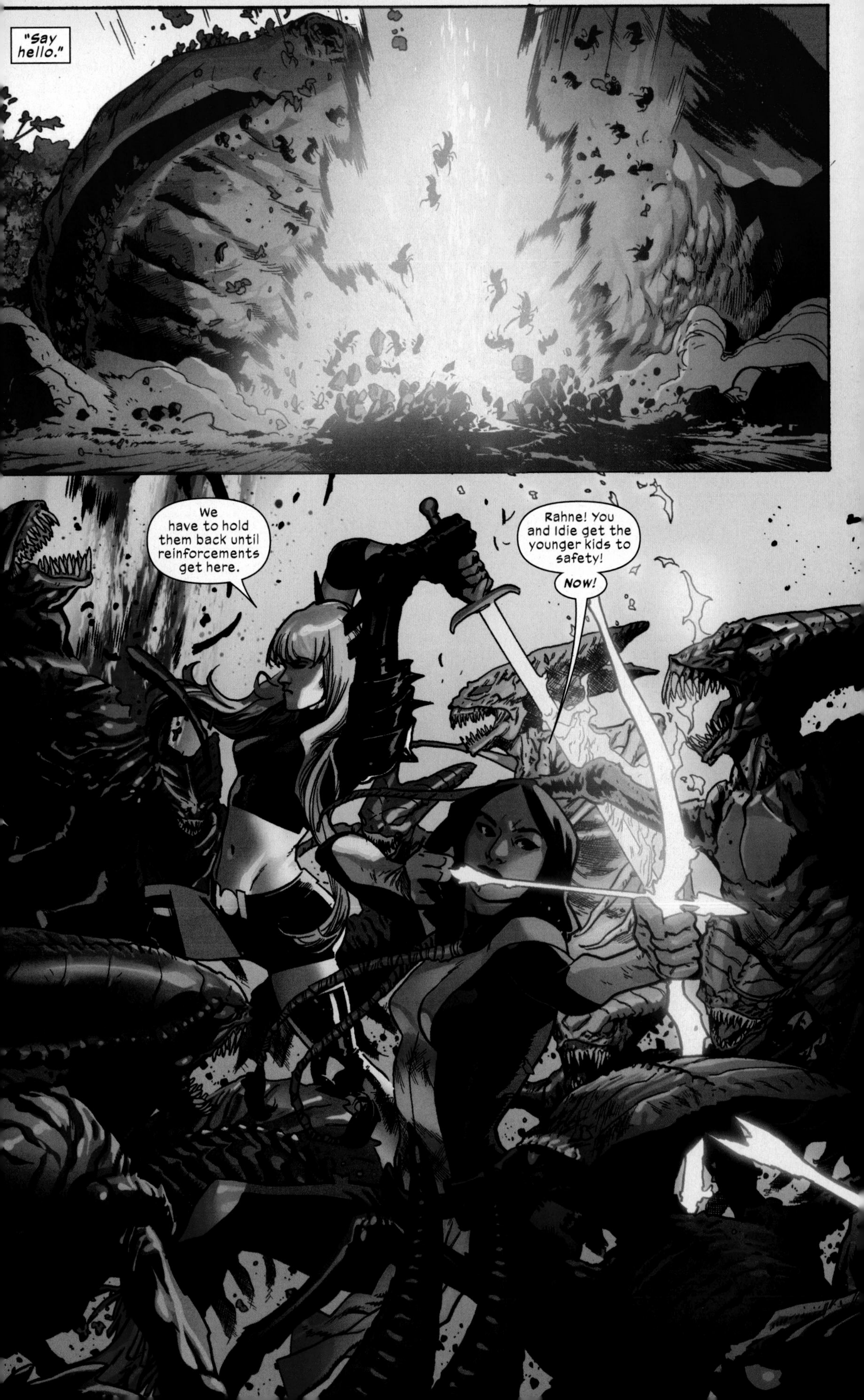
"Say hello."
We have to hold them back until reinforcements get here.
Rahne! You and Idie get the younger kids to safety!
NOW!

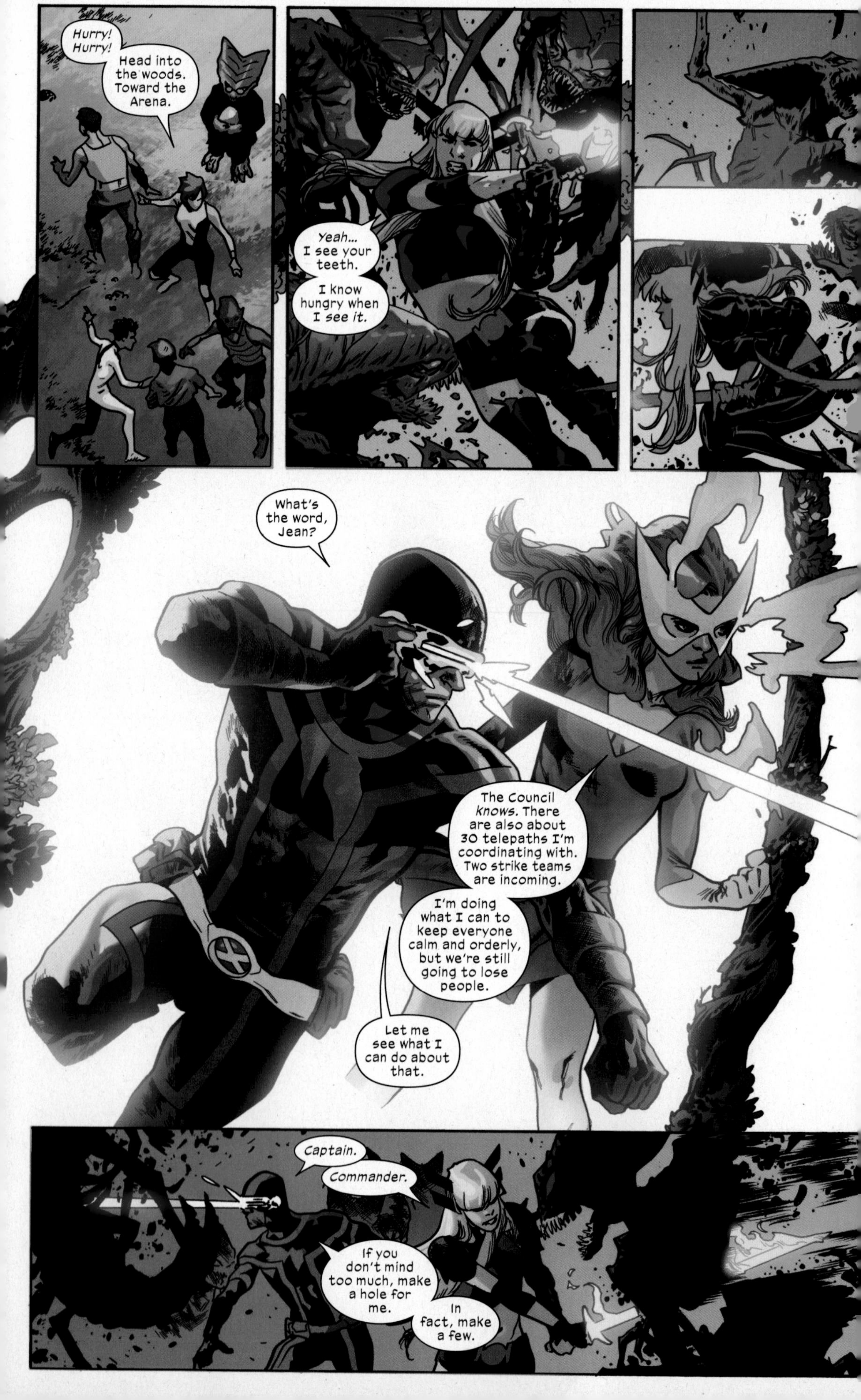
Hurry! Hurry!
Head into the woods. Toward the Arena.
Yeah... I see your teeth.
I know hungry when I see it.
What's the word, Jean?
The Council knows. There are also about 30 telepaths I'm coordinating with. Two strike teams are incoming.
I'm doing what I can to keep everyone calm and orderly, but we're still going to lose people.
Let me see what I can do about that.
Captain.
Commander.
If you don't mind too much, make a hole for me.
In fact, make a few.

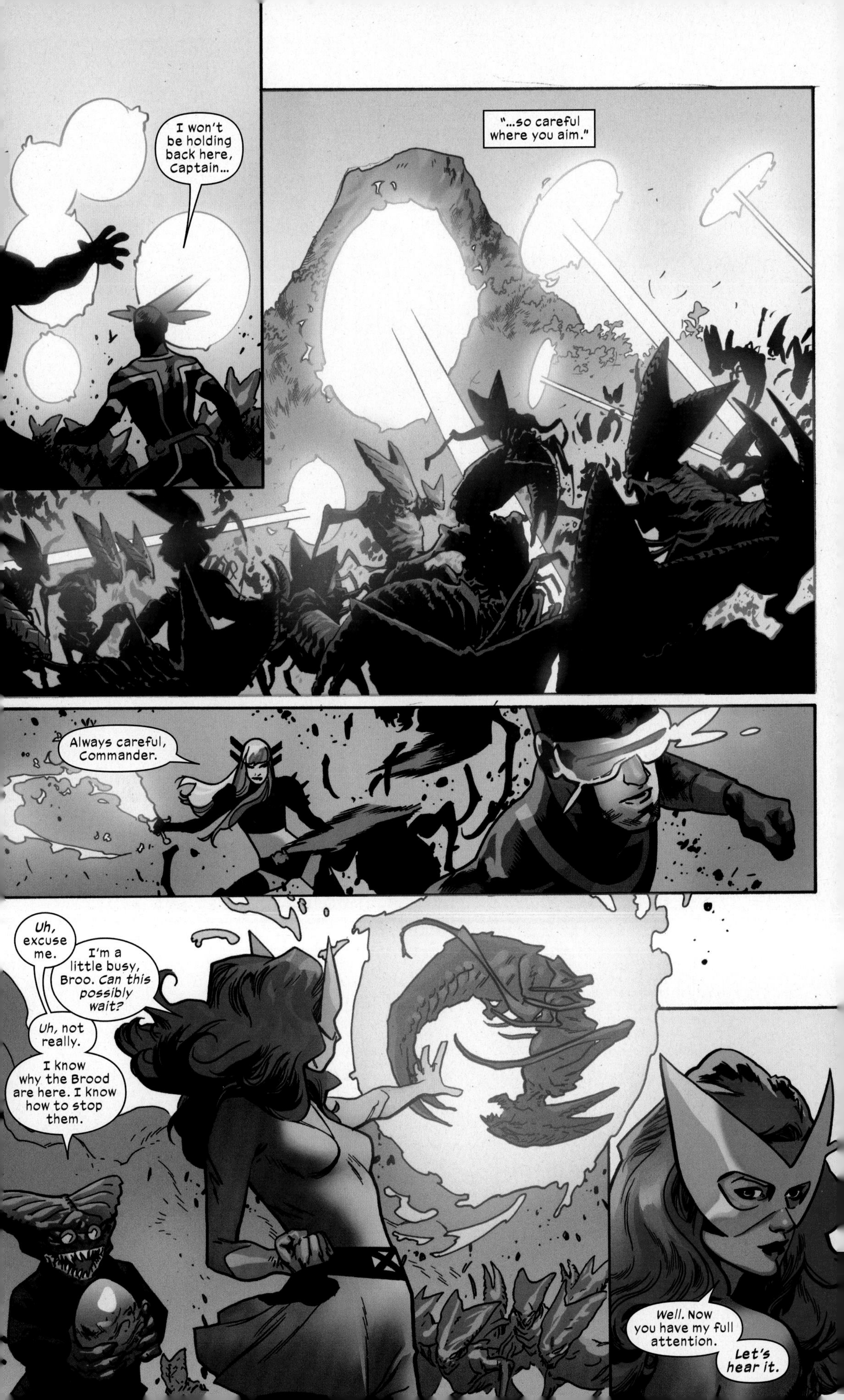
I won't be holding back here, Captain...
"...so careful where you aim."
Always careful, Commander.
Uh, excuse me.
I'm a little busy, Broo. Can this possibly wait?
Uh, not really.
I know why the Brood are here. I know how to stop them.
Well. Now you have my full attention.
Let's hear it.

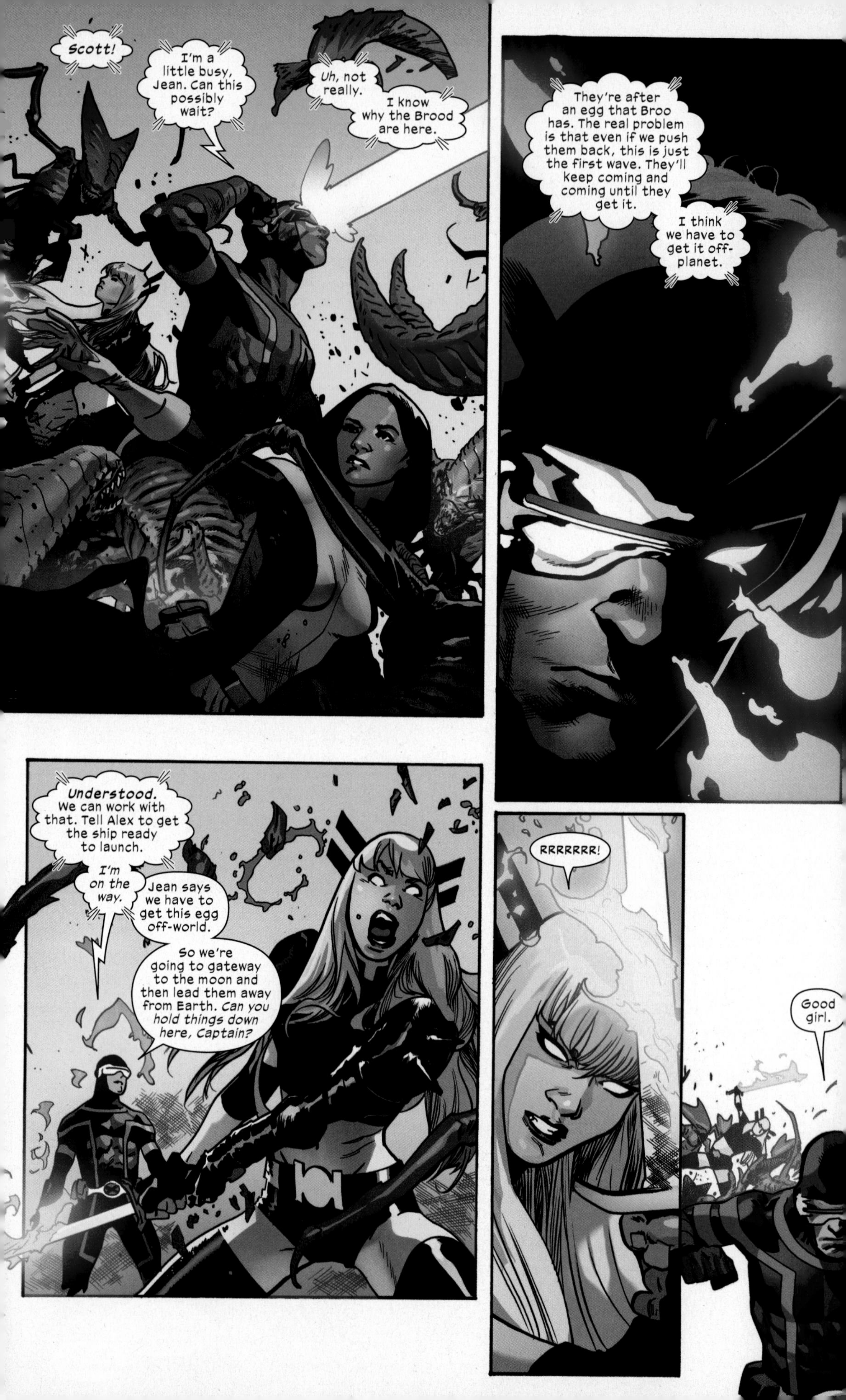
Scott!
I'm a little busy, Jean. Can this possibly wait?
Uh, not really.
I know why the Brood are here.
They're after an egg that Broo has. The real problem is that even if we push them back, this is just the first wave. They'll keep coming and coming until they get it.
I think we have to get it off-planet.
Understood. We can work with that. Tell Alex to get the ship ready to launch.
I'm on the way.
Jean says we have to get this egg off-world.
So we're going to gateway to the moon and then lead them away from Earth. Can you hold things down here, Captain?
RRRRRRR!
Good girl.

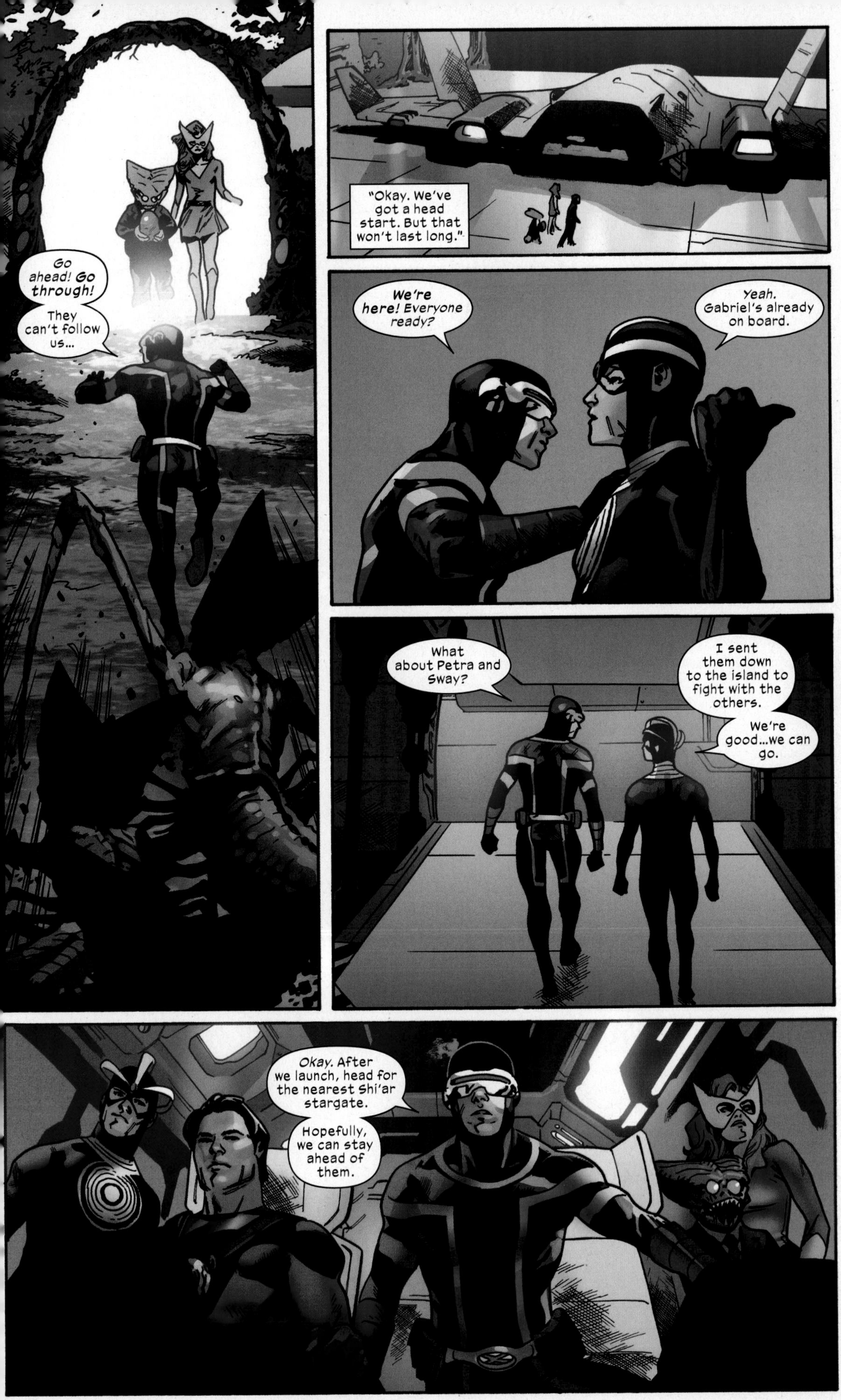

Go ahead! Go through!
They can't follow us...
"Okay. We've got a head start. But that won't last long."
We're here! Everyone ready?
Yeah. Gabriel's already on board.
What about Petra and Sway?
I sent them down to the island to fight with the others.
We're good...we can go.
Okay. After we launch, head for the nearest Shi'ar stargate.
Hopefully, we can stay ahead of them.

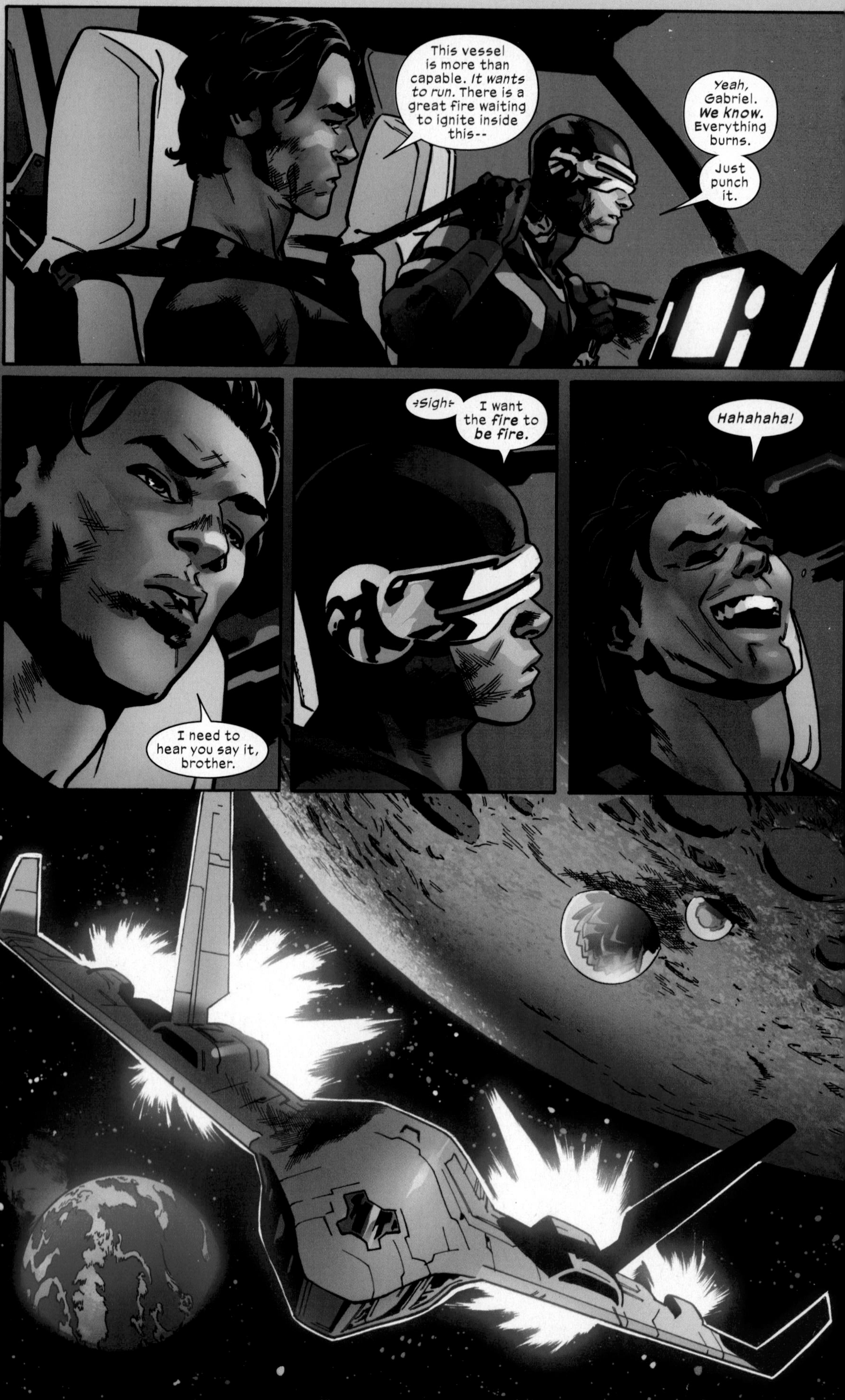
This vessel is more than capable. *It wants to run.* There is a great fire waiting to ignite inside this--
Yeah, Gabriel. ***We know.*** Everything burns.
Just punch it.
I need to hear you say it, brother.
Sigh
I want the *fire* to ***be fire.***
Hahahaha!

[00.SHI'AR........B]
[00...............R]

SHI'AR BATTLE RECORD

[Empire]...............[BR]
[......]...............[UP]

RE[redacted]E FAULT

An[redacted]r-action report of the events surrounding the War of Kings an[redacted] death of Lilandra Neramani.

[1[redacted]
GL[redacted]TOR [Kallark]: Crowned Majestor of the empire after the [redacted]or exile of a Neramani heir. Former Superguardian and [redacted] of the Imperial Guard.

UPDATE: GLADIATOR has recently signaled his desire to surrender the imperial throne to Xandra Neramani, the genetic offspring of Lilandra Neramani and Charles Xavier.

[2]
BLACK BOLT [Blackagar Boltagon]: Killed at the conclusion of the war when a T-bomb detonated, ripping a hole in the fabric of space and time. This anomaly is known as the Fault, and nothing has ever escaped it.

UPDATE: He does not speak, so no one knows exactly how BLACK BOLT escaped from the Fault. Some say he died and returned as the MIDNIGHT KING. Others know better and understand the power of genetic prophecy. The will of a celestial messiah cannot be denied.

[3]
VULCAN [Gabriel Summers]: Also killed at the conclusion of the war when the T-bomb detonated. VULCAN was also believed to have perished in the Fault.

UPDATE: VULCAN never died.

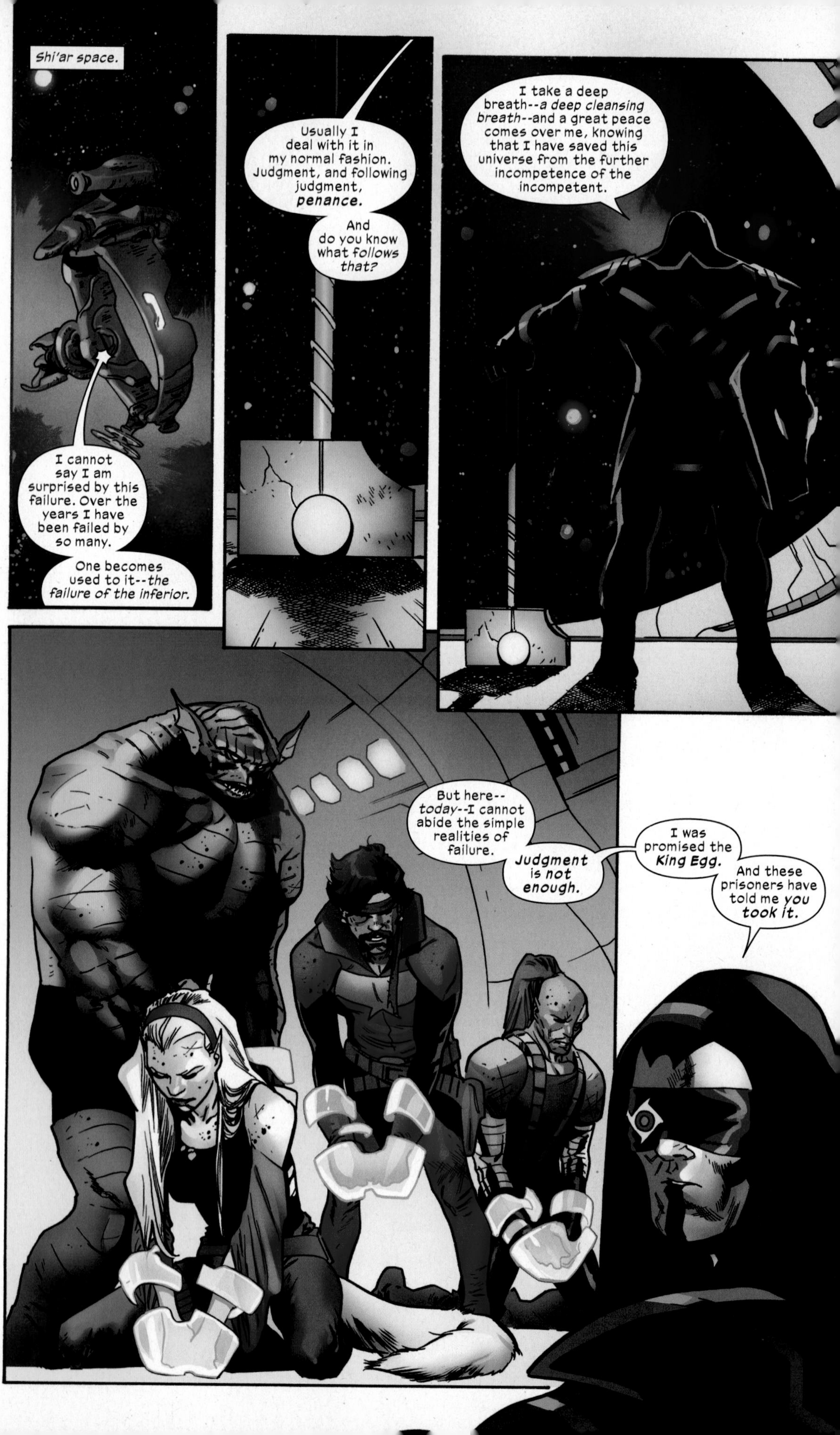
Shi'ar space.
I cannot say I am surprised by this failure. Over the years I have been failed by so many.
One becomes used to it--*the failure of the inferior.*
Usually I deal with it in my normal fashion. Judgment, and following judgment, **penance.**
And do you know what *follows* that?
I take a deep breath--*a deep cleansing breath*--and a great peace comes over me, knowing that I have saved this universe from the further incompetence of the incompetent.
But here--*today*--I cannot abide the simple realities of failure.
Judgment is **not enough.**
I was promised the **King Egg.**
And these prisoners have told me *you* **took it.**

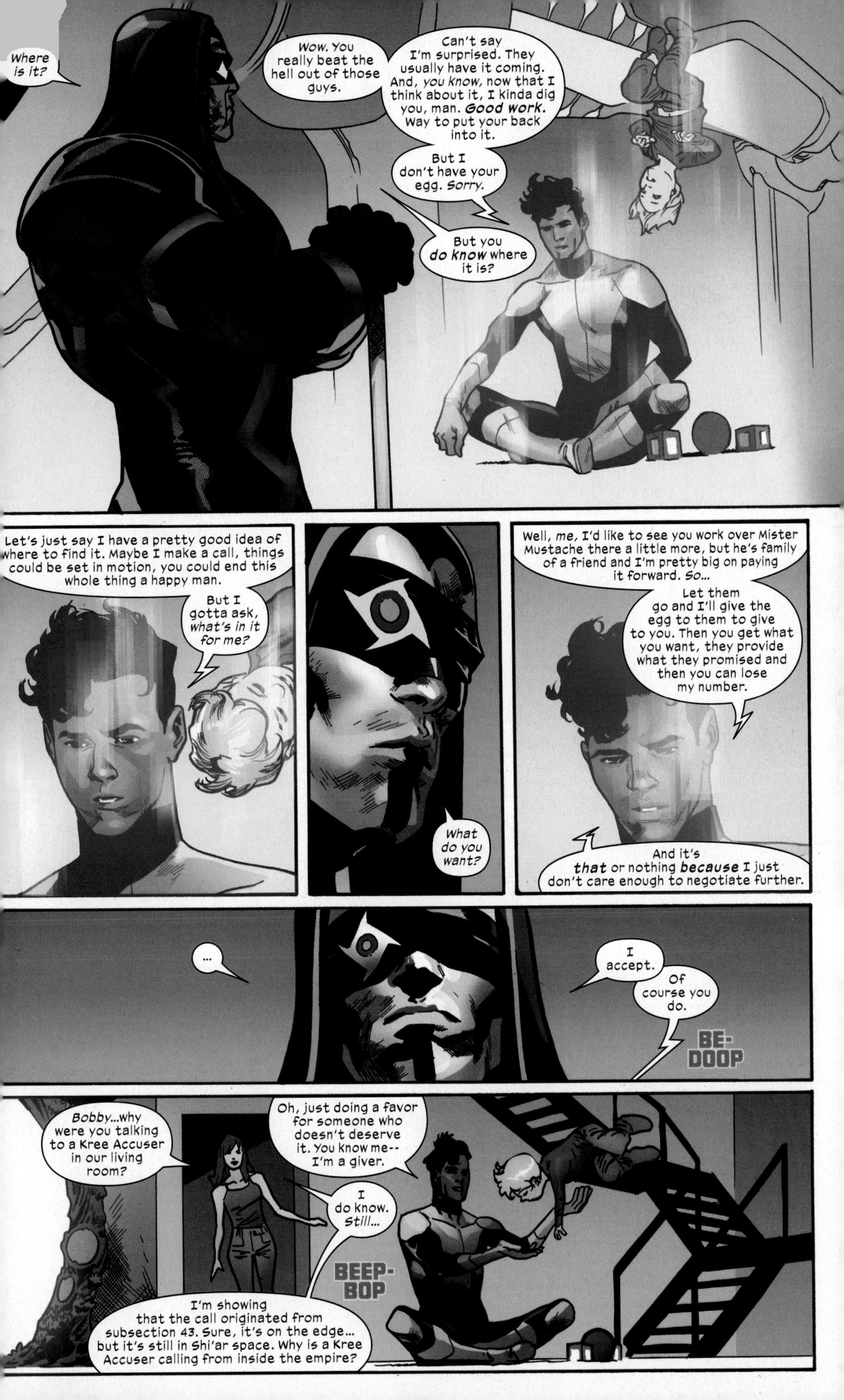

Where is it?
Wow. You really beat the hell out of those guys.
Can't say I'm surprised. They usually have it coming. And, you know, now that I think about it, I kinda dig you, man. Good work. Way to put your back into it.
But I don't have your egg. Sorry.
But you do know where it is?
Let's just say I have a pretty good idea of where to find it. Maybe I make a call, things could be set in motion, you could end this whole thing a happy man.
But I gotta ask, what's in it for me?
What do you want?
Well, me, I'd like to see you work over Mister Mustache there a little more, but he's family of a friend and I'm pretty big on paying it forward. So...
Let them go and I'll give the egg to them to give to you. Then you get what you want, they provide what they promised and then you can lose my number.
And it's that or nothing because I just don't care enough to negotiate further.
...
I accept.
Of course you do.
BE-DOOP
Bobby...why were you talking to a Kree Accuser in our living room?
Oh, just doing a favor for someone who doesn't deserve it. You know me-- I'm a giver.
I do know. Still...
BEEP-BOP
I'm showing that the call originated from subsection 43. Sure, it's on the edge... but it's still in Shi'ar space. Why is a Kree Accuser calling from inside the empire?

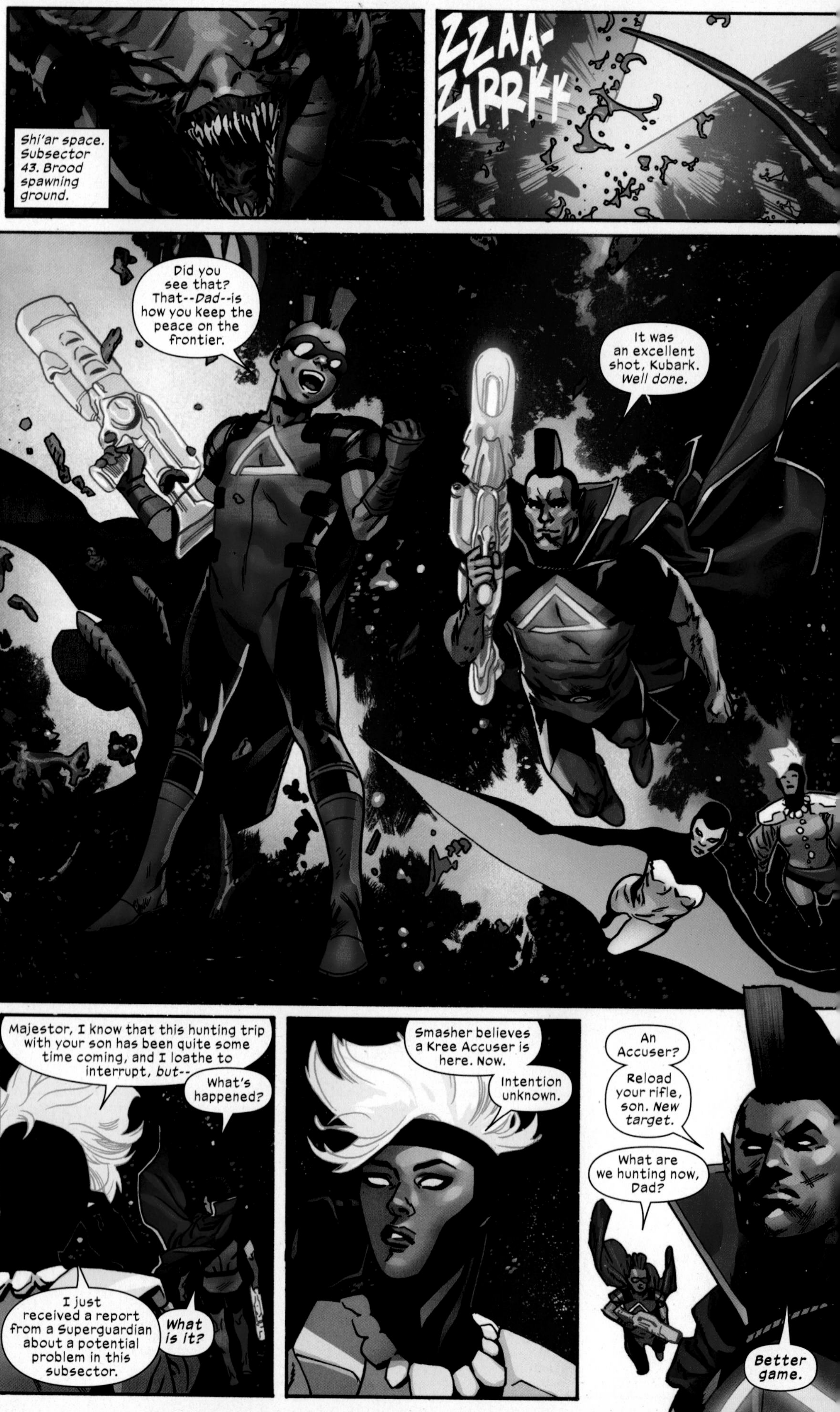
Shi'ar space. Subsector 43. Brood spawning ground.
ZZAA-ZARRKK
Did you see that? That--Dad--is how you keep the peace on the frontier.
It was an excellent shot, Kubark. Well done.
Majestor, I know that this hunting trip with your son has been quite some time coming, and I loathe to interrupt, but--
What's happened?
I just received a report from a Superguardian about a potential problem in this subsector.
What is it?
Smasher believes a Kree Accuser is here. Now.
Intention unknown.
An Accuser?
Reload your rifle, son. New target.
What are we hunting now, Dad?
Better game.

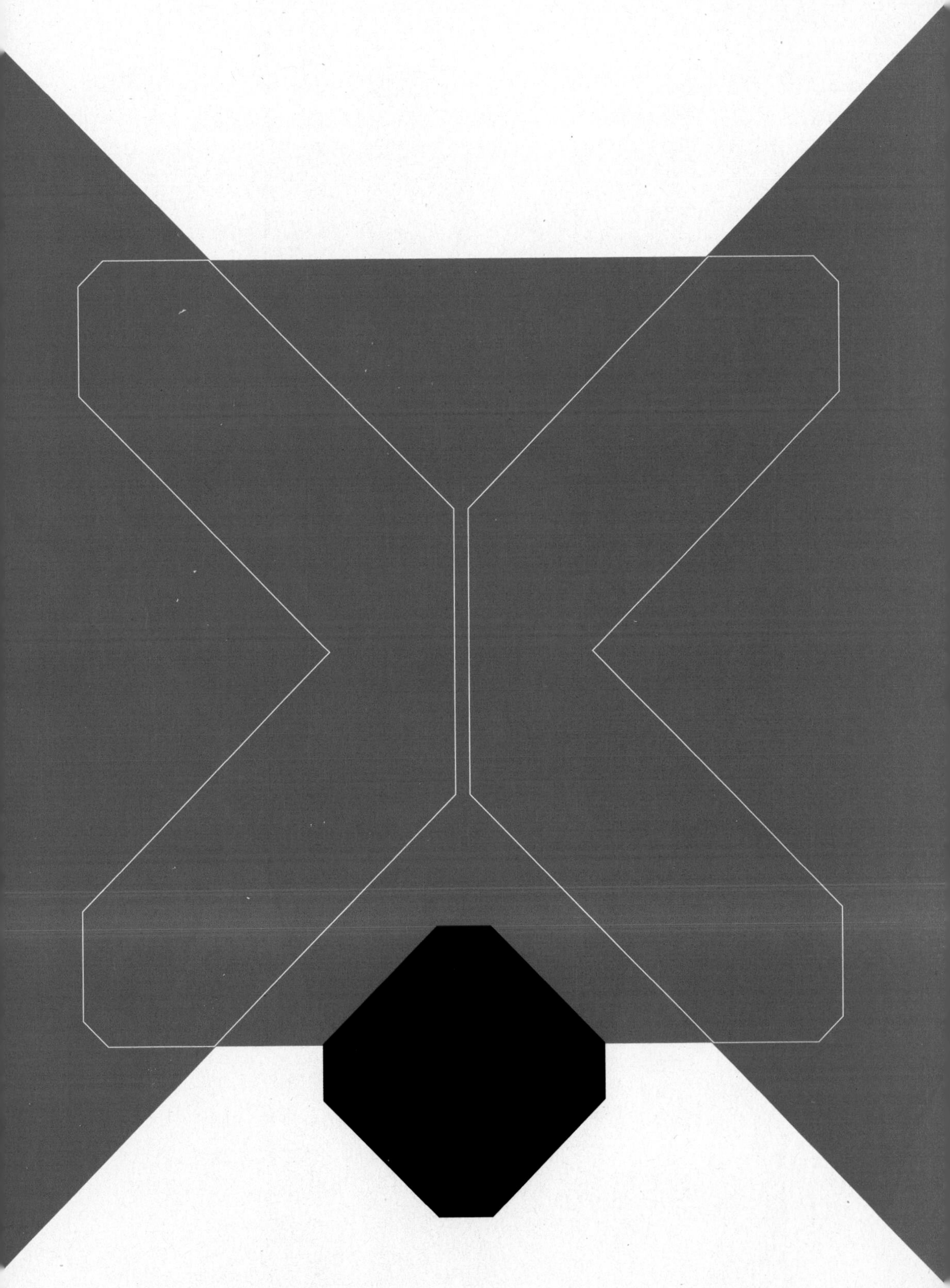

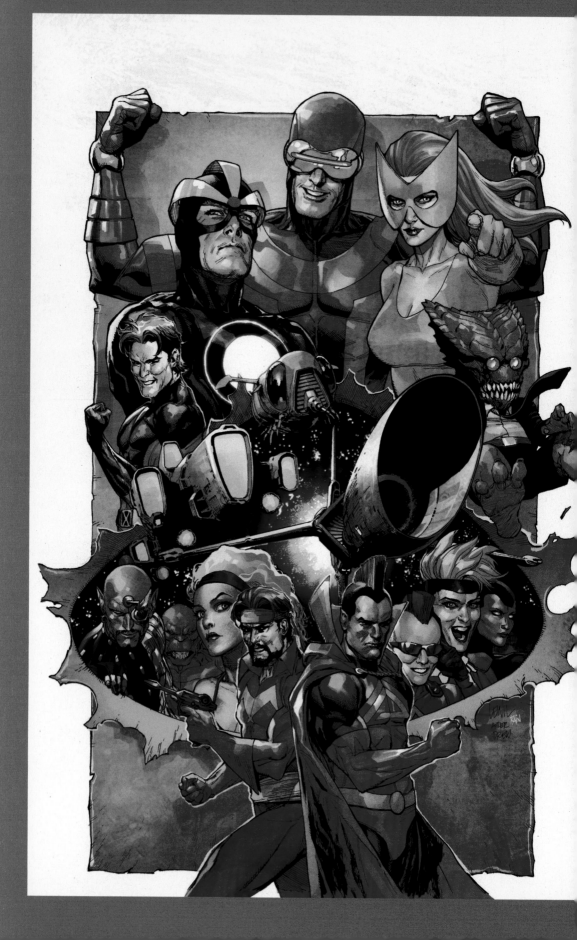

The King Egg

Then.
Hala.
The Kree Empire.

Where did you find them?

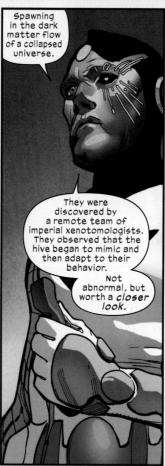

Spawning in the dark matter flow of a collapsed universe.

They were discovered by a remote team of imperial xenotomologists. They observed that the hive began to mimic and then adapt to their behavior.

Not abnormal, but worth a *closer look.*

It was only after they realized that the creatures were luring, trapping and parasitically consuming members of the team that they understood they were dealing with an *ancient, highly adaptive, aggressive species.*

And so it was brought to our attention, and from us, the information flowed to you.

Adaptive how?

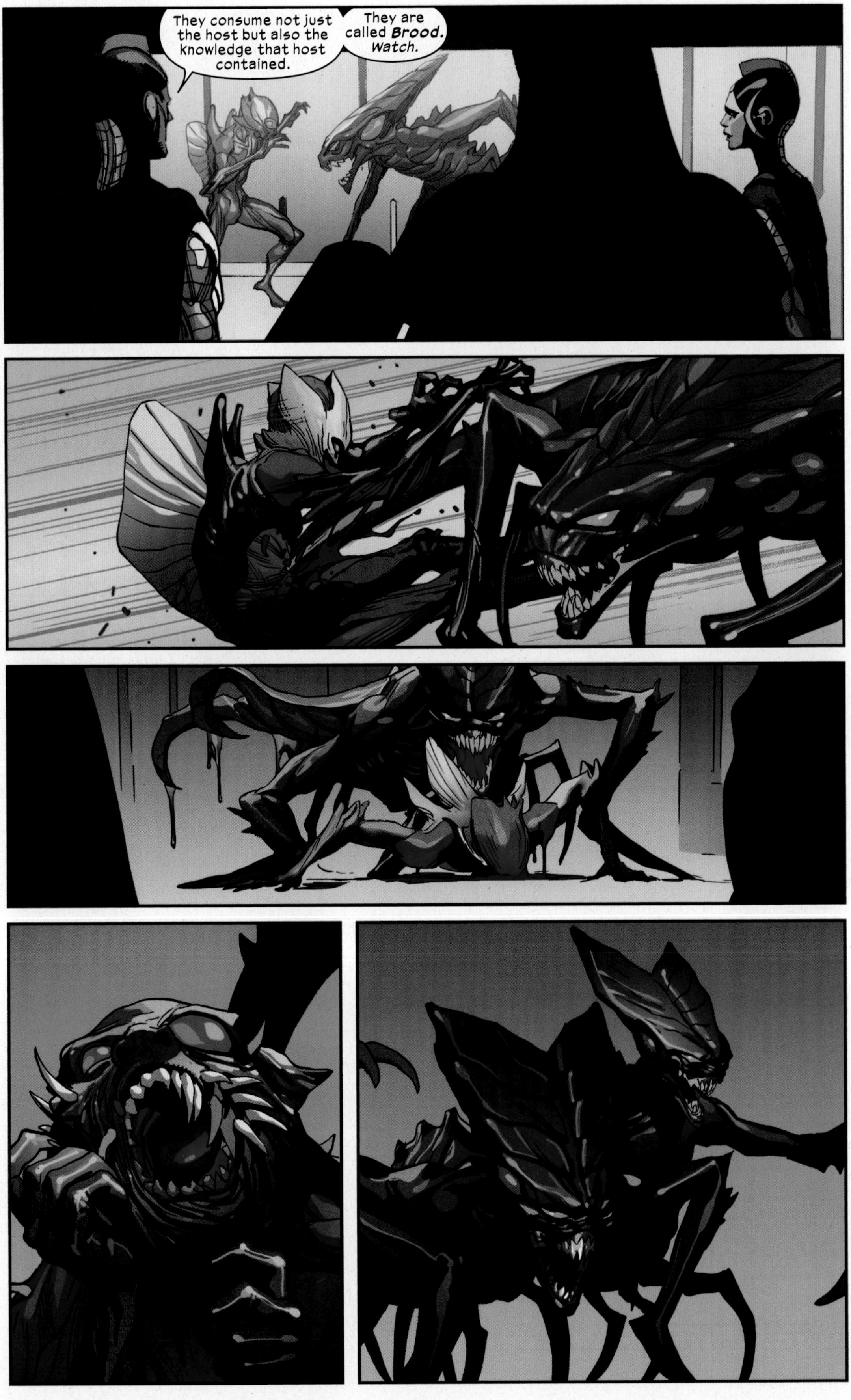
They consume not just the host but also the knowledge that host contained.
They are called Brood. Watch.

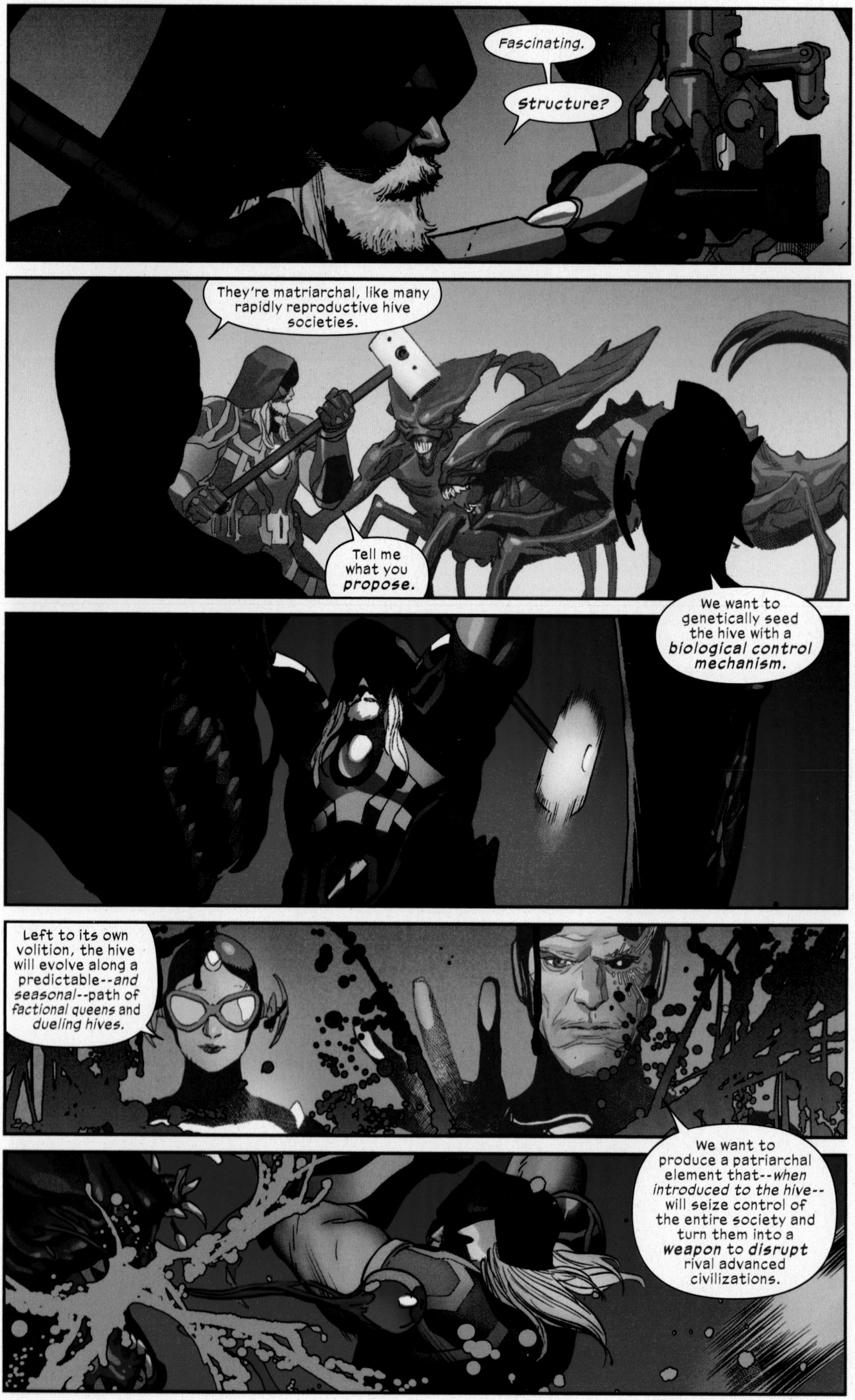
Fascinating.
Structure?
They're matriarchal, like many rapidly reproductive hive societies.
Tell me what you *propose.*
We want to genetically seed the hive with a *biological control mechanism.*
Left to its own volition, the hive will evolve along a predictable--*and seasonal*--path of *factional queens* and *dueling hives.*
We want to produce a patriarchal element that--*when introduced to the hive*--will seize control of the entire society and turn them into a **weapon** to **disrupt** rival advanced civilizations.

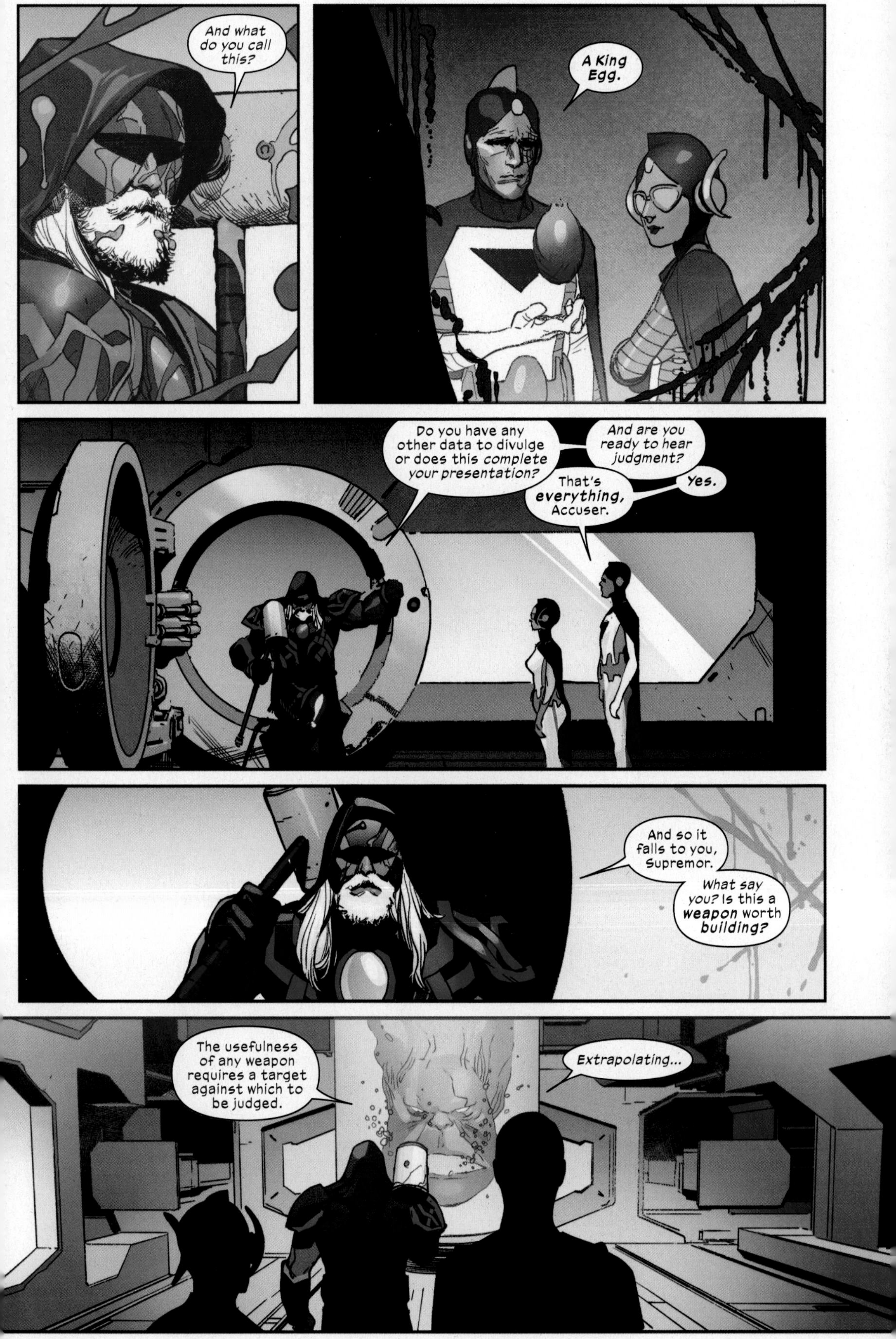
And what do you call this?
A King Egg.
Do you have any other data to divulge or does this complete your presentation?
And are you ready to hear judgment?
That's everything, Accuser.
Yes.
And so it falls to you, Supremor.
What say you? Is this a weapon worth building?
The usefulness of any weapon requires a target against which to be judged.
Extrapolating...

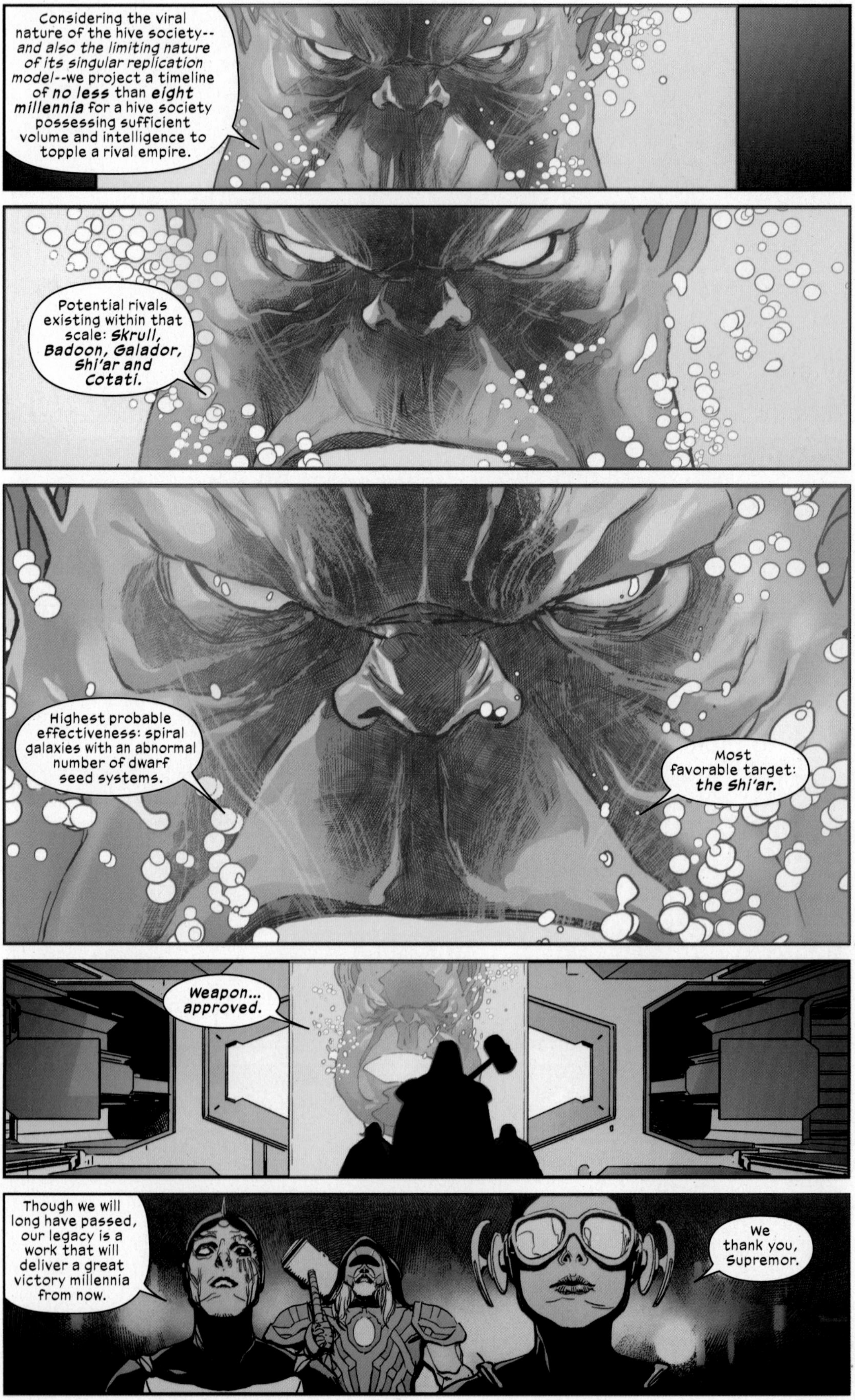

Considering the viral nature of the hive society--and also the limiting nature of its singular replication model--we project a timeline of no less than eight millennia for a hive society possessing sufficient volume and intelligence to topple a rival empire.
Potential rivals existing within that scale: Skrull, Badoon, Galador, Shi'ar and Cotati.
Highest probable effectiveness: spiral galaxies with an abnormal number of dwarf seed systems.
Most favorable target: the Shi'ar.
Weapon... approved.
Though we will long have passed, our legacy is a work that will deliver a great victory millennia from now.
We thank you, Supremor.

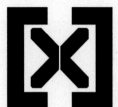

[kra_[0.9]
[koa_[0.9]

[kra_[0.X]
[koa_[0.X]

THE KING EGG

The New Mutants brought a King Egg home from space -- unfortunately, the King Egg brings with it trillions of hungry Brood. Now the X-Men have taken the King Egg off Earth, but the Brood aren't the only ones after it. A Kree Accuser took the Starjammers hostage, holding them in exchange for information...and unwittingly exposing his presence in Shi'ar space. Now Gladiator, Kid Gladiator and the Imperial Guard are after him. And everyone's about to run into one another. Let's see how this goes...

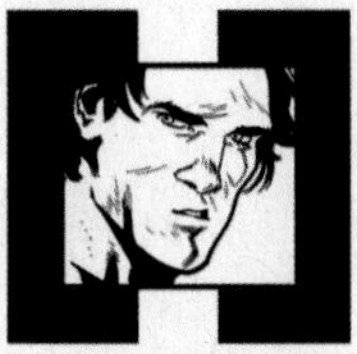
Vulcan

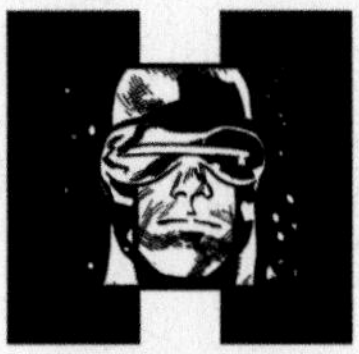
Cyclops

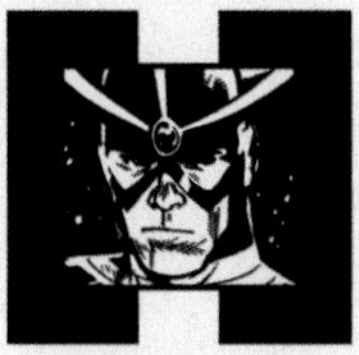
Havok

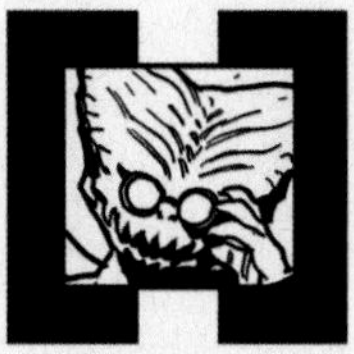
Broo

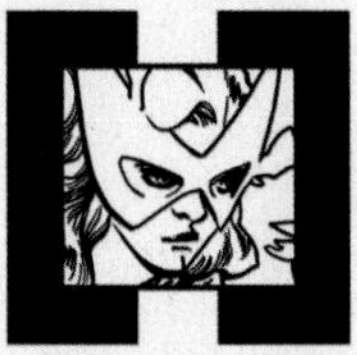
Jean Grey

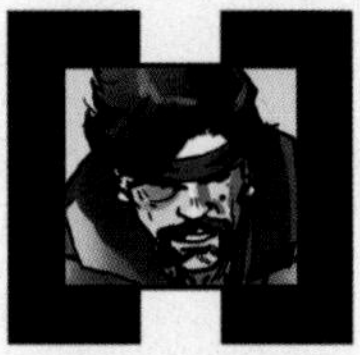
Corsair

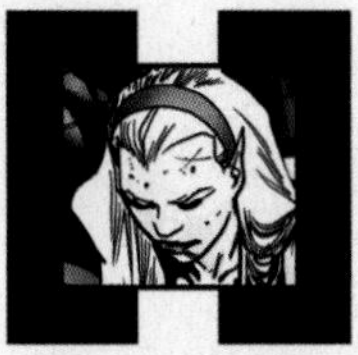
Hepzibah

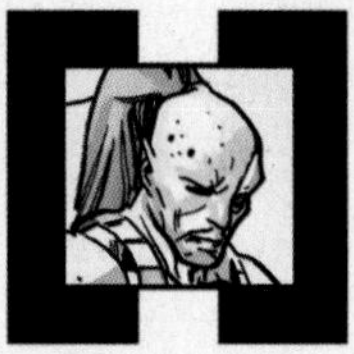
Raza

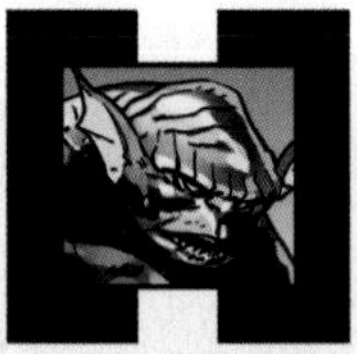
Ch'od

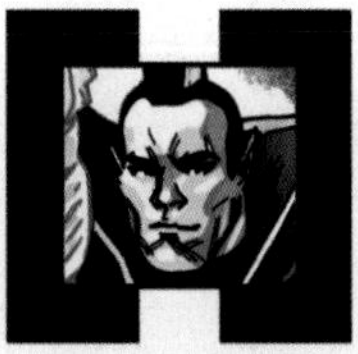
Gladiator

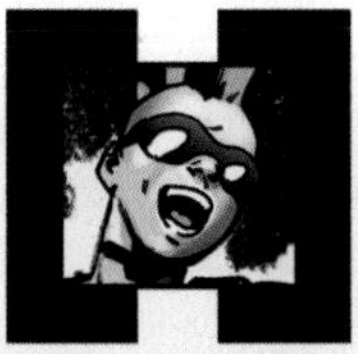
Kid Gladiator

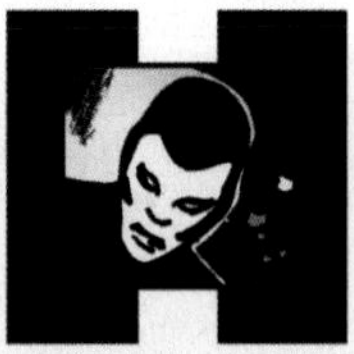
Manta

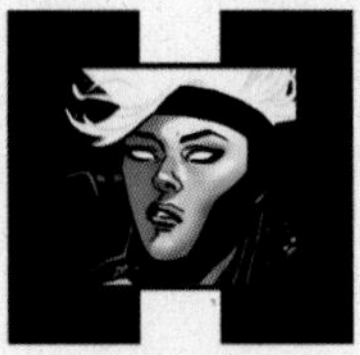
Oracle

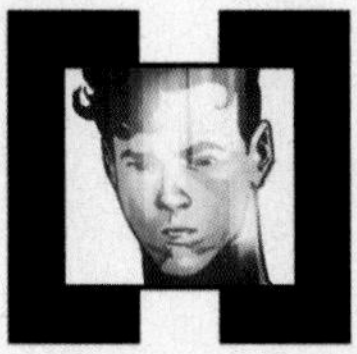
Sunspot

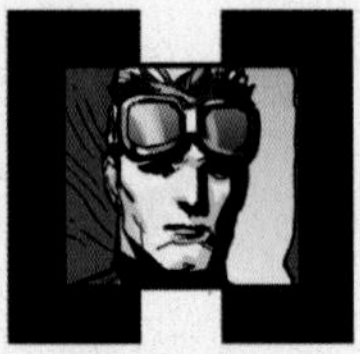
Cannonball

[kra_[0.9]...]
[koa_[0.9]...]

[A._New_World]

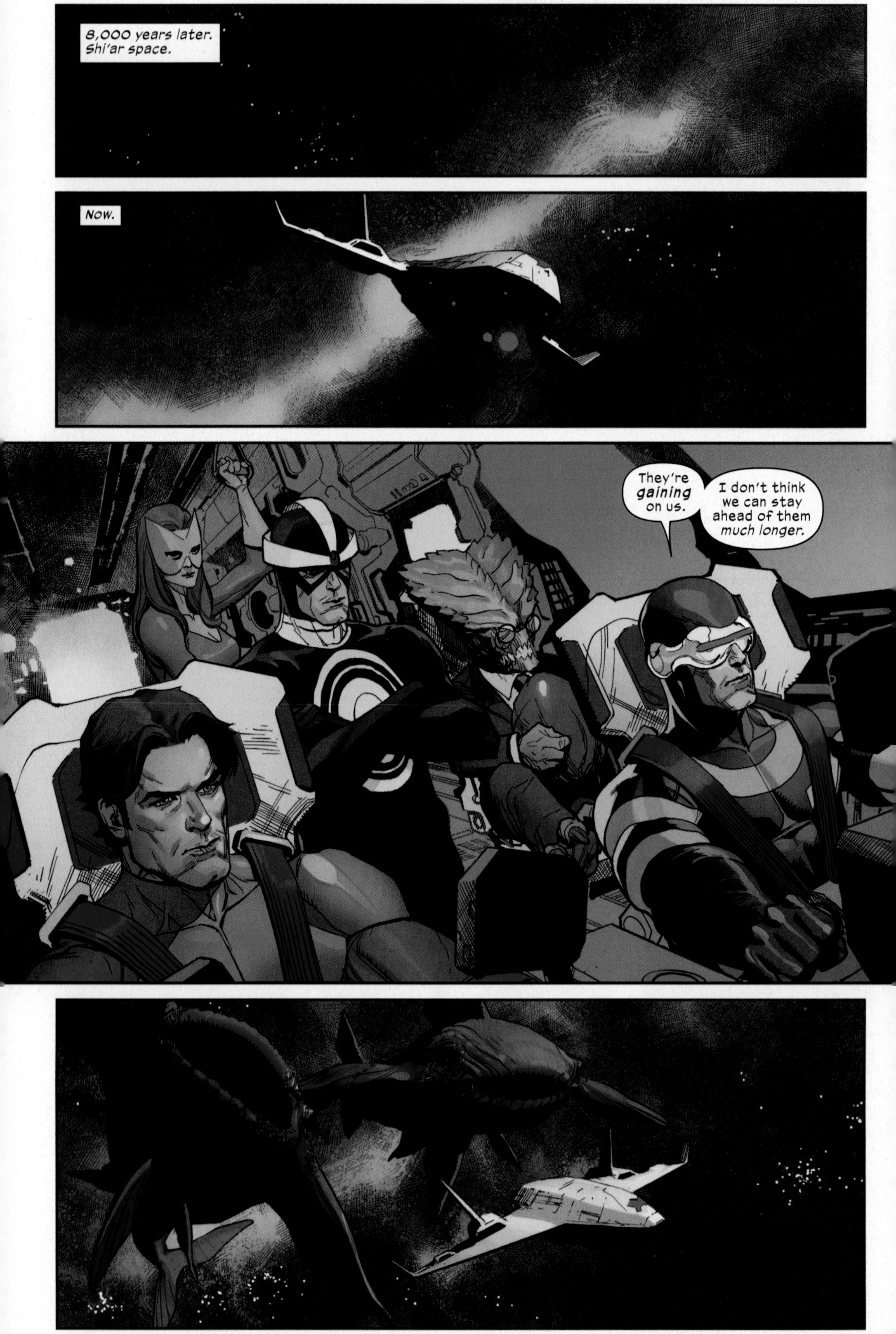
8,000 years later. Shi'ar space.
Now.
They're gaining on us.
I don't think we can stay ahead of them much longer.

I don't think we need to worry about who's *behind us*, Scott.

Look!

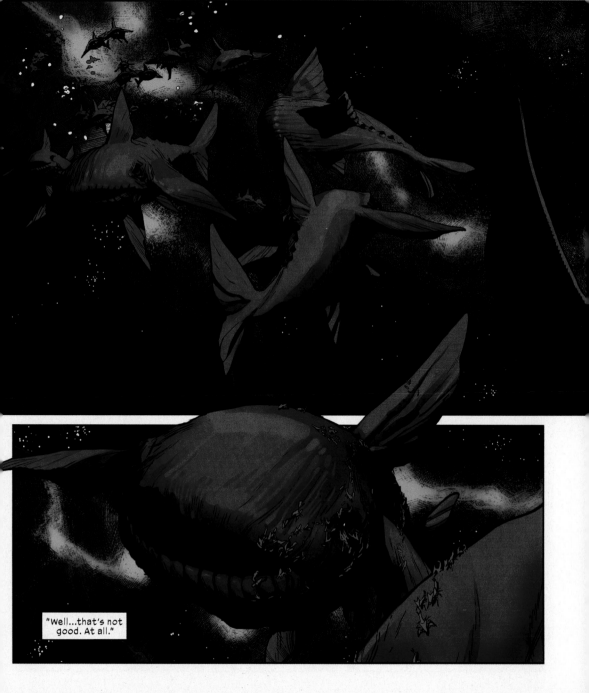

"Well...that's not good. At all."

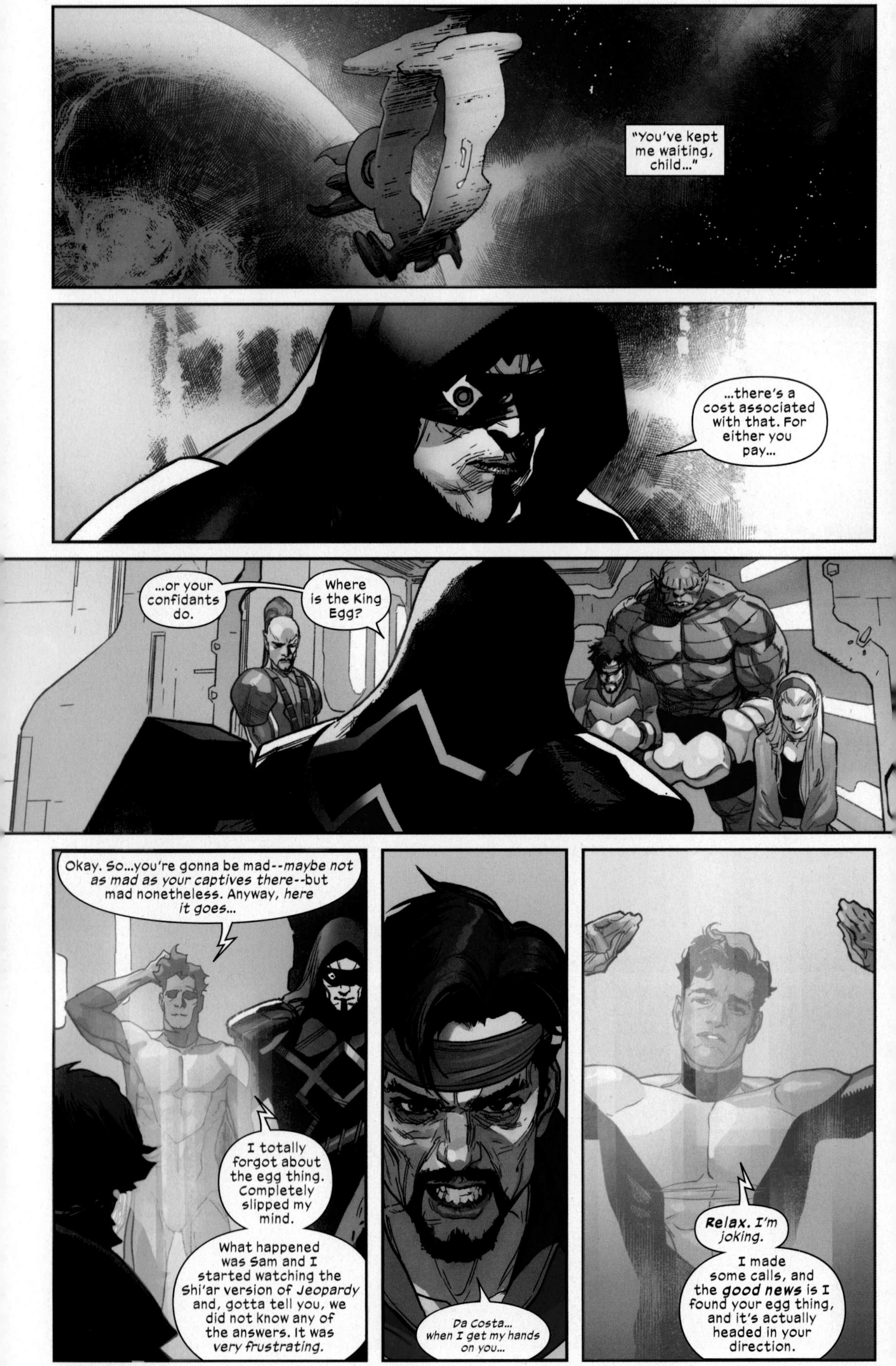
"You've kept me waiting, child..."
...there's a cost associated with that. For either you pay...
...or your confidants do.
Where is the King Egg?
Okay. So...you're gonna be mad--*maybe not as mad as your captives there*--but mad nonetheless. Anyway, *here it goes...*
I totally forgot about the egg thing. Completely slipped my mind.
What happened was Sam and I started watching the Shi'ar version of *Jeopardy* and, gotta tell you, we did not know any of the answers. It was *very frustrating.*
Da Costa... when I get my hands on you...
Relax. *I'm joking.*
I made some calls, and the ***good news*** is I found your egg thing, and it's actually headed in your direction.

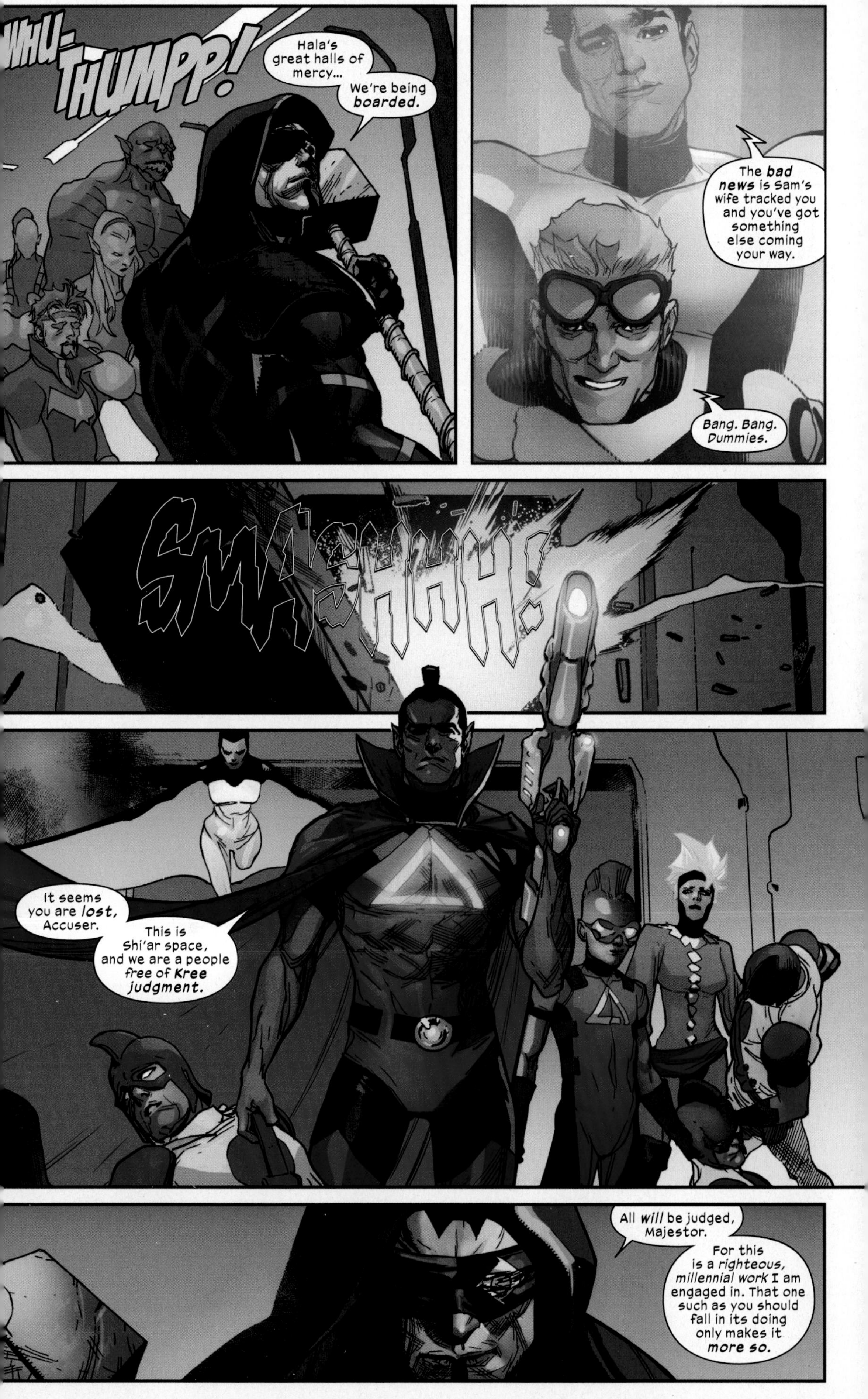
WHU-THUMPP!
Hala's great halls of mercy...
We're being boarded.
The bad news is Sam's wife tracked you and you've got something else coming your way.
Bang. Bang. Dummies.
SMASHHH!
It seems you are lost, Accuser.
This is Shi'ar space, and we are a people free of Kree judgment.
All will be judged, Majestor.
For this is a righteous, millennial work I am engaged in. That one such as you should fall in its doing only makes it more so.

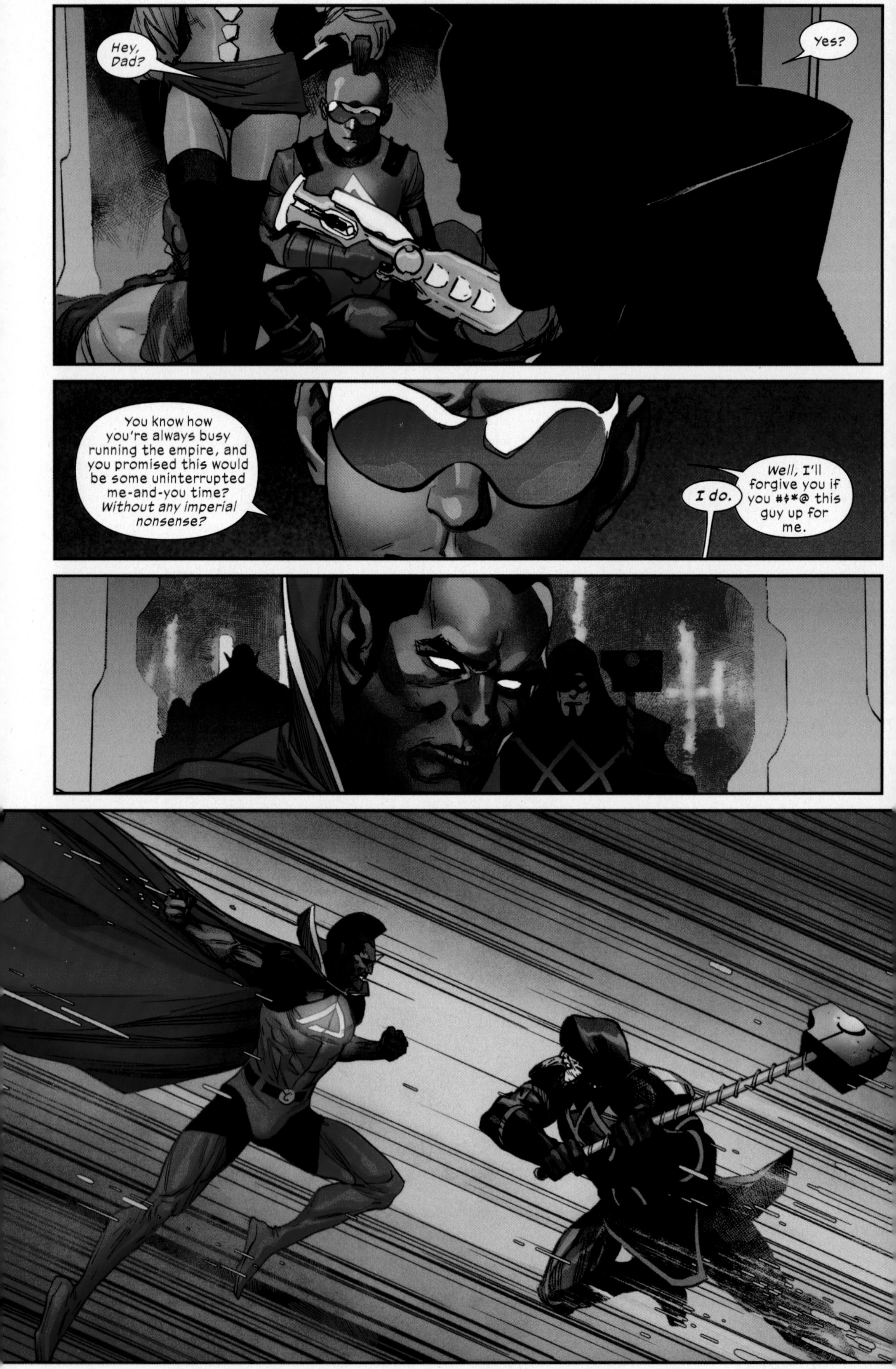
Hey, Dad?
Yes?
You know how you're always busy running the empire, and you promised this would be some uninterrupted me-and-you time? Without any imperial nonsense?
I do.
Well, I'll forgive you if you #$*@ this guy up for me.

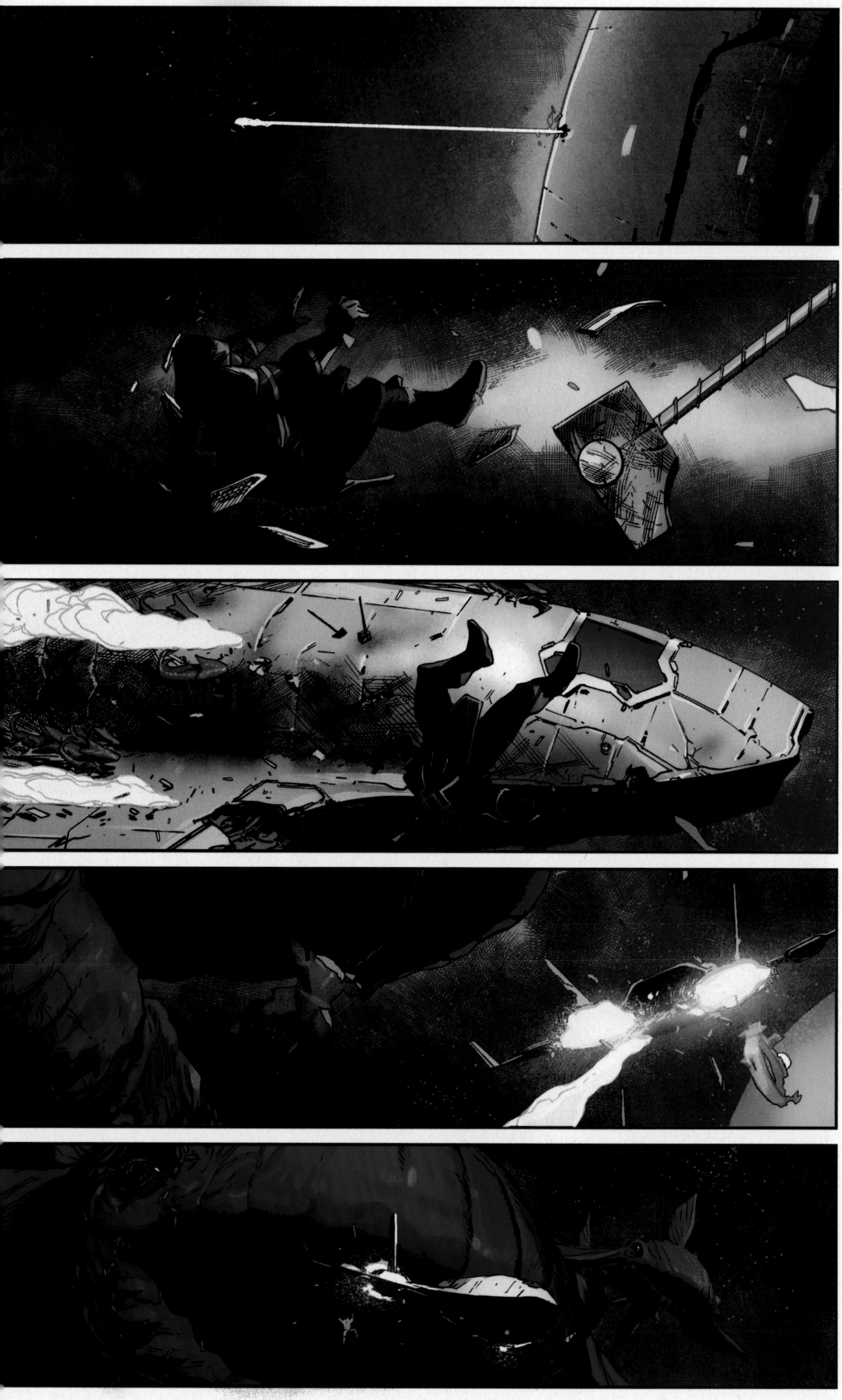

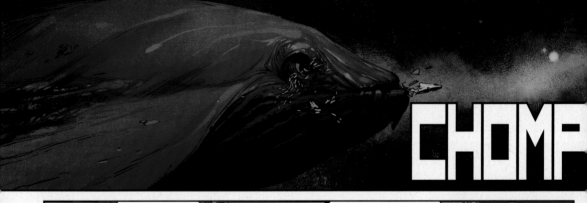

CHOMP

Can't hold it. **We're going down.**

It looks like we have two choices. That station or the planetoid it's orbiting.

Head for the planet. Bigger canvas to work with...

...and that station's gonna get chewed up by the Brood in our wake. Alex?

On it.

To the unidentified station we're approaching.

If you can, you need to evacuate immediately-- there's a Brood swarm on our--

Dad? What the--

I know it's not the reunion you were expecting, son...but we can catch up later.

Right now I need to know if you happen to have a Brood King Egg on you.

We do.

Ah, so that's what this is about. A King Egg. *Now I* understand.

Are you landing on the planet below?

Landing?

"Not likely."

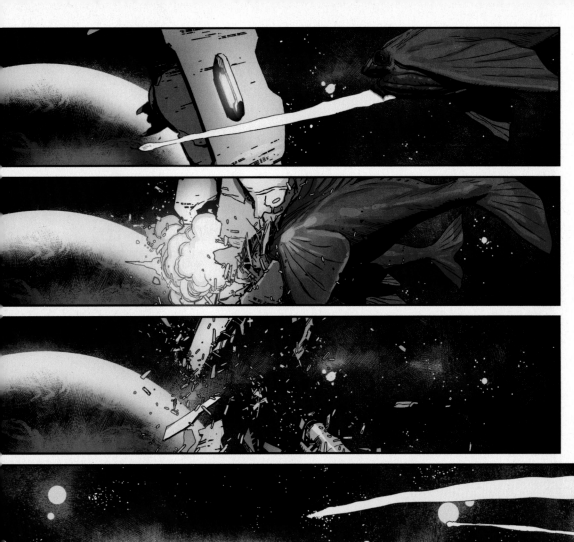

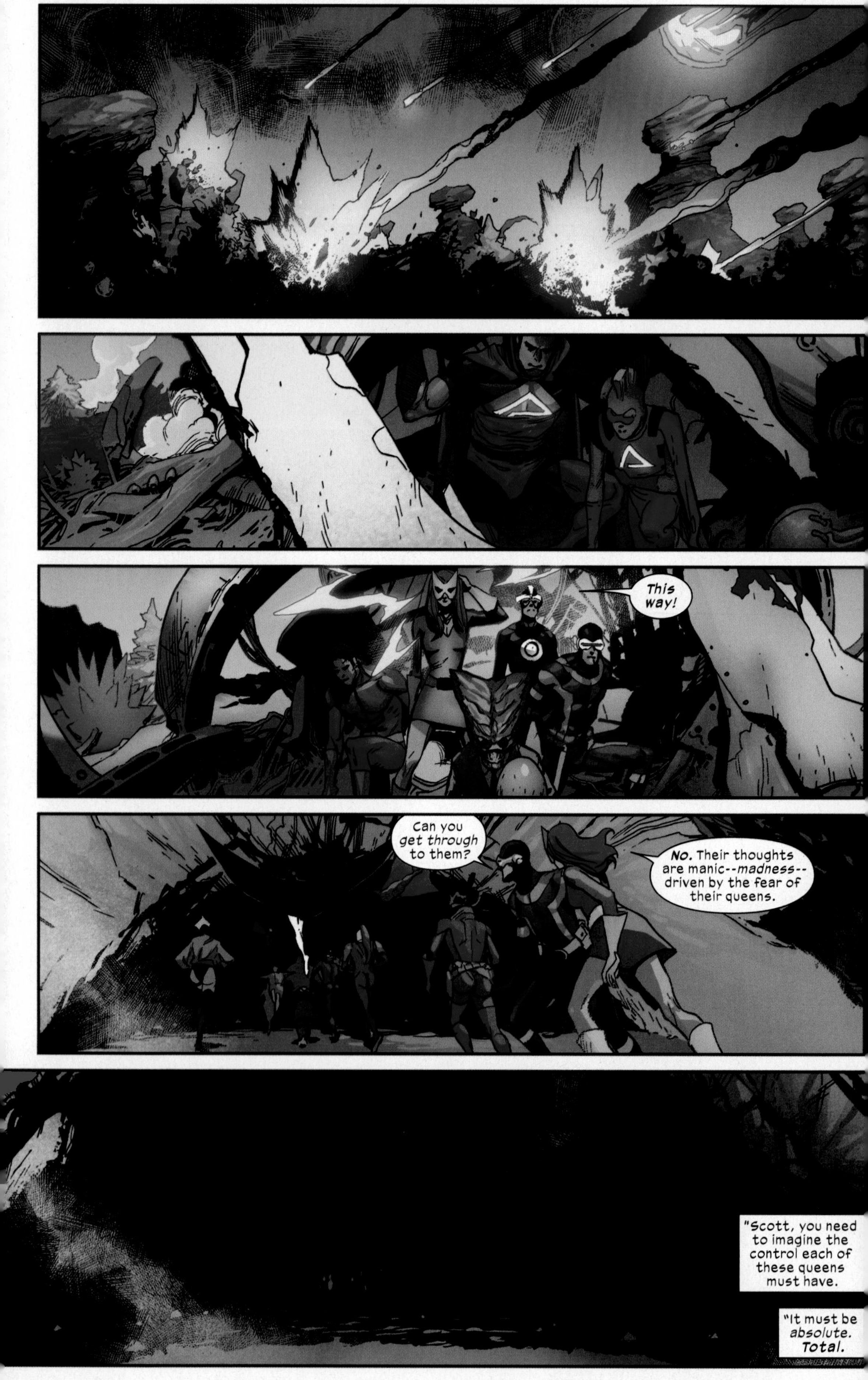
This way!
Can you get through to them?
No. Their thoughts are manic--madness--driven by the fear of their queens.
"Scott, you need to imagine the control each of these queens must have.
"It must be absolute. Total.

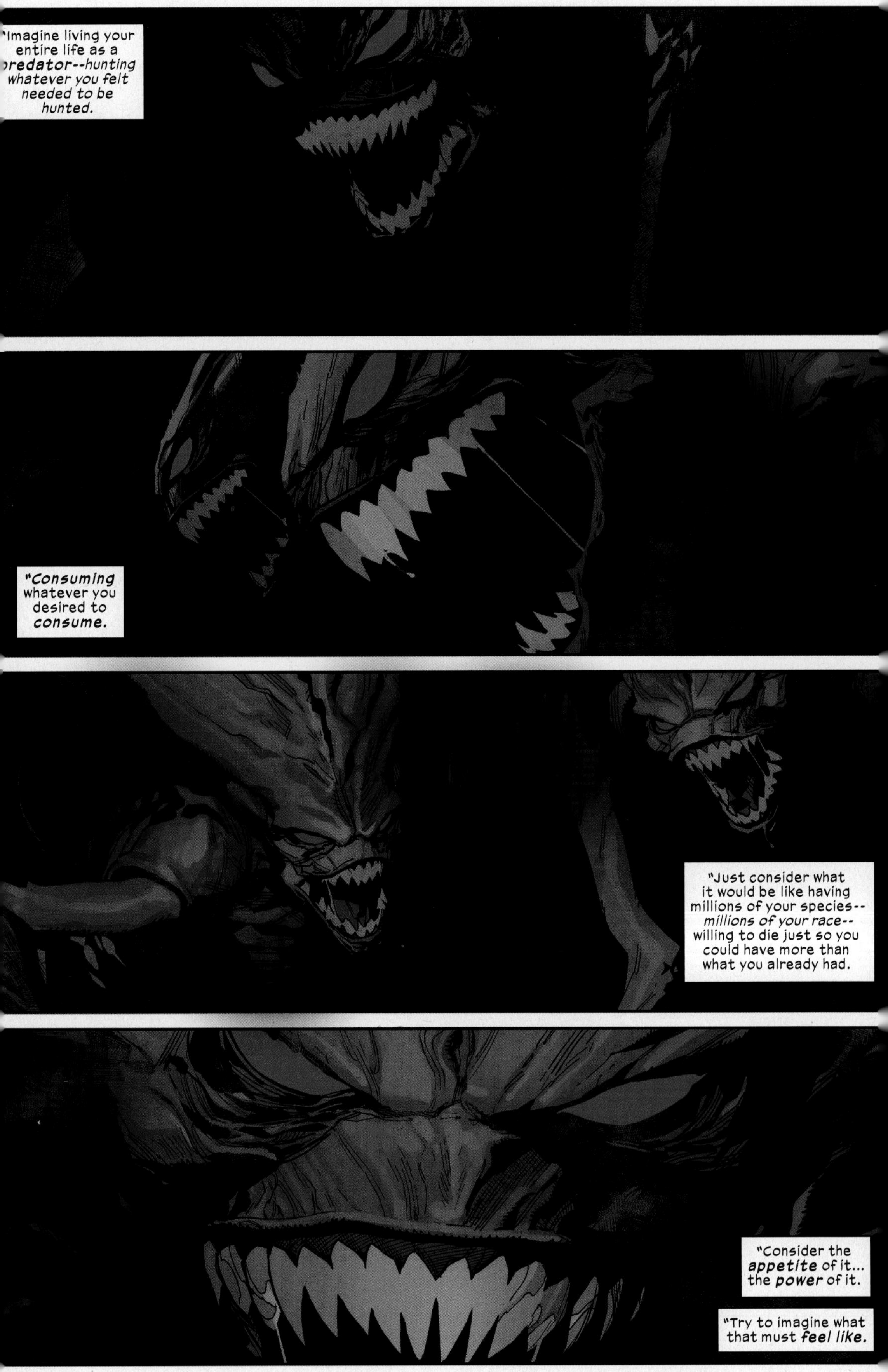
"Imagine living your entire life as a predator--hunting whatever you felt needed to be hunted.
"Consuming whatever you desired to consume.
"Just consider what it would be like having millions of your species--millions of your race--willing to die just so you could have more than what you already had.
"Consider the appetite of it... the power of it.
"Try to imagine what that must feel like.

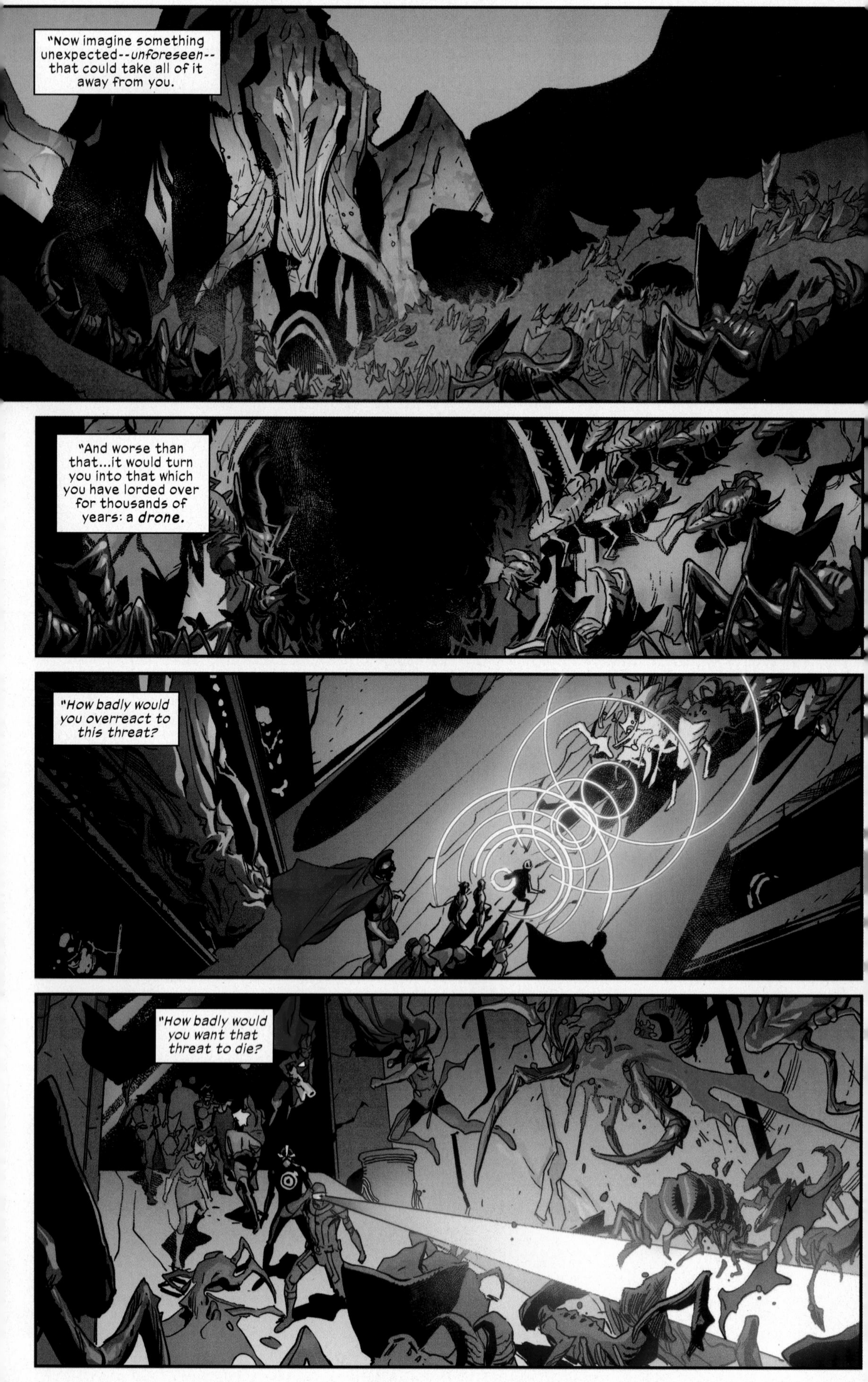
"Now imagine something unexpected--*unforeseen*--that could take all of it away from you.
"And worse than that...it would turn you into that which you have lorded over for thousands of years: a ***drone.***
"How badly would you overreact to this threat?
"How badly would you want that threat to die?

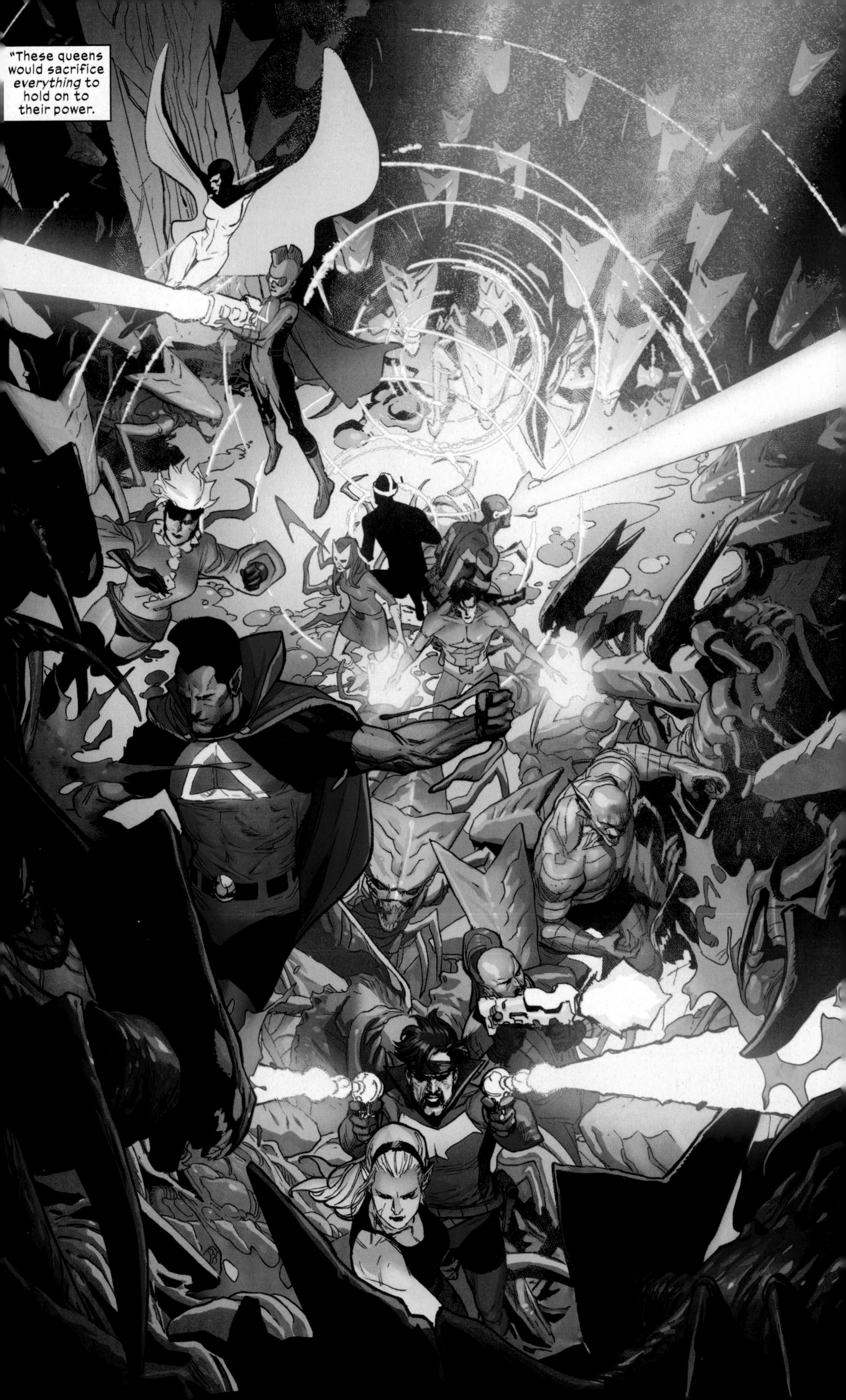
"These queens would sacrifice *everything* to hold on to their power.

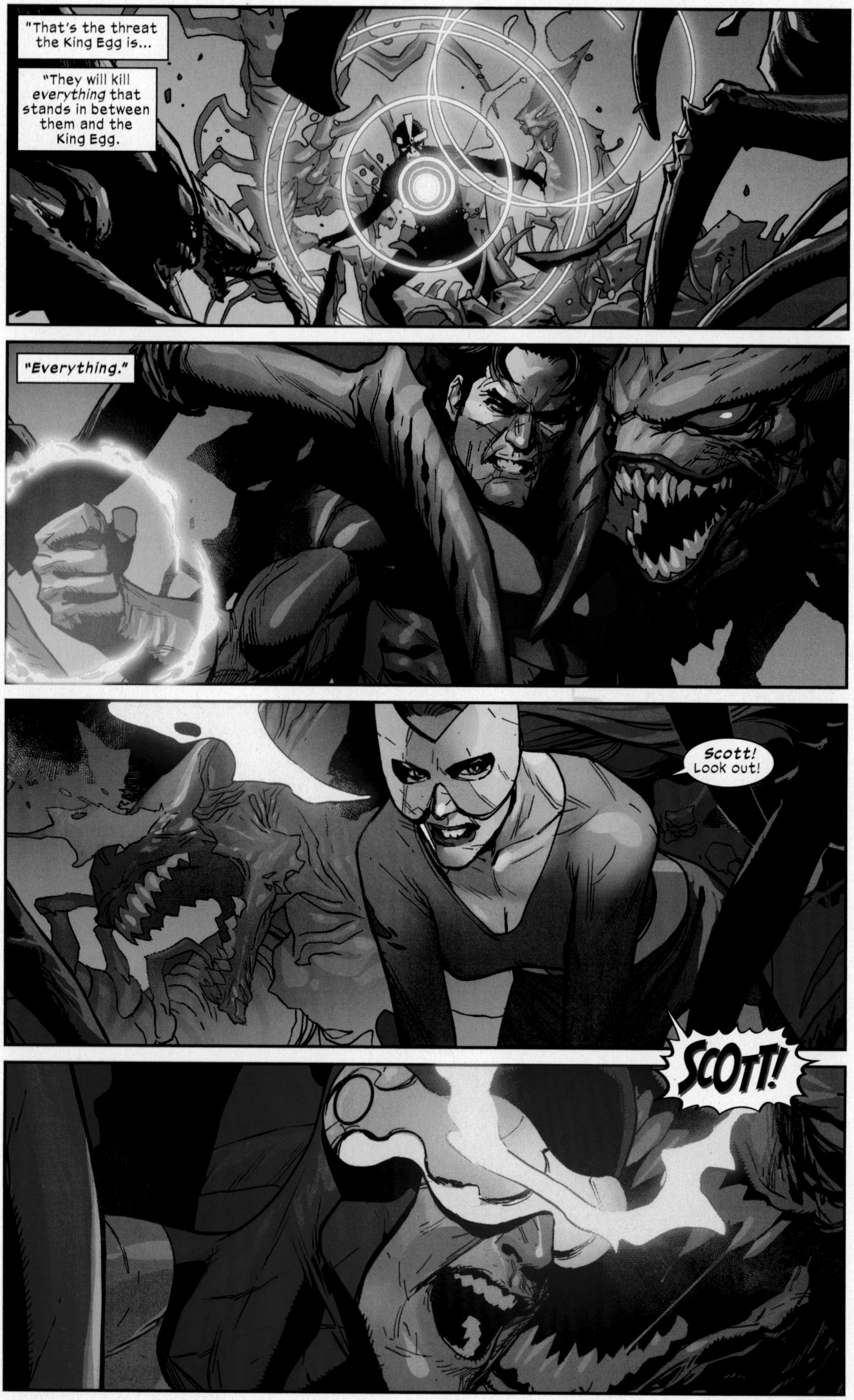
"That's the threat the King Egg is...
"They will kill *everything* that stands in between them and the King Egg.
"*Everything.*"
Scott! Look out!
SCOTT!

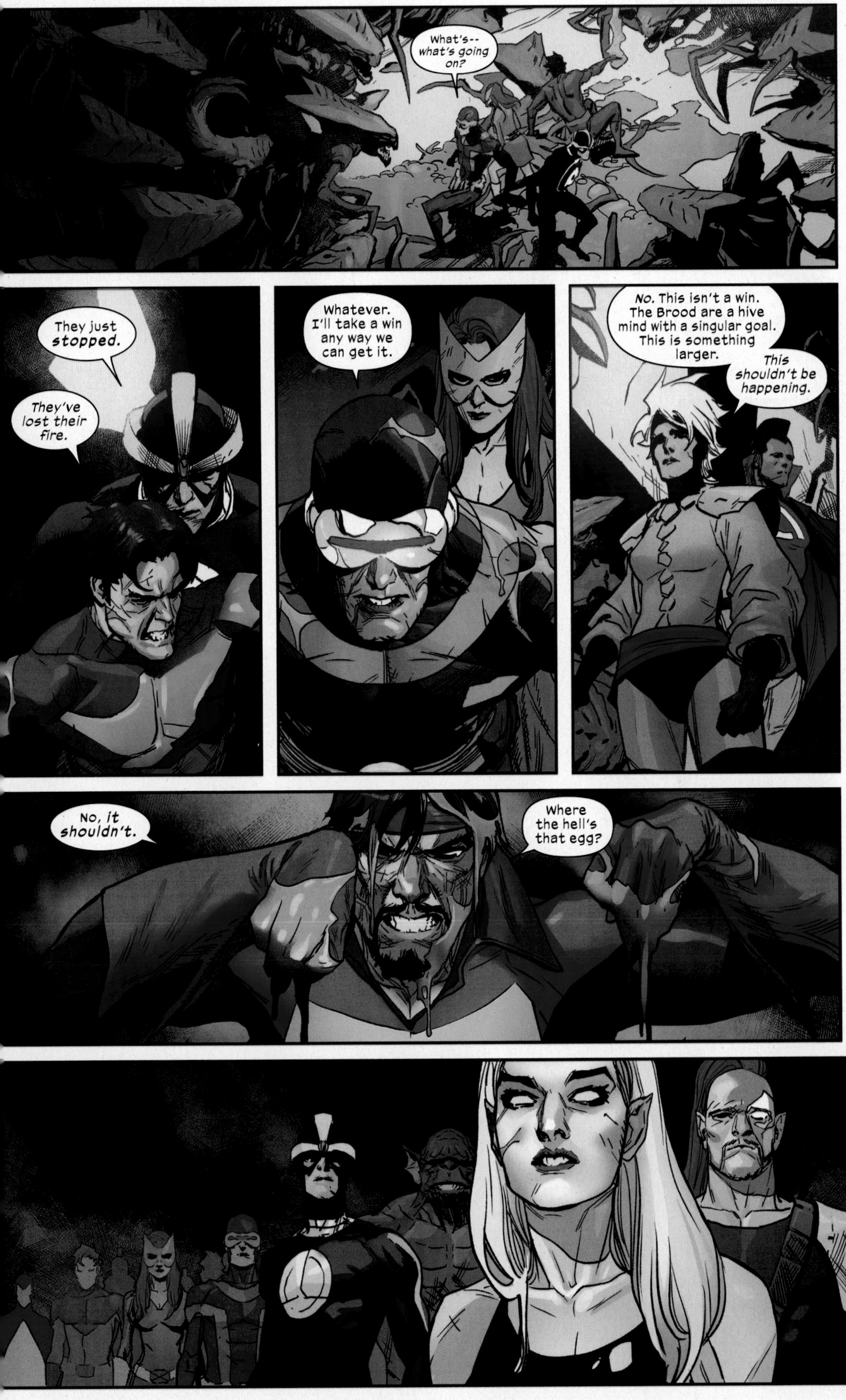
What's--
what's going
on?
They just *stopped.*
They've lost their fire.
Whatever. I'll take a win any way we can get it.
No. This isn't a win. The Brood are a hive mind with a singular goal. This is something larger.
This shouldn't be happening.
No, *it shouldn't.*
Where the hell's that egg?

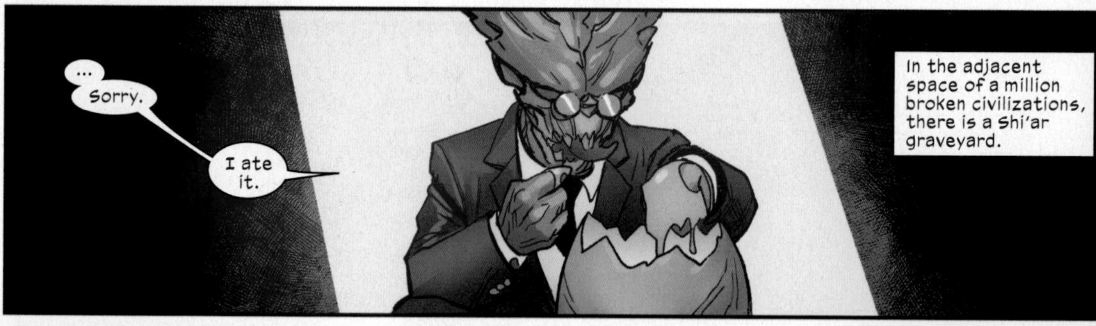
...
Sorry.
I ate it.
In the adjacent space of a million broken civilizations, there is a Shi'ar graveyard.

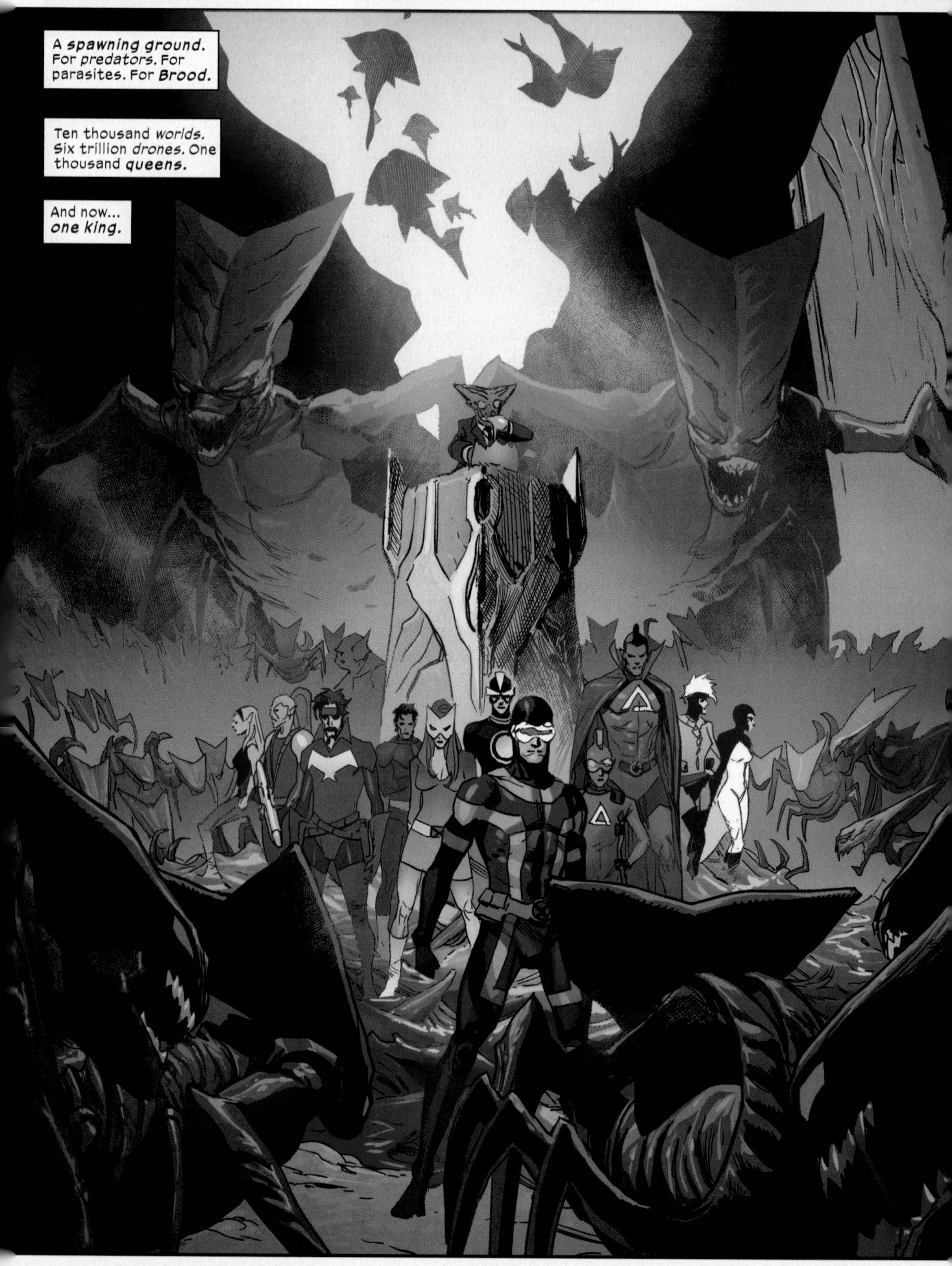
A *spawning ground.* For *predators.* For parasites. For *Brood.*
Ten thousand *worlds.* Six trillion *drones.* One thousand *queens.*
And now... *one king.*

THE EYES OF THE SUPREMOR

RE: A report from the secret order of Black Judges regarding the creation of a weaponized slave catalyst for hive species.

POTENTIAL SEED SPECIES:

```
- Tal Ba-Rii.............[failure from process : extinct]
- Sidri.................[failure from mind structure]
- Scatter...............[success : minor]
- Phalanx...............[failure from adaptivity]
- Gu'Knoiss.............[failure from biological integrity : extinct]
- Brood.................[success : major]
```

BROOD

Regarded as this universe's first galactic predators, the Brood entered this reality through the dark matter flow of a collapsing universe. Being extra-universal, little is known about the origins of the alpha hive, but close study implies manufacture. This presents several injection complications based on species design.

The Brood have a matriarchal caste system, which is structured as follows: **Empress > Firstborn > Queen > Dwarf Queen > Drone.**

Careful study and beta testing of slave catalyst has resulted in the conclusion that a pheromone-based solution works best for total control, but species design means that it can only be injected at the Queen level of the hive.

That the entire militaristic class of Firstborn dies when the Empress does means that our weapon system can only be introduced at the death [or extermination] of the Brood Empress. After such an event [the death of an Empress], the nest wars between rival queens to determine who will assume control of the hive usually last several decades, giving us ample time to exercise the use of our weapon.

[NOTE: During the nest wars that determine the new Empress, the population of the entire Brood hive drops dramatically, so it is best used at the onset of succession.]

THE KING EGG

After several hundred years of testing and design, the Black Judges [the secret science wing of the Accusers] presented the Supreme Intelligence with a pheromone-based weapon built to hack the Brood caste system and seize control of the hive by reproducing and supercharging the pheromonal Empress effect.

[NOTE: Normally, the Empress controls the hive through a combination of pheromones and telepathic dominance. Out of necessity, our weapon supercharges the first since we cannot effectively replicate the second. The effect of this is a more compliant but less autonomous drone.]

The King Egg itself is a container for a serum that alters and enhances the biology of the King Egg host and will give the host control of the entire hive for an estimated 5-10 standard Kree cycles. The King Egg is activated by ingesting the serum contained inside the shell.

[NOTE: Production of a rival King Egg can disrupt the host's control of the hive.]

[Supremor..[_si]_01]
[1000 WI..[_si]_05]

[KING]..............[EGG]
[ver...............314_3]

[dawn_of_x]

[kra_]
[koa_]

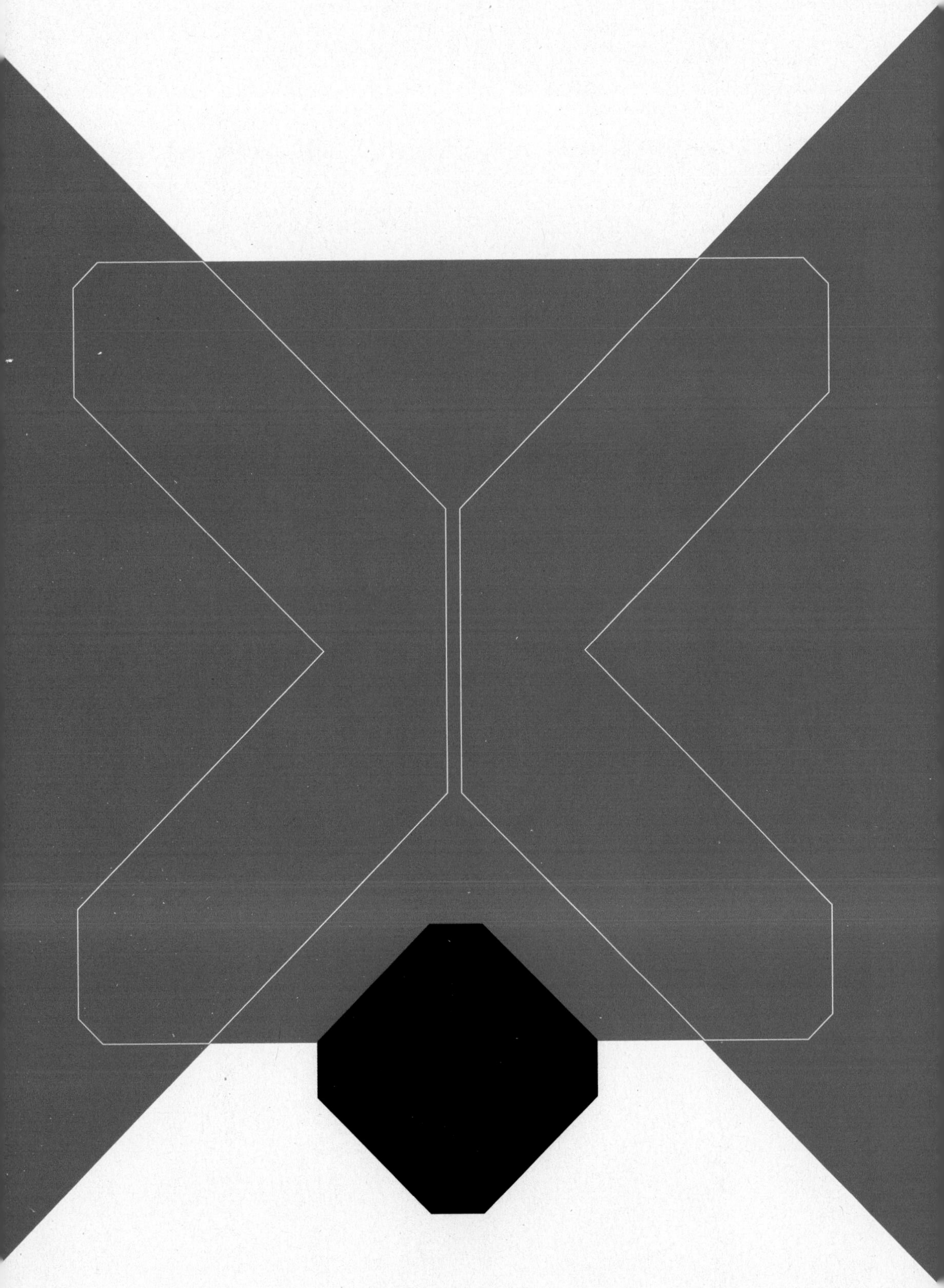

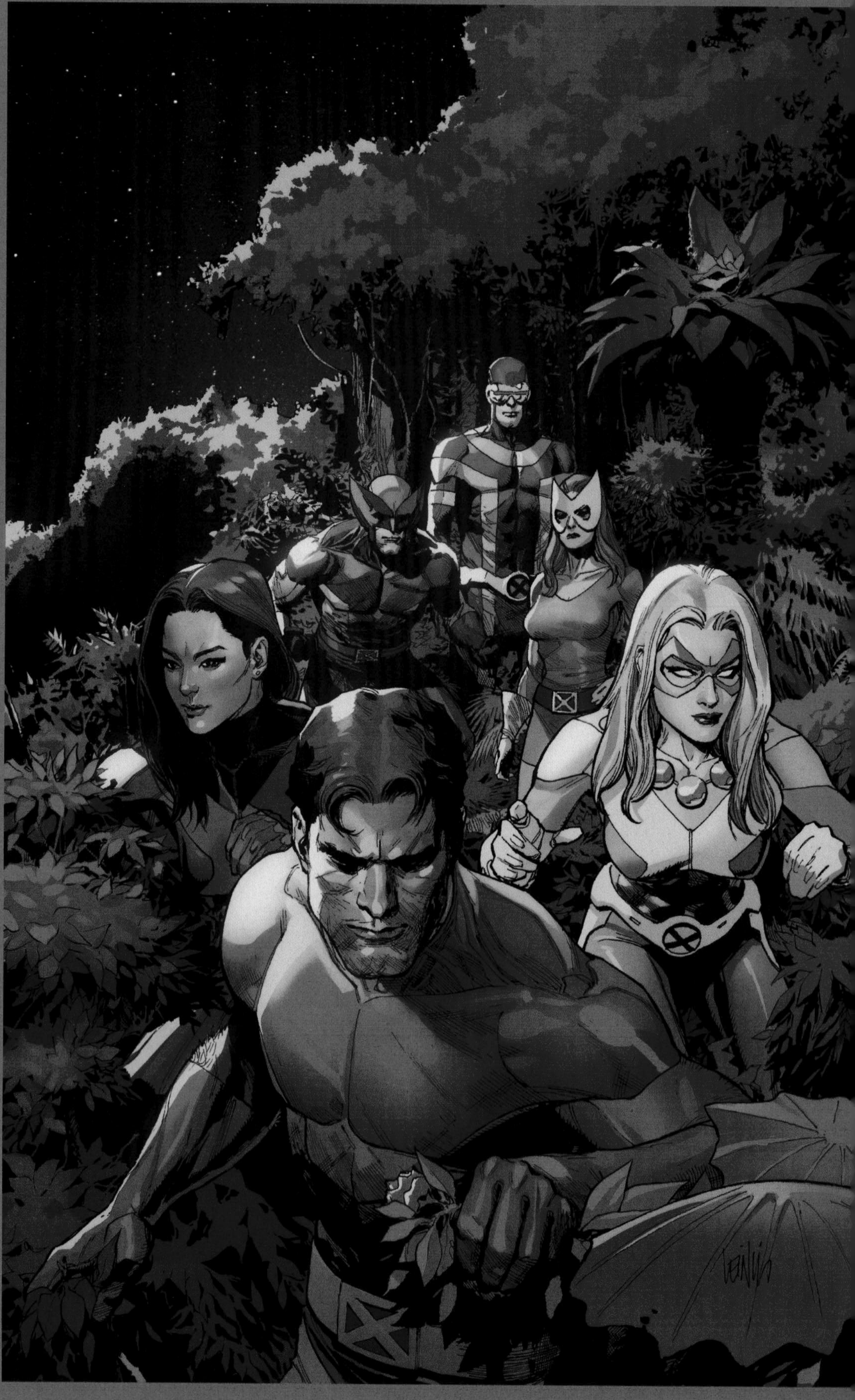

Fire

10

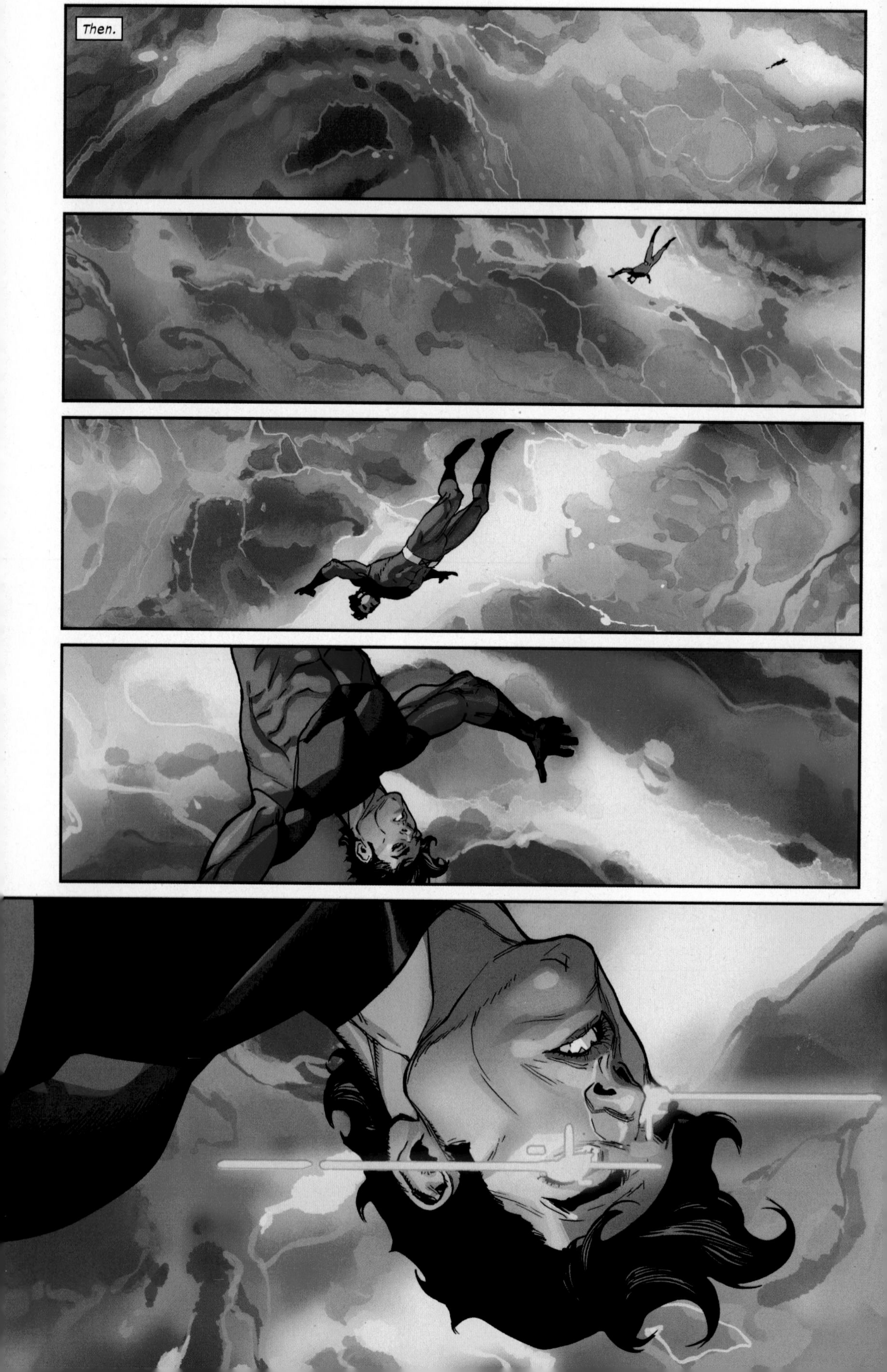
Then.

GENTLY...
THE CELESTIAL AVATAR ESCAPED-- THAT KING IS LOST TO US.
SO LET'S TAKE A BIT MORE CARE WITH THIS ONE.
HURKKK!

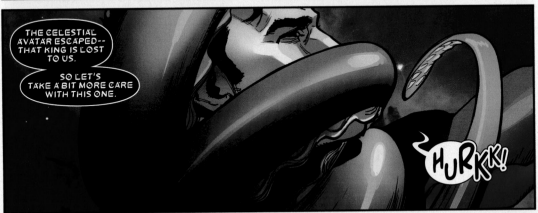

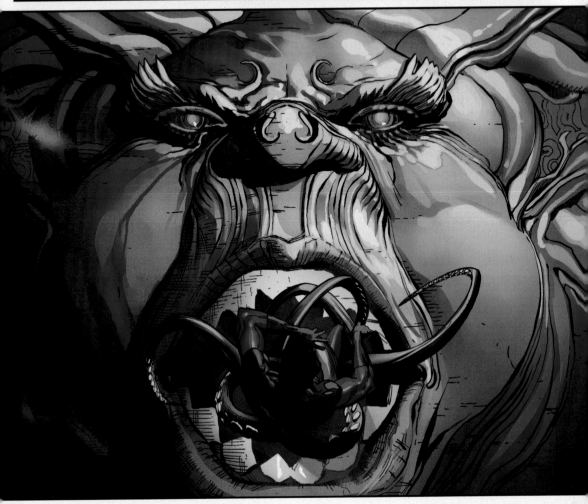

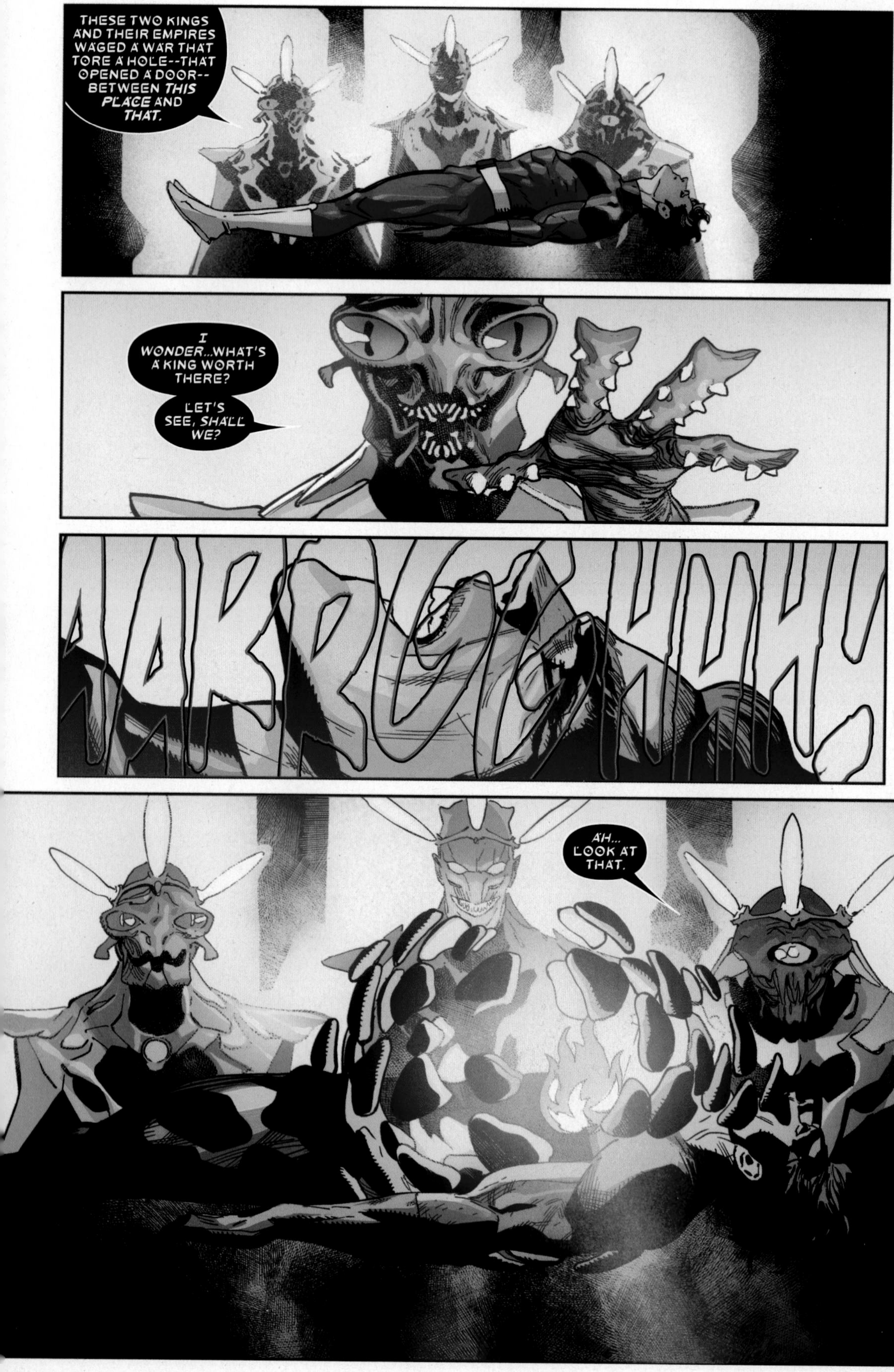
THESE TWO KINGS AND THEIR EMPIRES WAGED A WAR THAT TORE A HOLE--THAT OPENED A DOOR--BETWEEN *THIS PLACE* AND *THAT.*
I WONDER...WHAT'S A KING WORTH *THERE?*
LET'S SEE, *SHALL* WE?
AH... LOOK AT THAT.

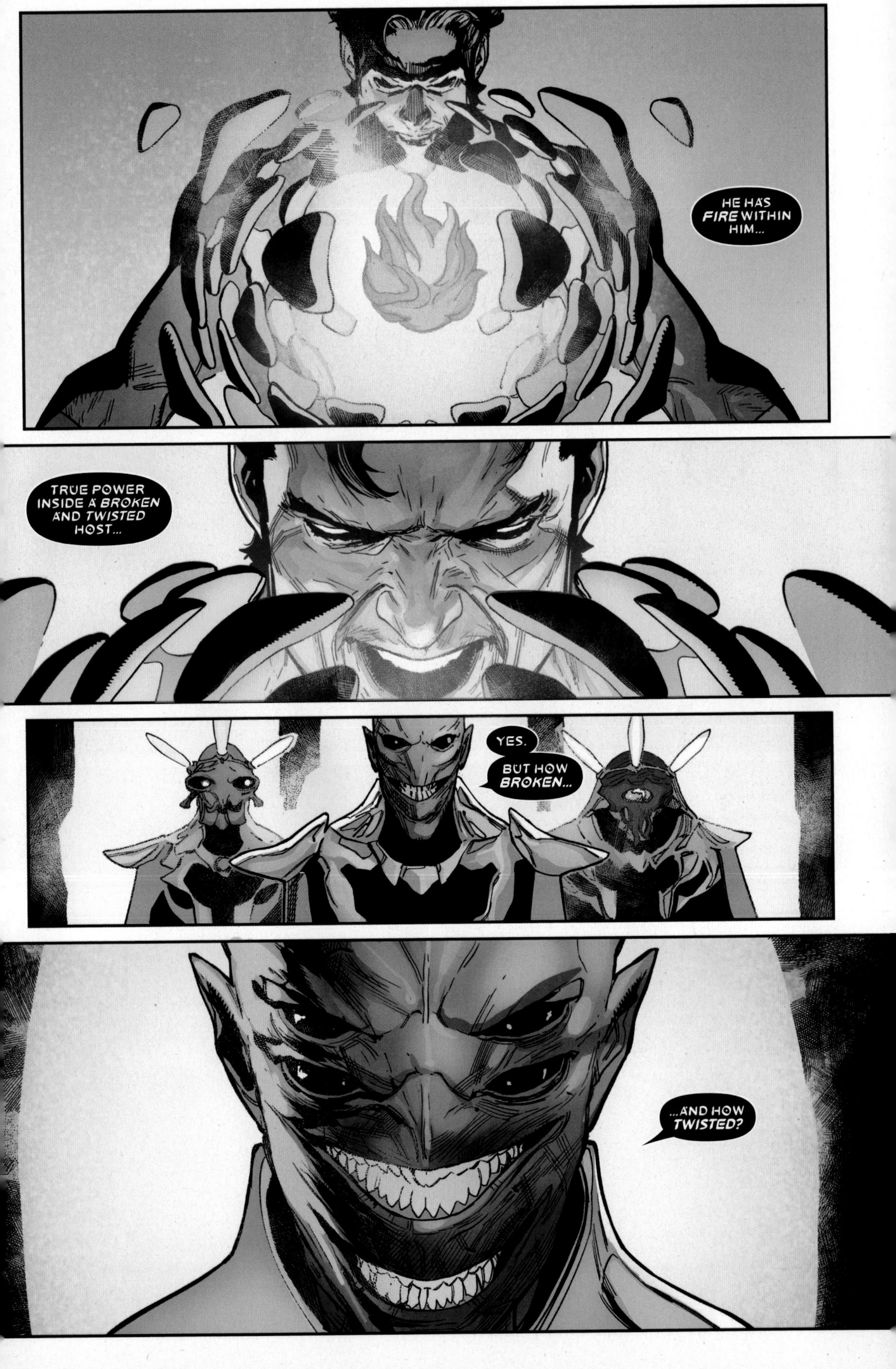
HE HAS *FIRE* WITHIN HIM...
TRUE POWER INSIDE A *BROKEN* AND *TWISTED* HOST...
YES.
BUT HOW *BROKEN*...
...AND HOW *TWISTED*?

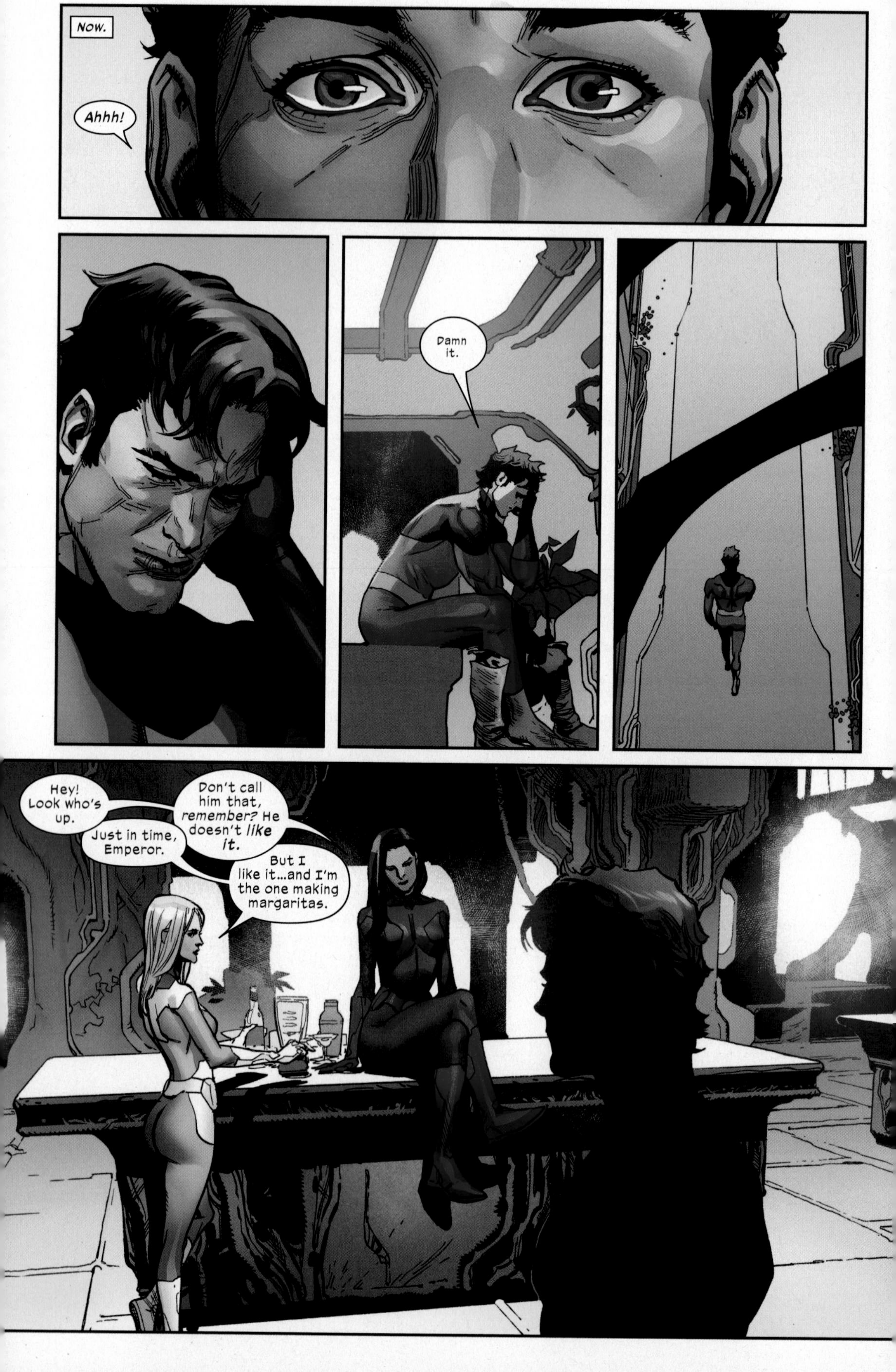

Now.
Ahhh!
Damn it.
Hey! Look who's up.
Don't call him that, *remember?* He doesn't *like it.*
Just in time, Emperor.
But I like it...and I'm the one making margaritas.

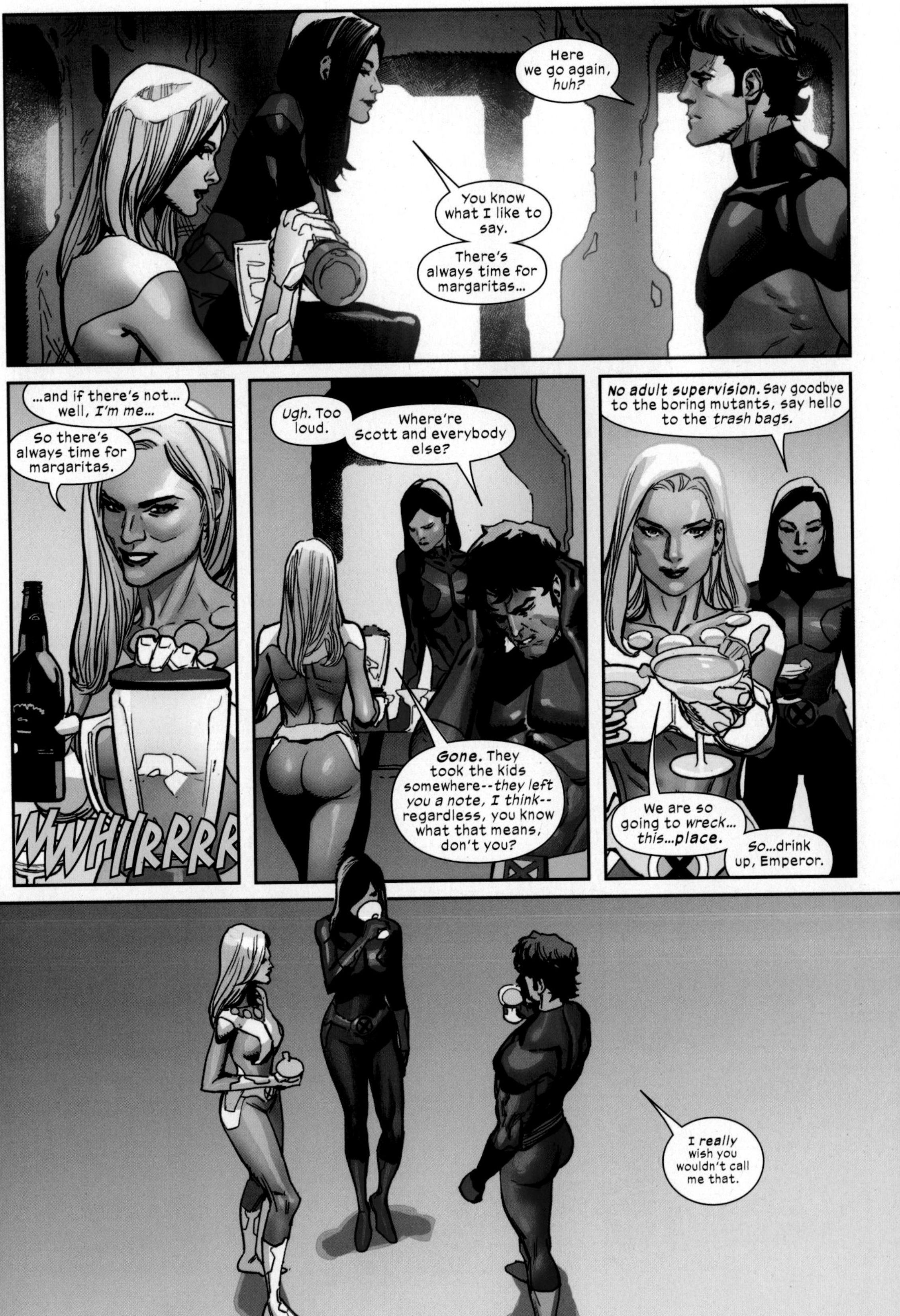
Here we go again, *huh?*
You know what I like to say.
There's always time for margaritas...
...and if there's not... well, *I'm me*...
So there's always time for margaritas.
WWHIRRRR
Ugh. Too loud.
Where're Scott and everybody else?
Gone. They took the kids somewhere--*they left you a note, I think*--regardless, you know what that means, don't you?
No adult supervision. Say goodbye to the boring mutants, say hello to the *trash bags.*
We are so going to *wreck*... *this*...***place.***
So...drink up, Emperor.
I ***really*** wish you wouldn't call me that.

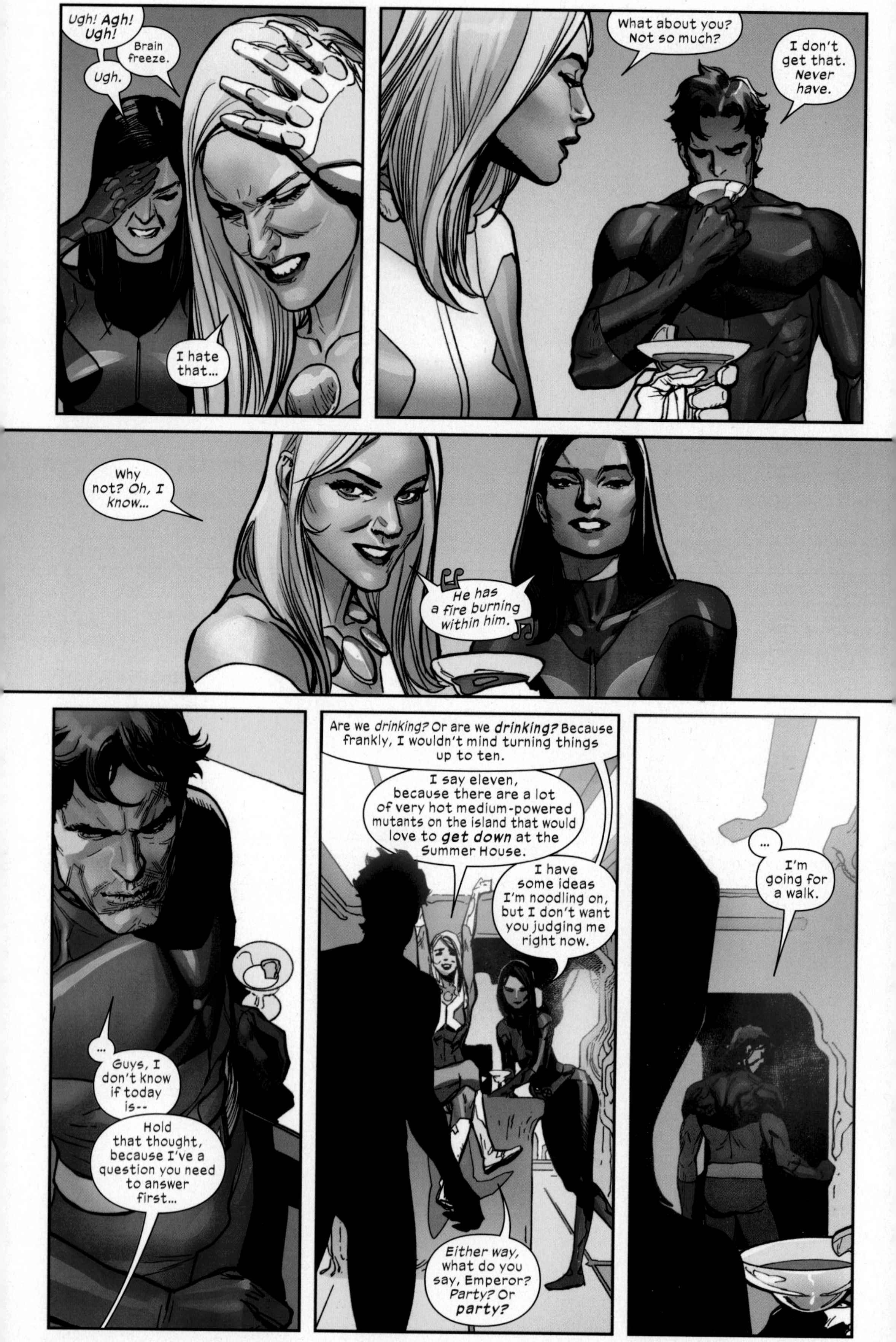
Ugh! Agh! Ugh!
Brain freeze.
Ugh.
I hate that...
What about you? Not so much?
I don't get that. Never have.
Why not? Oh, I know...
He has a fire burning within him.
...Guys, I don't know if today is--
Hold that thought, because I've a question you need to answer first...
Are we drinking? Or are we drinking? Because frankly, I wouldn't mind turning things up to ten.
I say eleven, because there are a lot of very hot medium-powered mutants on the island that would love to get down at the Summer House.
I have some ideas I'm noodling on, but I don't want you judging me right now.
Either way, what do you say, Emperor? Party? Or party?
...
I'm going for a walk.

[kra_[0.10]
[koa_[0.10]

[kra_[0.X]
[koa_[0.X]

EMPYRE

The Kree and Skrull empires have united under Emperor Hulkling to fight a common enemy: the Celestial Messiah Quoi and his plant-like Cotati, who have claimed Earth's Moon as their own!

Huh. Who do we know who lives on the Moon?

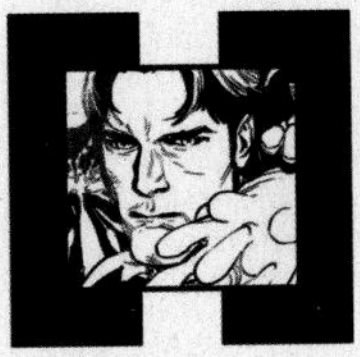

Vulcan

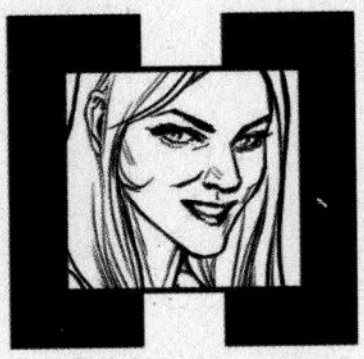

Petra

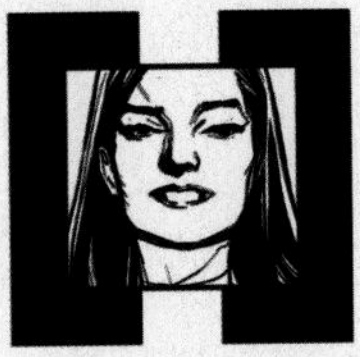

Sway

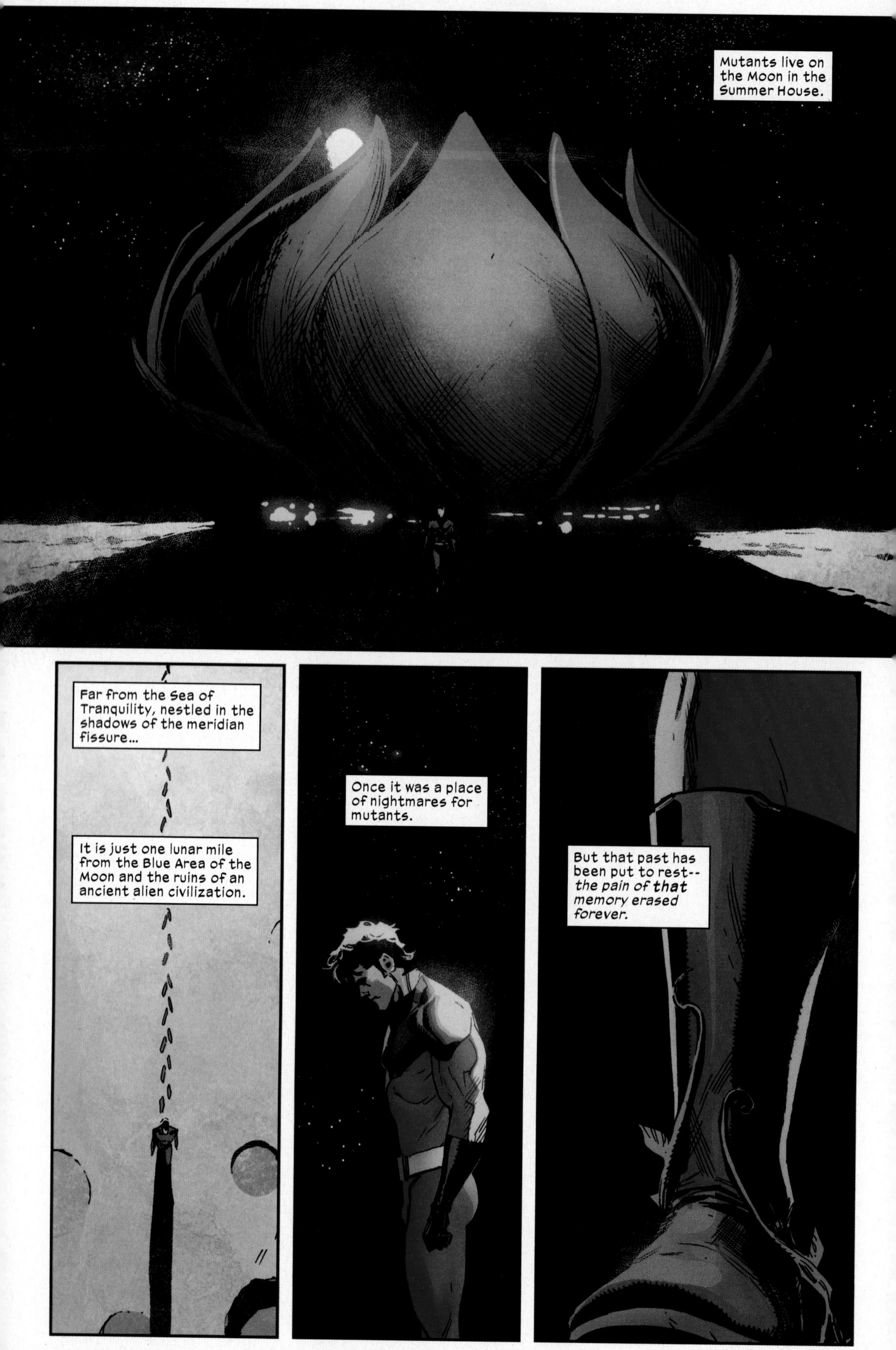
Mutants live on the Moon in the Summer House.
Far from the Sea of Tranquility, nestled in the shadows of the meridian fissure...
It is just one lunar mile from the Blue Area of the Moon and the ruins of an ancient alien civilization.
Once it was a place of nightmares for mutants.
But that past has been put to rest-- the pain of that memory erased forever.

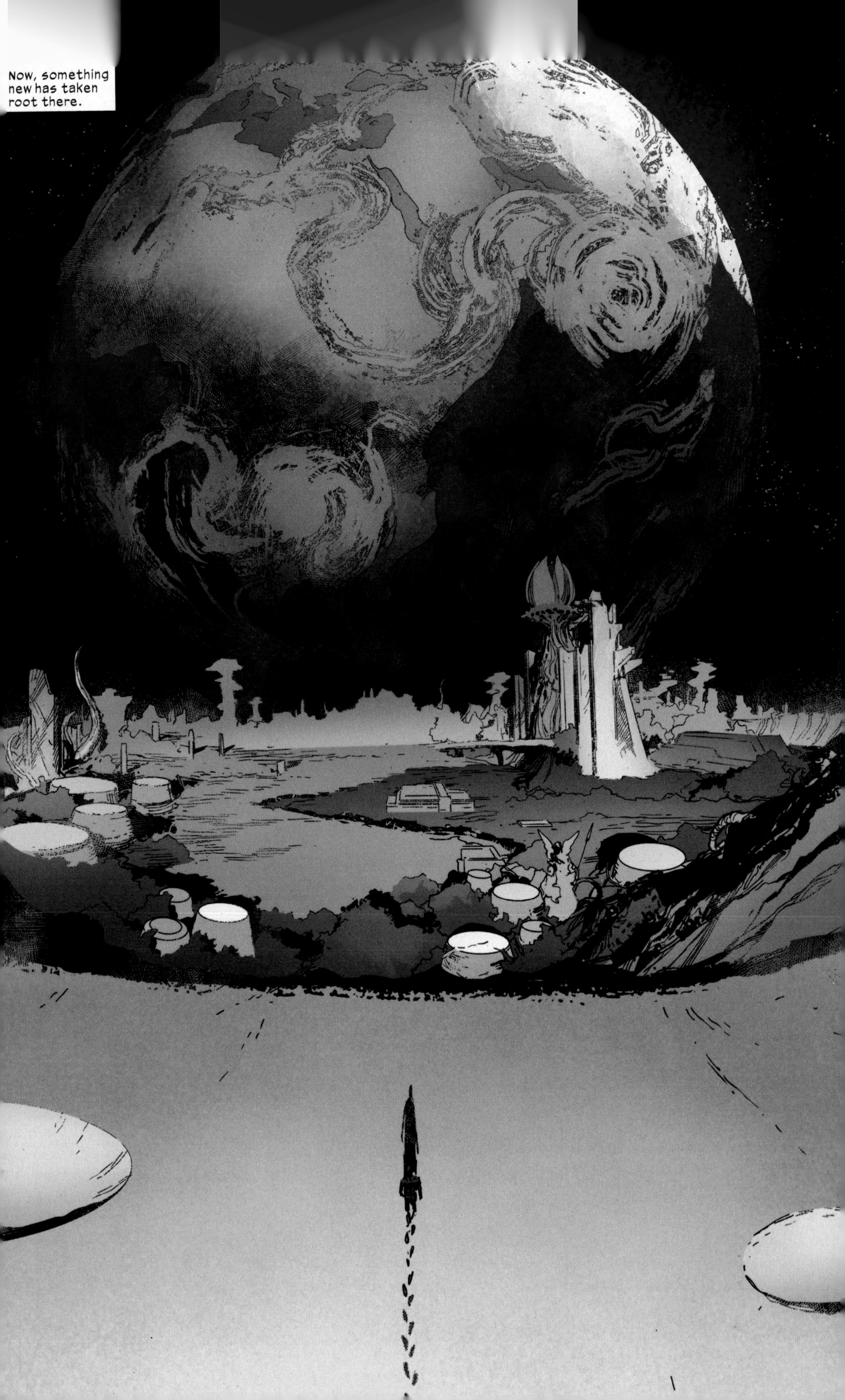
Now, something new has taken root there.

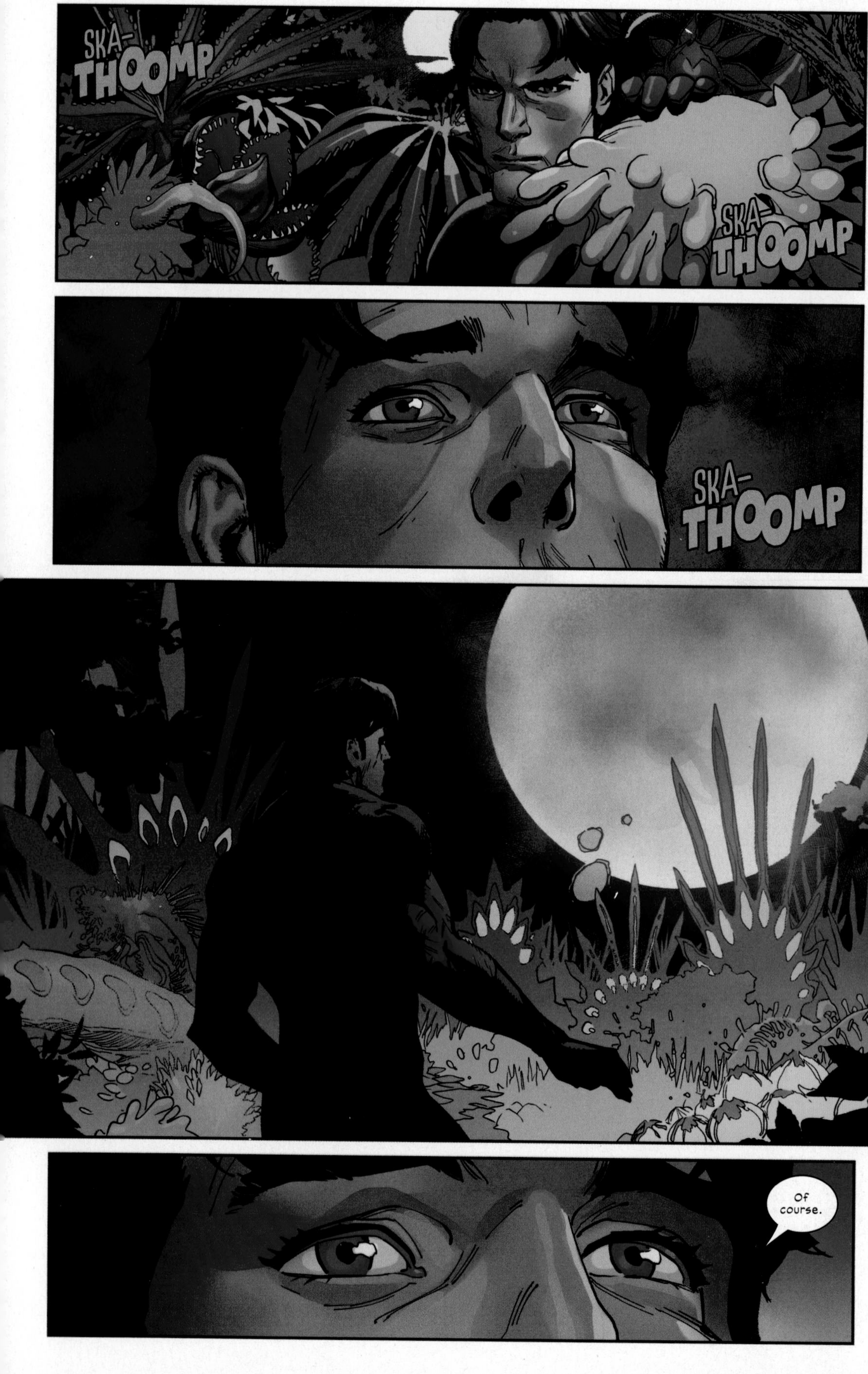
SKA-THOOMP
SKA-THOOMP
SKA-THOOMP
Of course.

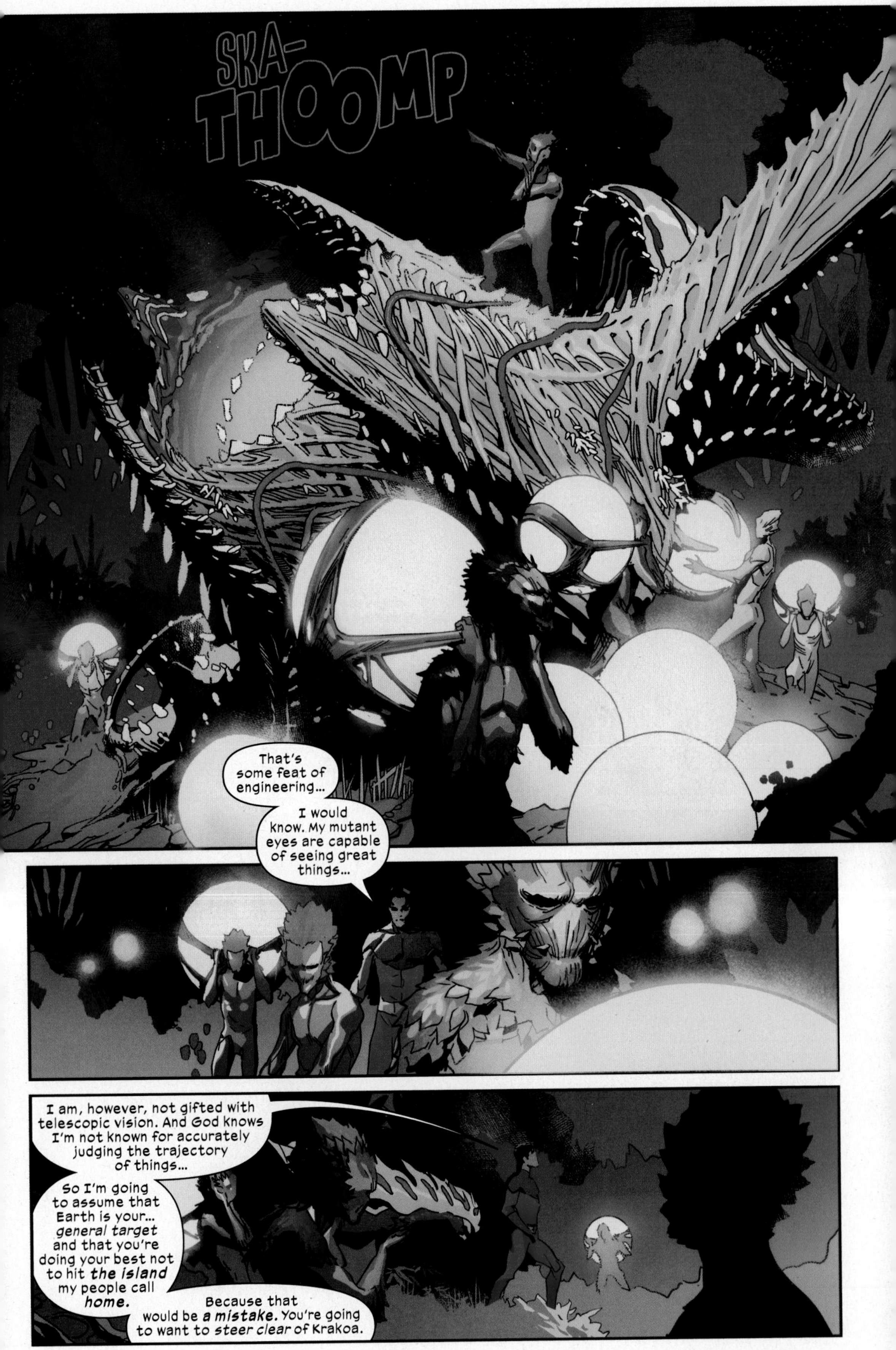

SKA-THOOMP
That's some feat of engineering...
I would know. My mutant eyes are capable of seeing great things...
I am, however, not gifted with telescopic vision. And God knows I'm not known for accurately judging the trajectory of things...
So I'm going to assume that Earth is your... *general target* and that you're doing your best not to hit ***the island*** my people call ***home.***
Because that would be ***a mistake.*** You're going to want to *steer clear* of Krakoa.

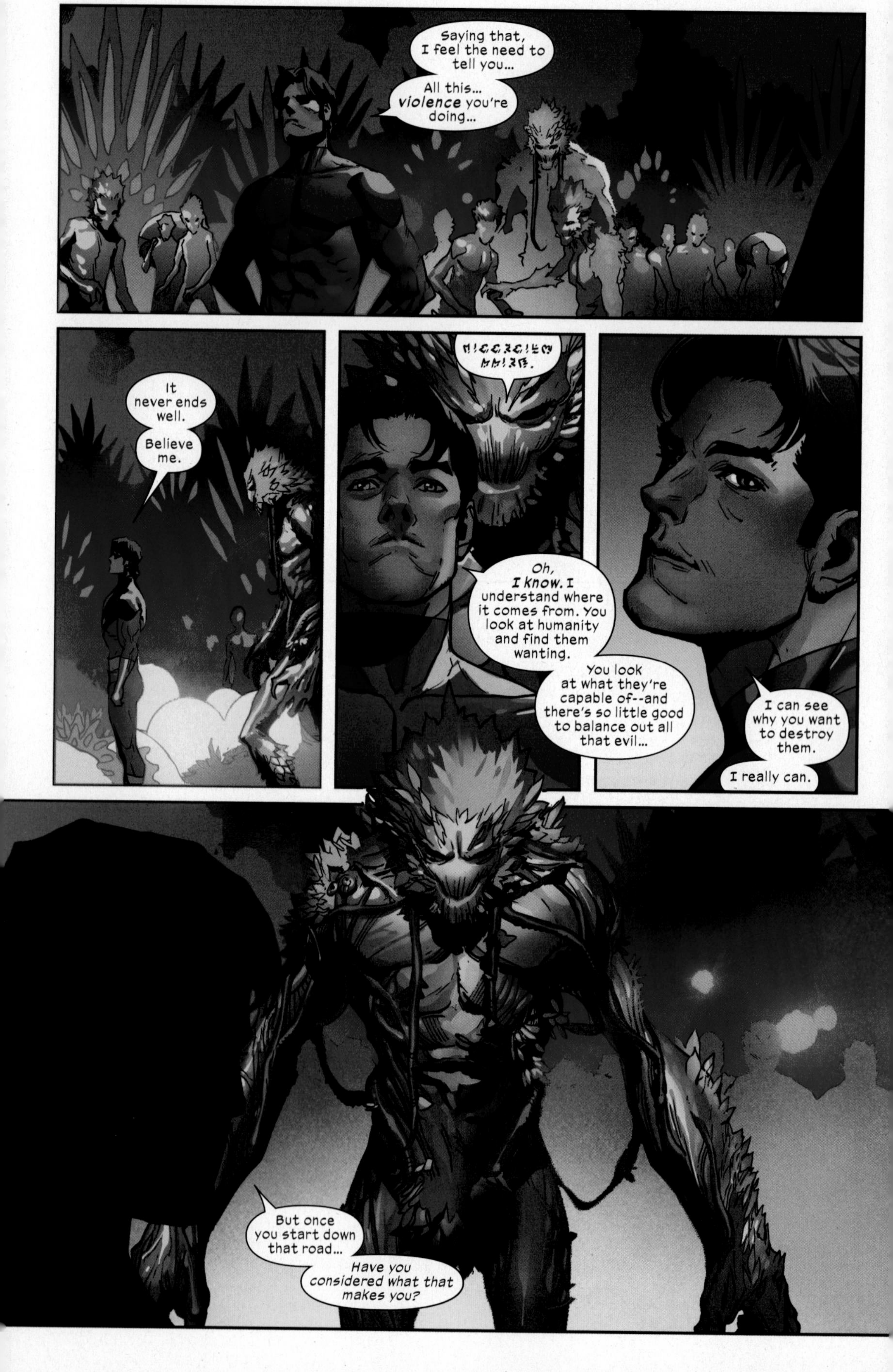
Saying that, I feel the need to tell you...
All this... *violence* you're doing...
It never ends well.
Believe me.
Oh, *I know.* I understand where it comes from. You look at humanity and find them wanting.
You look at what they're capable of--and there's so little good to balance out all that evil...
I can see why you want to destroy them.
I really can.
But once you start down that road...
Have you considered what that makes you?

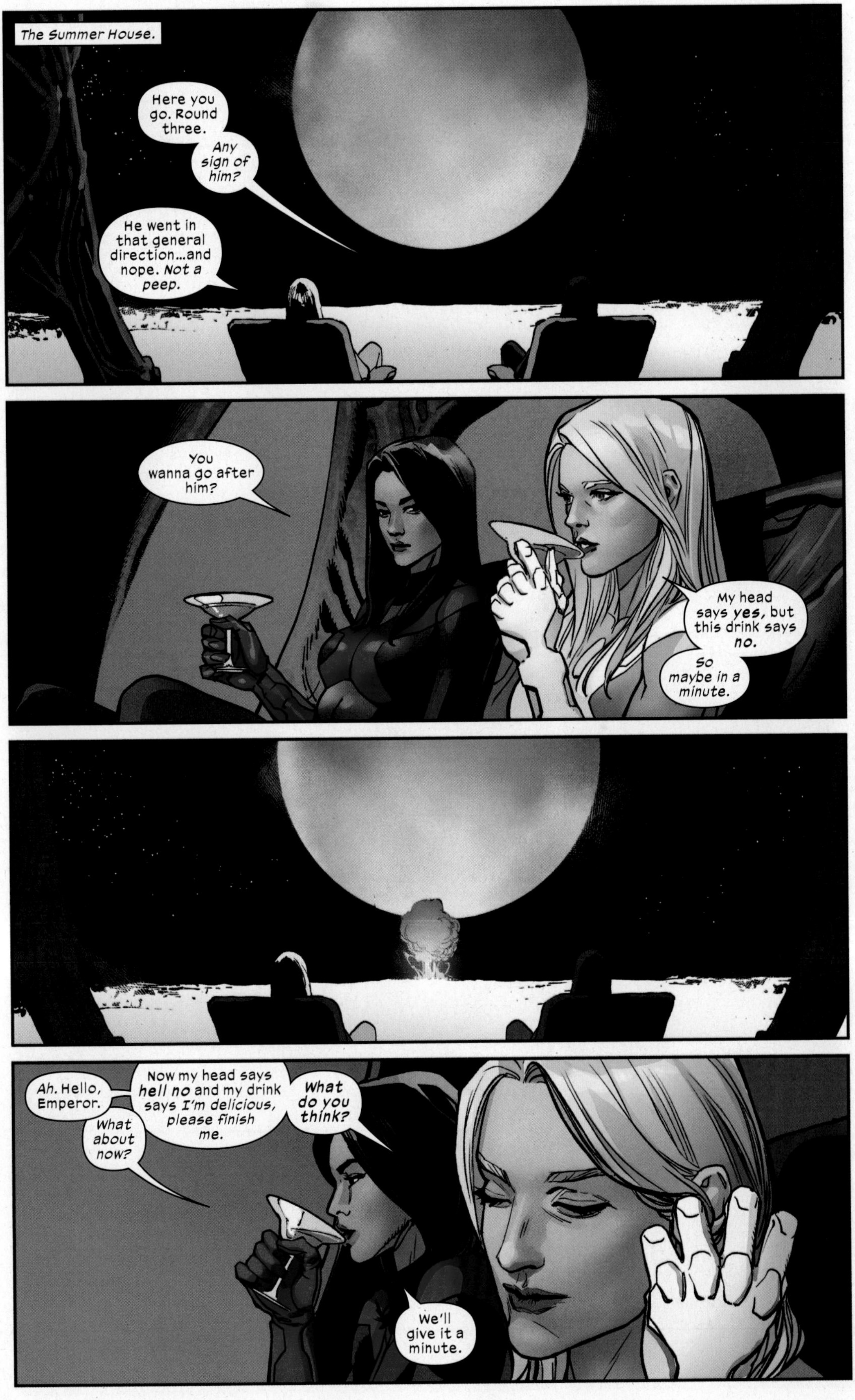

The Summer House.
Here you go. Round three.
Any sign of him?
He went in that general direction...and nope. Not a peep.
You wanna go after him?
My head says yes, but this drink says no.
So maybe in a minute.
Ah. Hello, Emperor.
What about now?
Now my head says hell no and my drink says I'm delicious, please finish me.
What do you think?
We'll give it a minute.

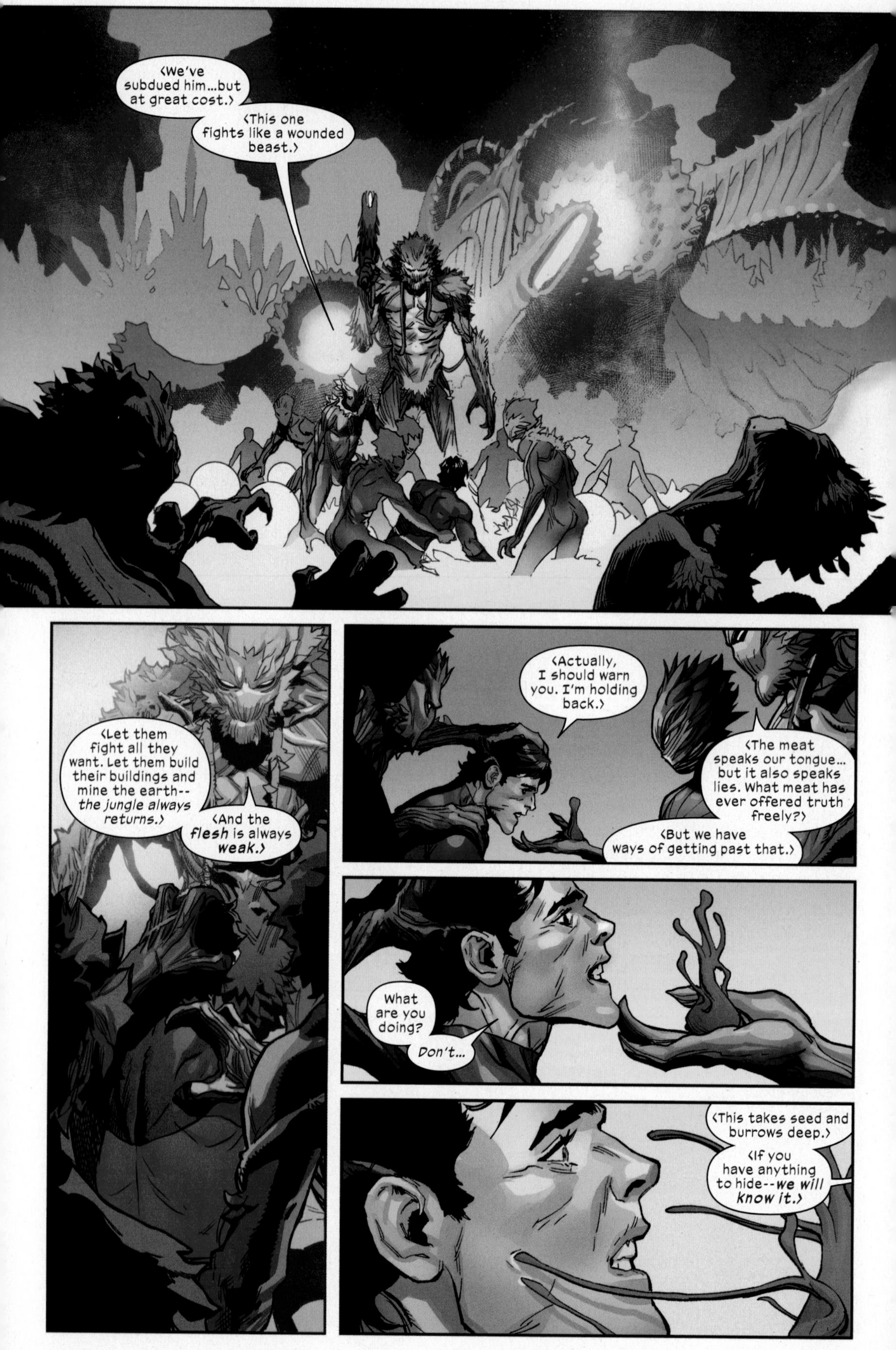
‹We've subdued him...but at great cost.›
‹This one fights like a wounded beast.›
‹Let them fight all they want. Let them build their buildings and mine the earth--*the jungle always* returns.›
‹And the *flesh* is always **weak.**›
‹Actually, I should warn you. I'm holding back.›
‹The meat speaks our tongue... but it also speaks lies. What meat has ever offered truth freely?›
‹But we have ways of getting past that.›
What are you doing?
Don't...
‹This takes seed and burrows deep.›
‹If you have anything to hide--***we will know it.***›

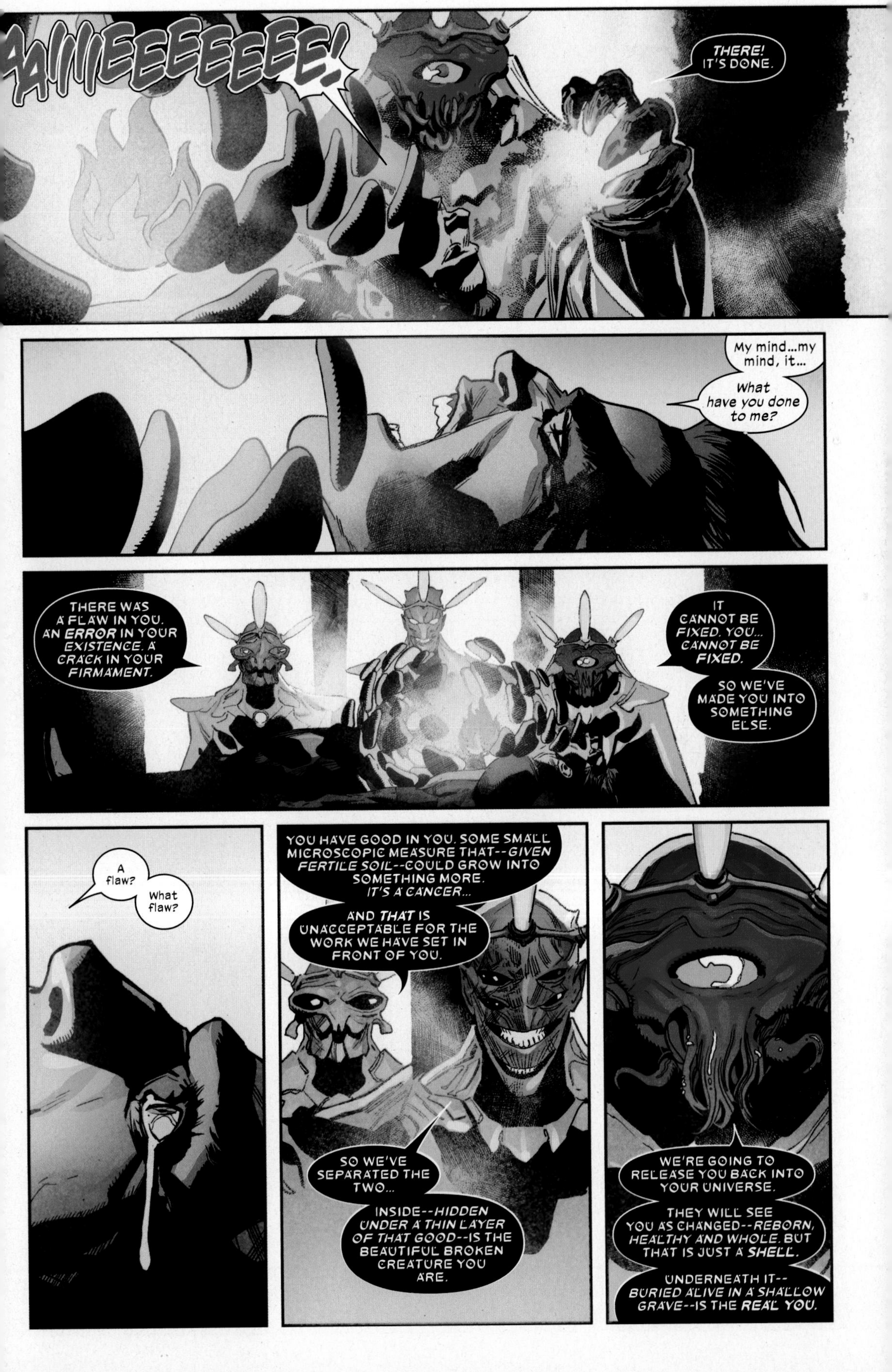
AAIIIIEEEEEEEE!
THERE! IT'S DONE.
My mind...my mind, it...
What have you done to me?
THERE WAS A FLAW IN YOU. AN ERROR IN YOUR EXISTENCE. A CRACK IN YOUR FIRMAMENT.
IT CANNOT BE FIXED. YOU... CANNOT BE FIXED.
SO WE'VE MADE YOU INTO SOMETHING ELSE.
A flaw?
What flaw?
YOU HAVE GOOD IN YOU. SOME SMALL MICROSCOPIC MEASURE THAT--GIVEN FERTILE SOIL--COULD GROW INTO SOMETHING MORE. IT'S A CANCER...
AND THAT IS UNACCEPTABLE FOR THE WORK WE HAVE SET IN FRONT OF YOU.
SO WE'VE SEPARATED THE TWO...
INSIDE--HIDDEN UNDER A THIN LAYER OF THAT GOOD--IS THE BEAUTIFUL BROKEN CREATURE YOU ARE.
WE'RE GOING TO RELEASE YOU BACK INTO YOUR UNIVERSE.
THEY WILL SEE YOU AS CHANGED--REBORN, HEALTHY AND WHOLE. BUT THAT IS JUST A SHELL.
UNDERNEATH IT--BURIED ALIVE IN A SHALLOW GRAVE--IS THE REAL YOU.

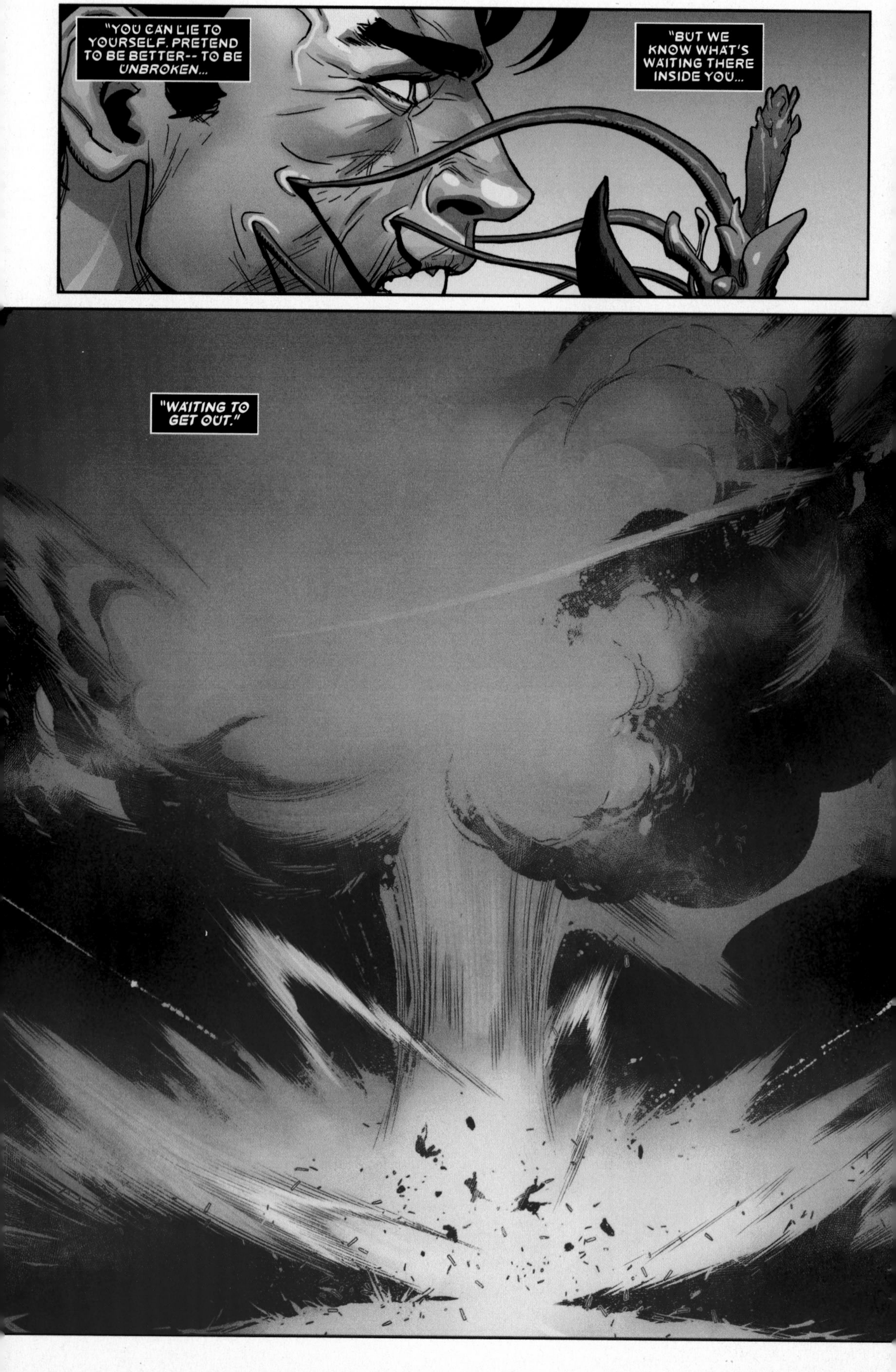
"YOU CAN LIE TO YOURSELF. PRETEND TO BE BETTER-- TO BE UNBROKEN...
"BUT WE KNOW WHAT'S WAITING THERE INSIDE YOU...
"WAITING TO GET OUT."

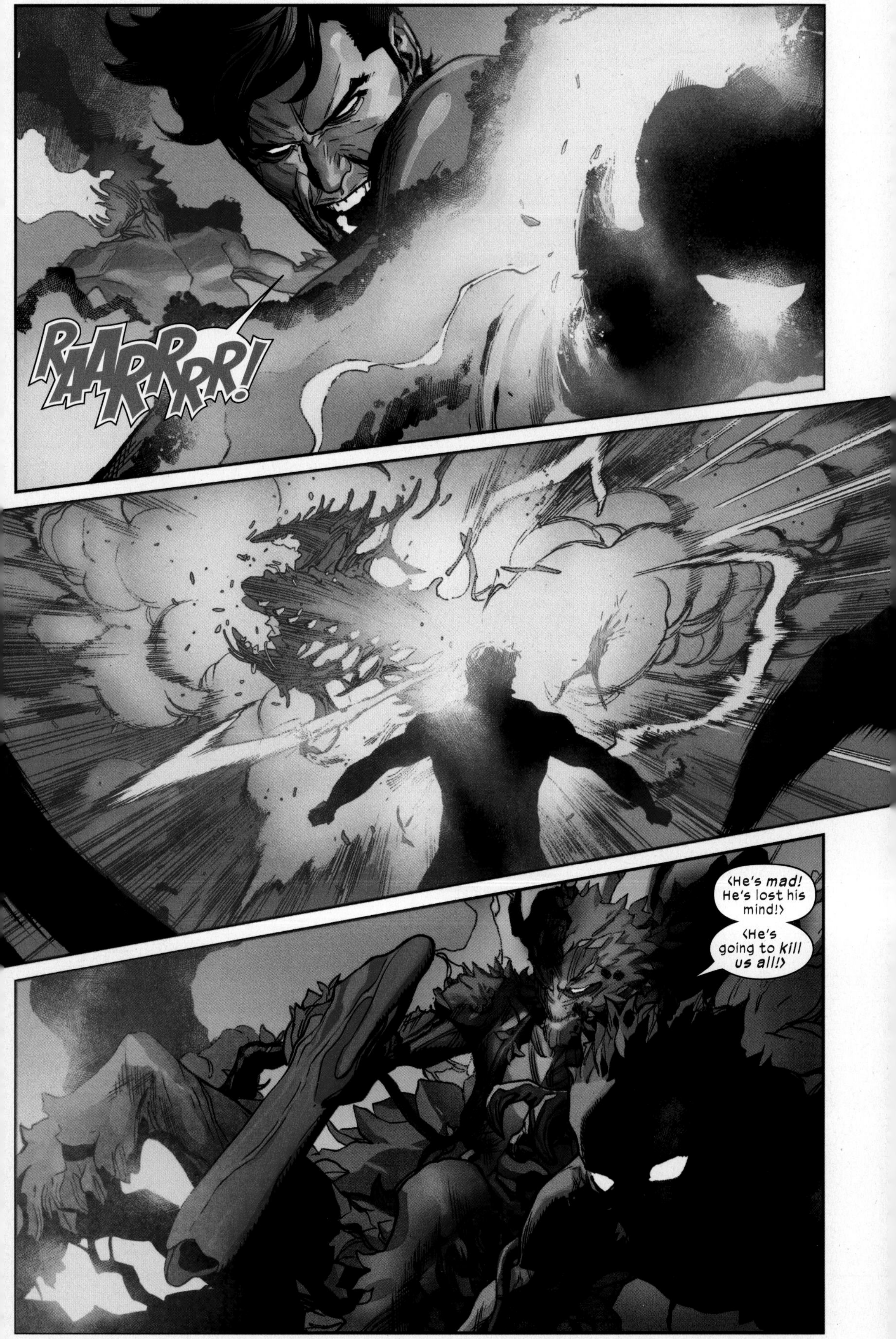
RAARRRR!
‹He's *mad!* He's lost his mind!›
‹He's going to *kill us all!*›

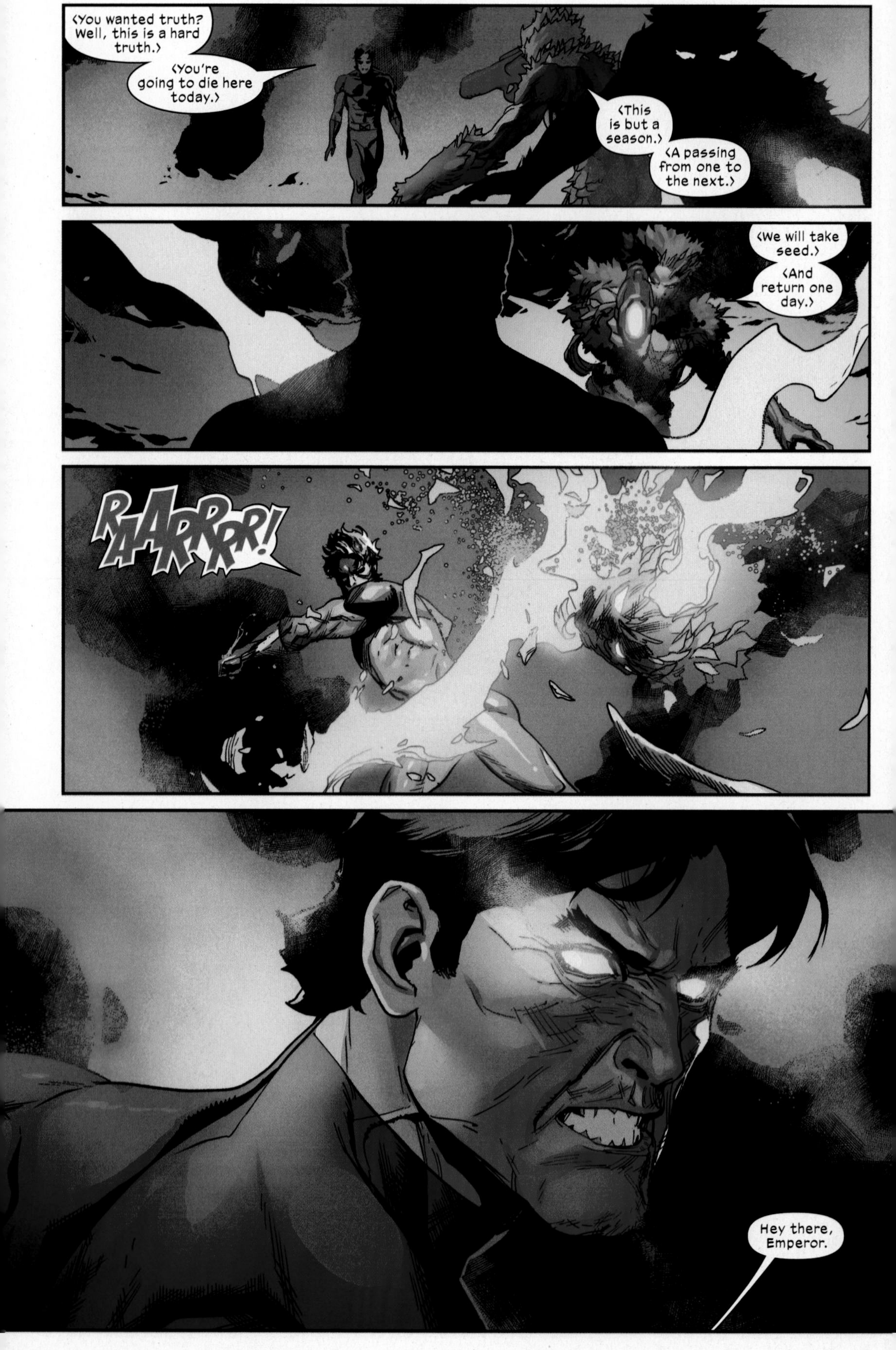
‹You wanted truth? Well, this is a hard truth.›
‹You're going to die here today.›
‹This is but a season.›
‹A passing from one to the next.›
‹We will take seed.›
‹And return one day.›
RAARRRR!
Hey there, Emperor.

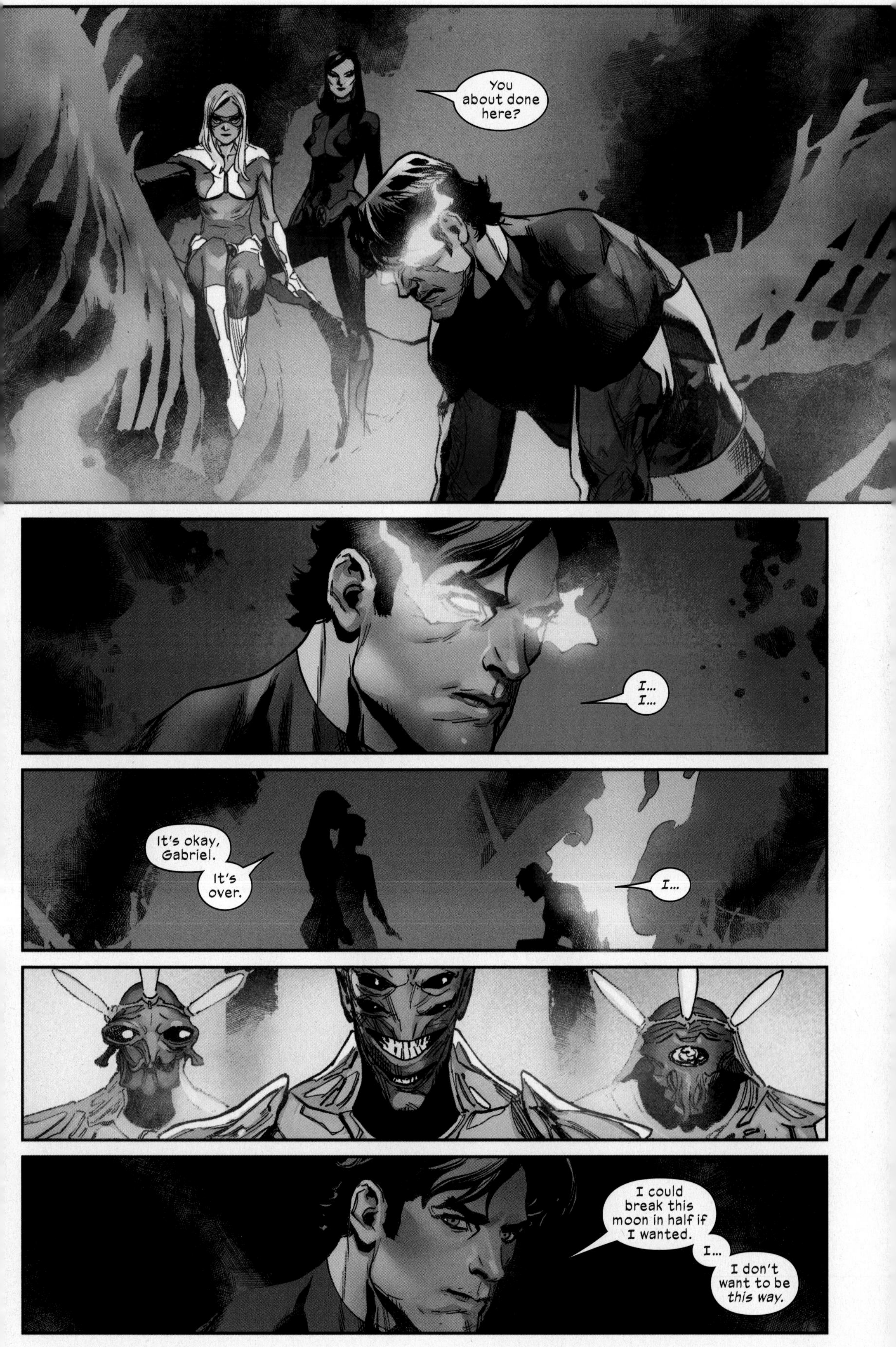
You about done here?
I... I...
It's okay, Gabriel.
It's over.
I...
I could break this moon in half if I wanted.
I...
I don't want to be *this way.*

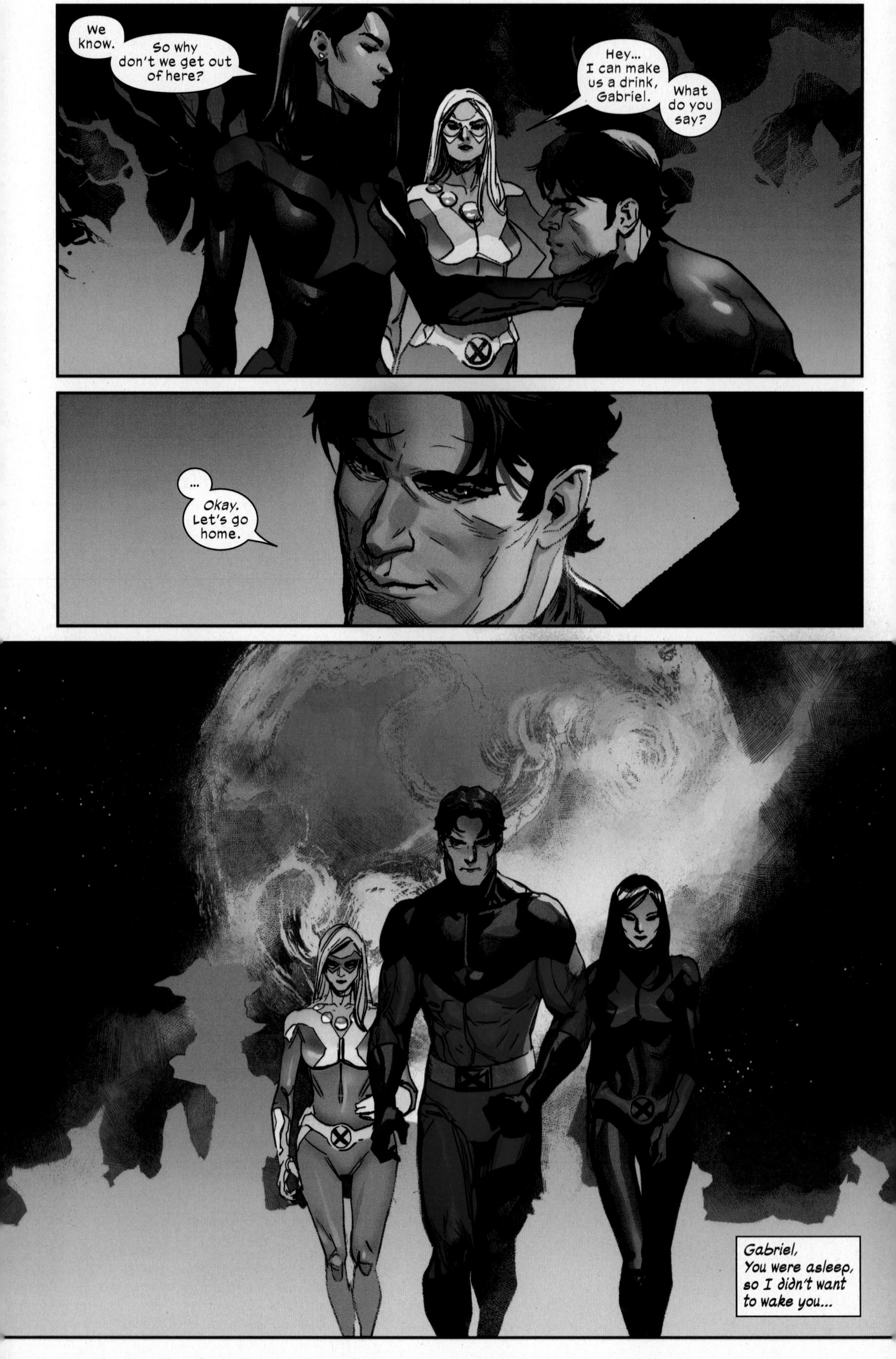

We know.
So why don't we get out of here?
Hey... I can make us a drink, Gabriel.
What do you say?
... Okay. Let's go home.
Gabriel, You were asleep, so I didn't want to wake you...

Jean and I are taking the kids to Chandilore for the day. I know we've talked about you getting out and not just staying at the house, and I really think you should reconsider it.

I know coming back here to Shi'ar space was out of the question-- maybe it shouldn't be--but doing the same thing over and over, each and every day, makes it hard to become someone new. I know that deep down that's what you want.

And, hey, I promise I'll be with you the whole way. Come fire, come war, come anything that would stand in the way. You're safe, because you're with family.

We'll probably be home after dinner.

Love,
Scott.

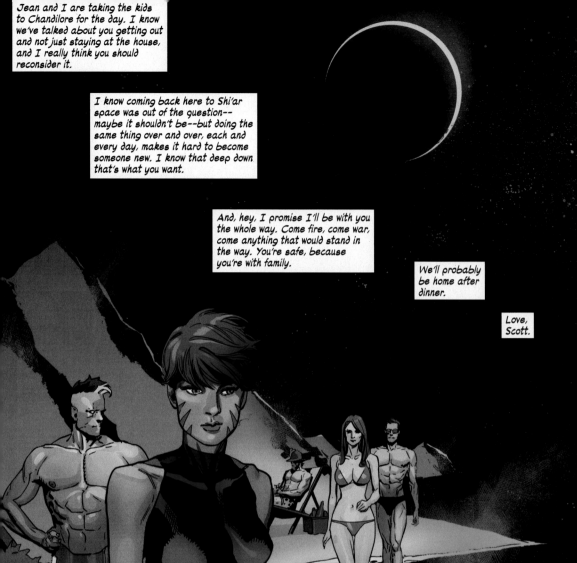

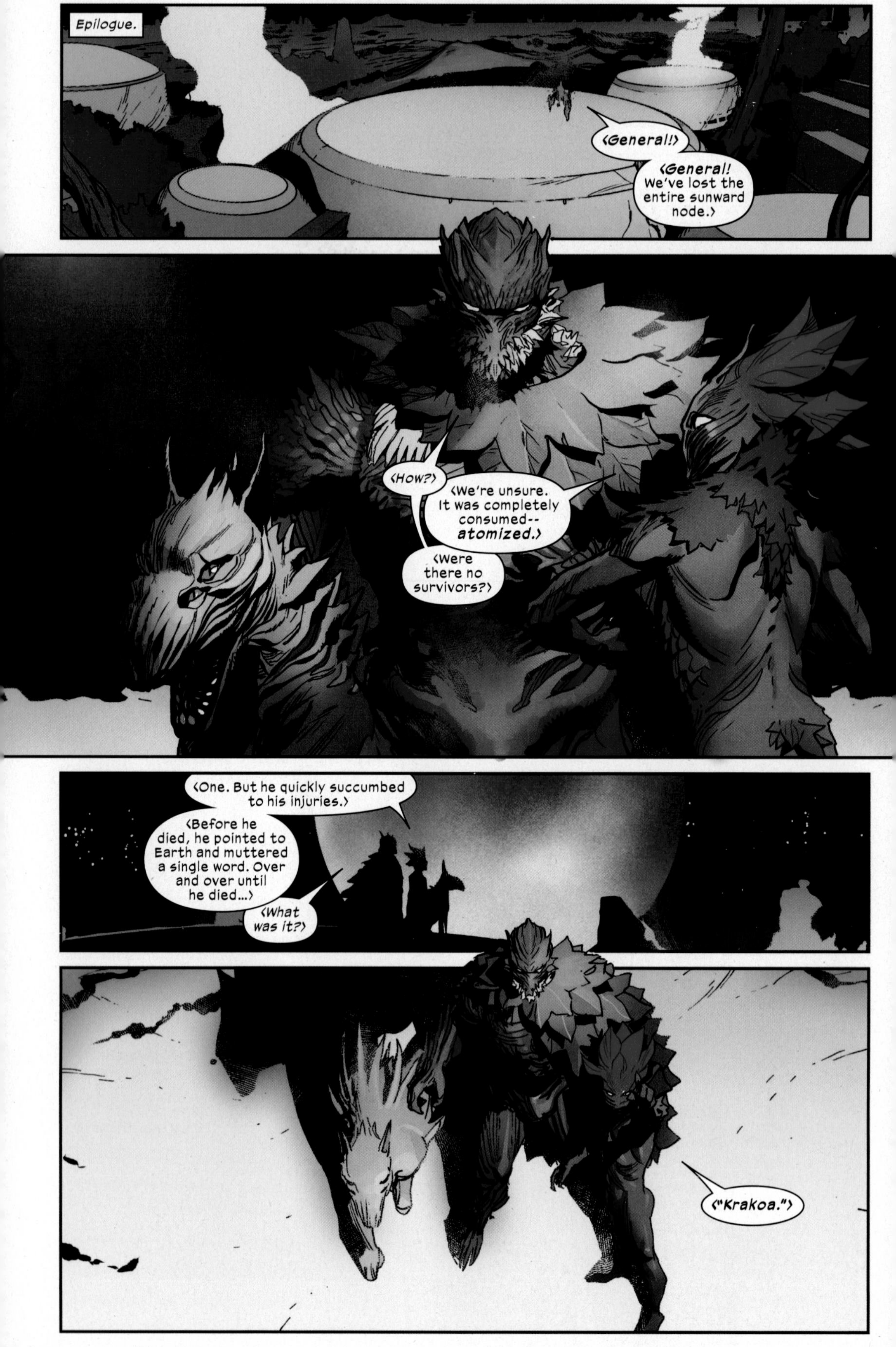

Epilogue.
<General!>
<General! We've lost the entire sunward node.>
<How?>
<We're unsure. It was completely consumed-- atomized.>
<Were there no survivors?>
<One. But he quickly succumbed to his injuries.>
<Before he died, he pointed to Earth and muttered a single word. Over and over until he died...>
<What was it?>
<"Krakoa.">

[dawn_of_x]

[kra_]
[koa_]

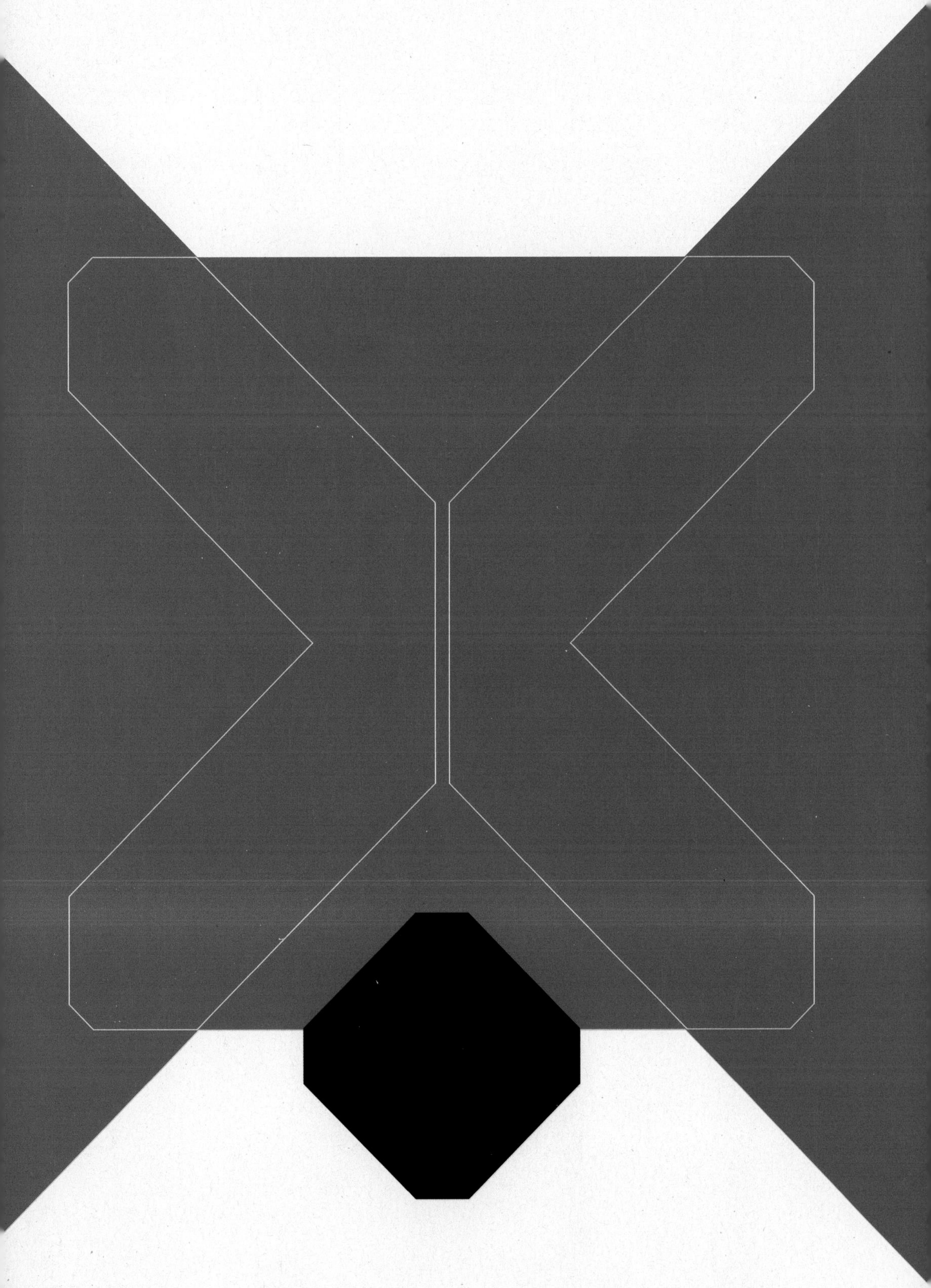

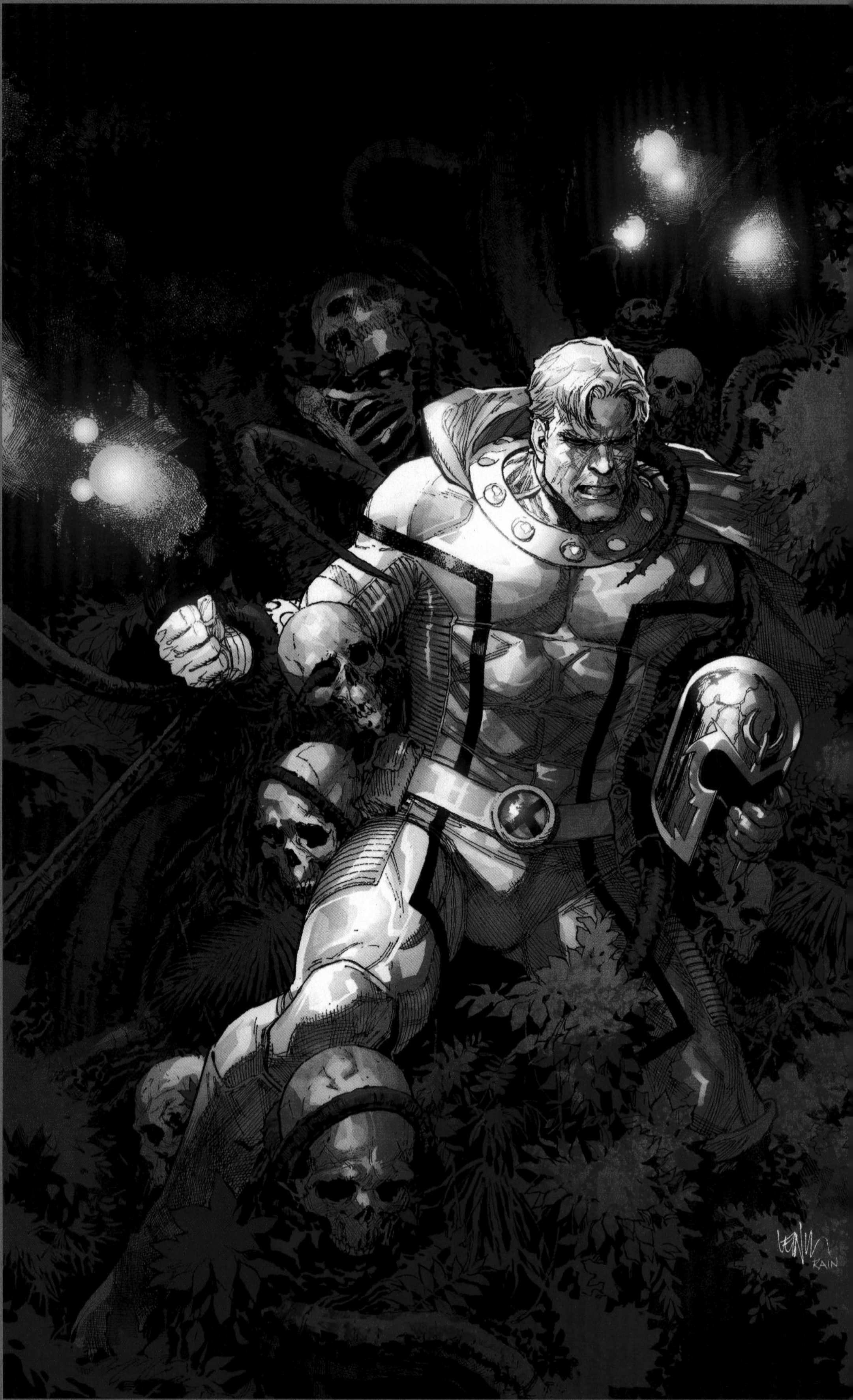
RAIN

One War, One Mutant

11

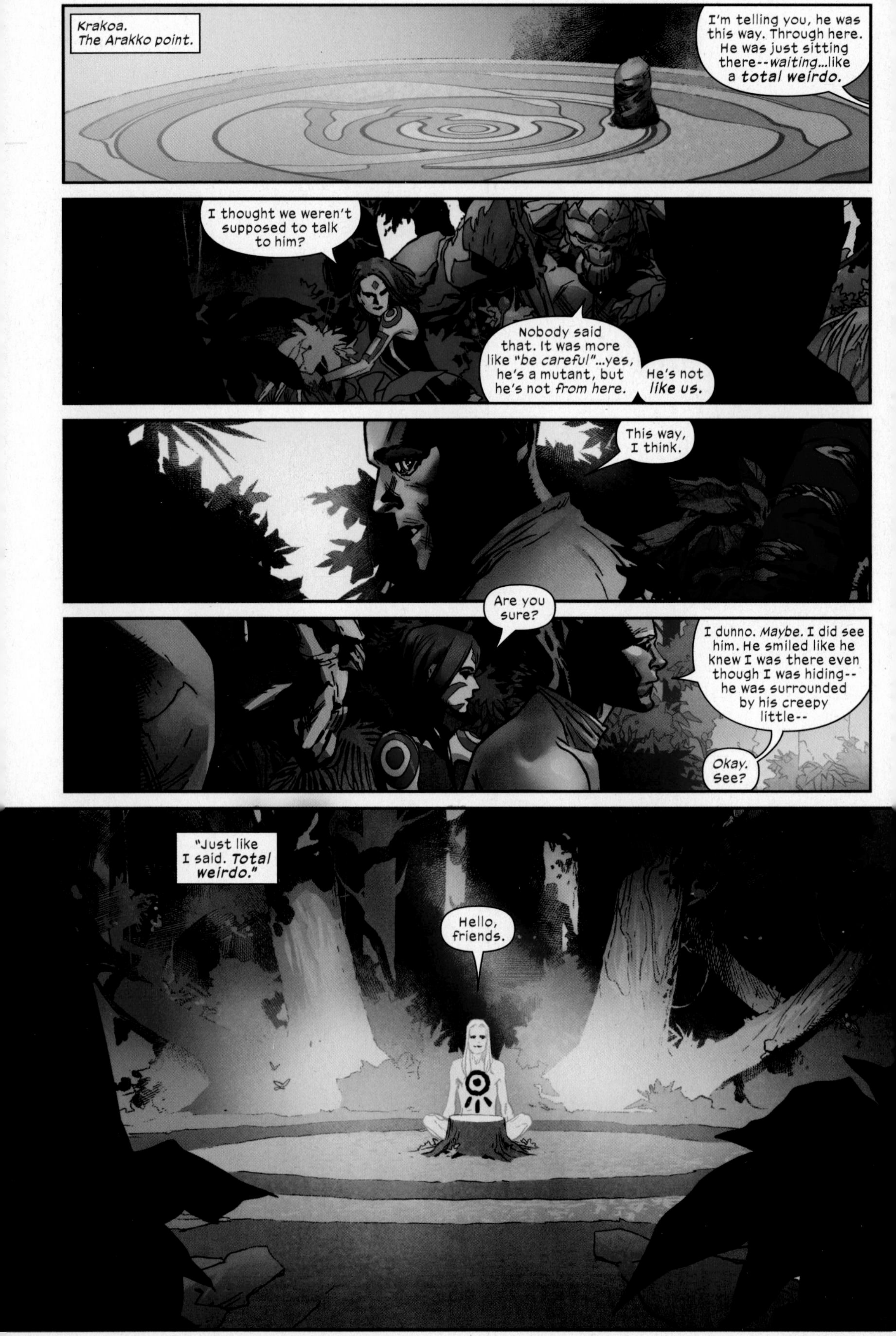
Krakoa.
The Arakko point.
I'm telling you, he was this way. Through here. He was just sitting there--*waiting*...like a **total weirdo.**
I thought we weren't supposed to talk to him?
Nobody said that. It was more like "*be careful*"...yes, he's a mutant, but he's not *from here.*
He's not **like us.**
This way, I think.
Are you sure?
I dunno. *Maybe.* I did see him. He smiled like he knew I was there even though I was hiding--he was surrounded by his creepy little--
Okay. See?
"Just like I said. ***Total weirdo.***"
Hello, friends.

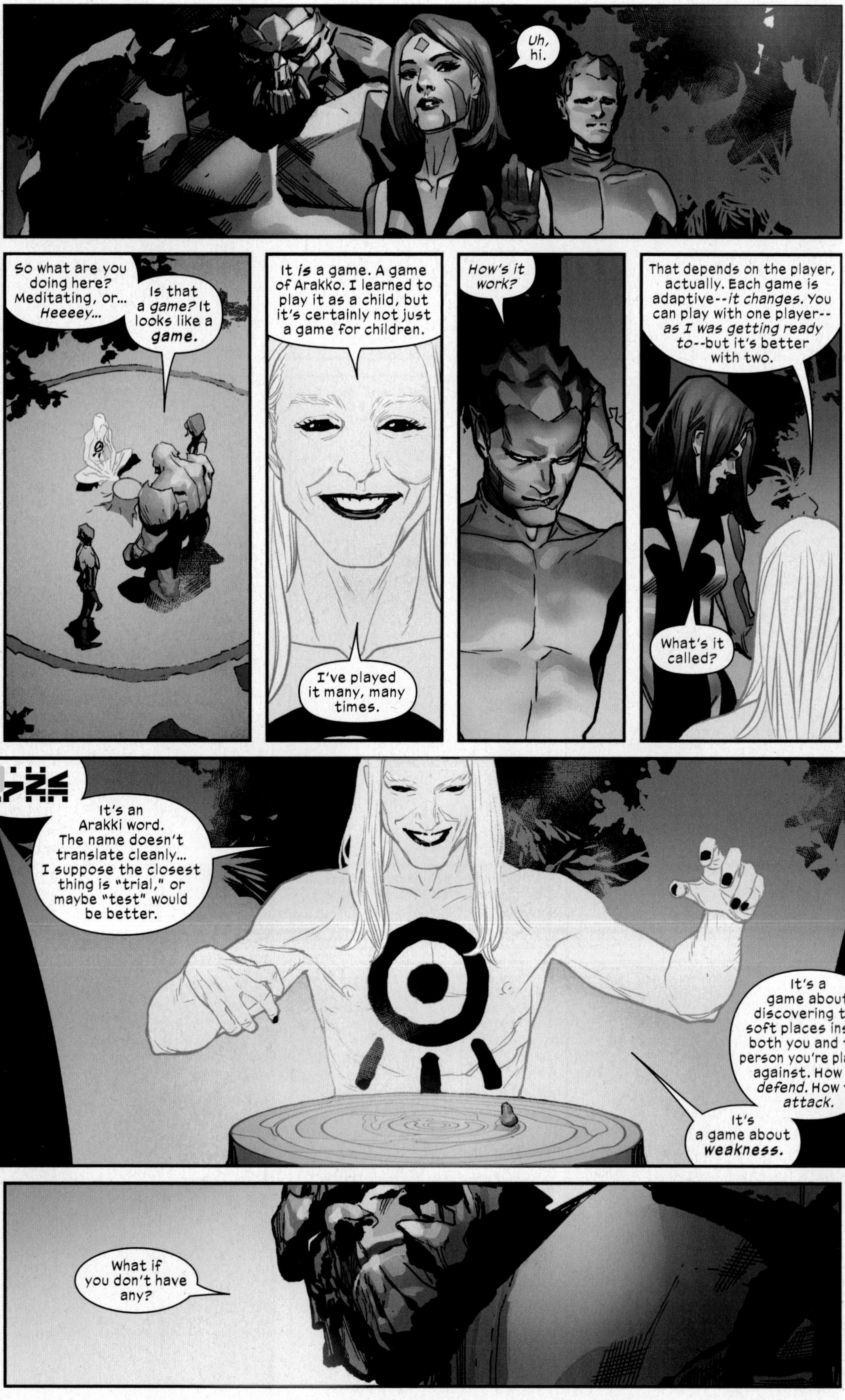

Uh, hi.
So what are you doing here? Meditating, or... Heeeey...
Is that a game? It looks like a game.
It is a game. A game of Arakko. I learned to play it as a child, but it's certainly not just a game for children.
I've played it many, many times.
How's it work?
That depends on the player, actually. Each game is adaptive--it changes. You can play with one player--as I was getting ready to--but it's better with two.
What's it called?
It's an Arakki word. The name doesn't translate cleanly... I suppose the closest thing is "trial," or maybe "test" would be better.
It's a game about discovering the soft places inside both you and the person you're playing against. How to defend. How to attack.
It's a game about weakness.
What if you don't have any?

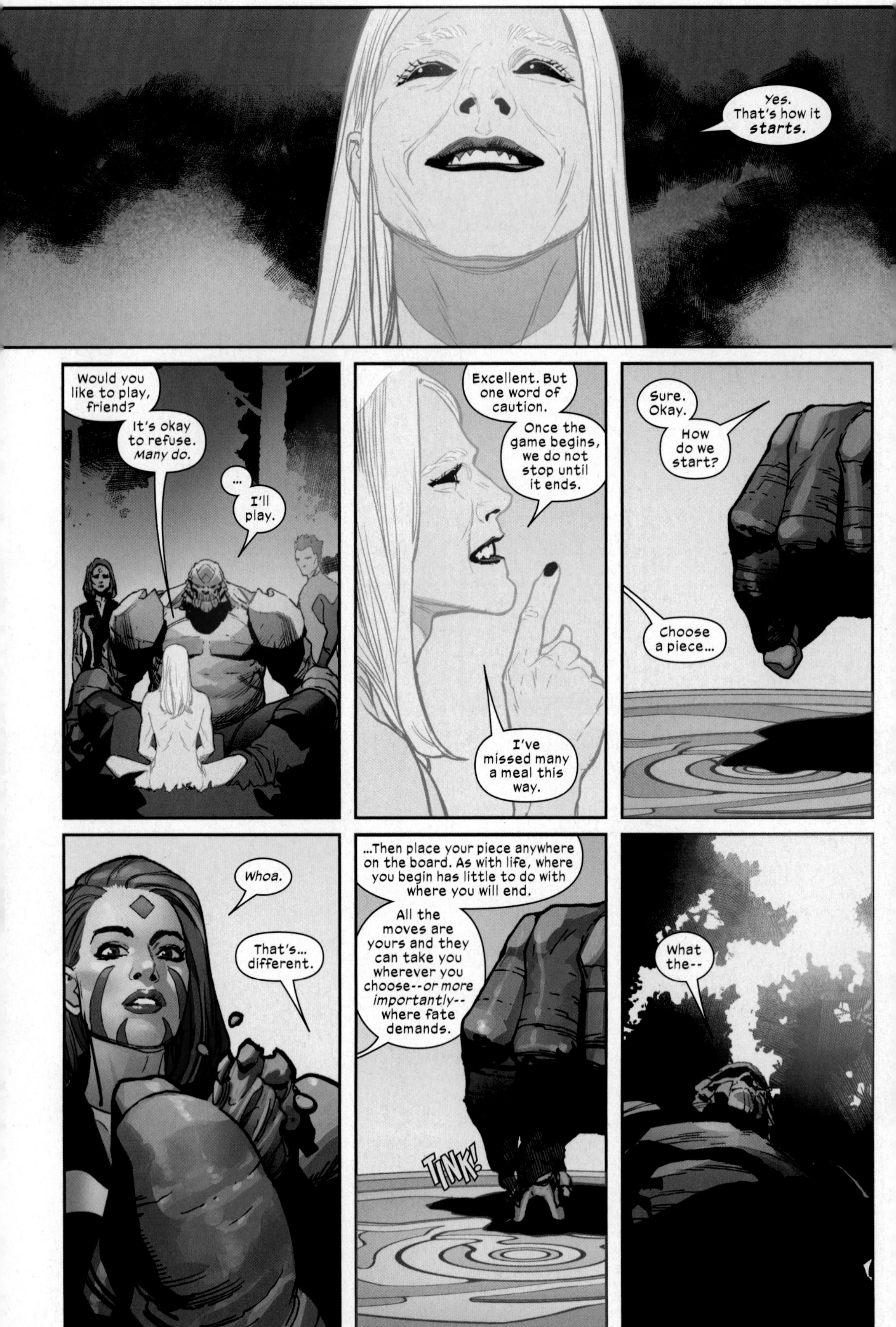
Yes. That's how it starts.
Would you like to play, friend?
It's okay to refuse. Many do.
...
I'll play.
Excellent. But one word of caution.
Once the game begins, we do not stop until it ends.
I've missed many a meal this way.
Sure. Okay.
How do we start?
Choose a piece...
Whoa.
That's... different.
...Then place your piece anywhere on the board. As with life, where you begin has little to do with where you will end.
All the moves are yours and they can take you wherever you choose--or more importantly--where fate demands.
TINK!
What the--

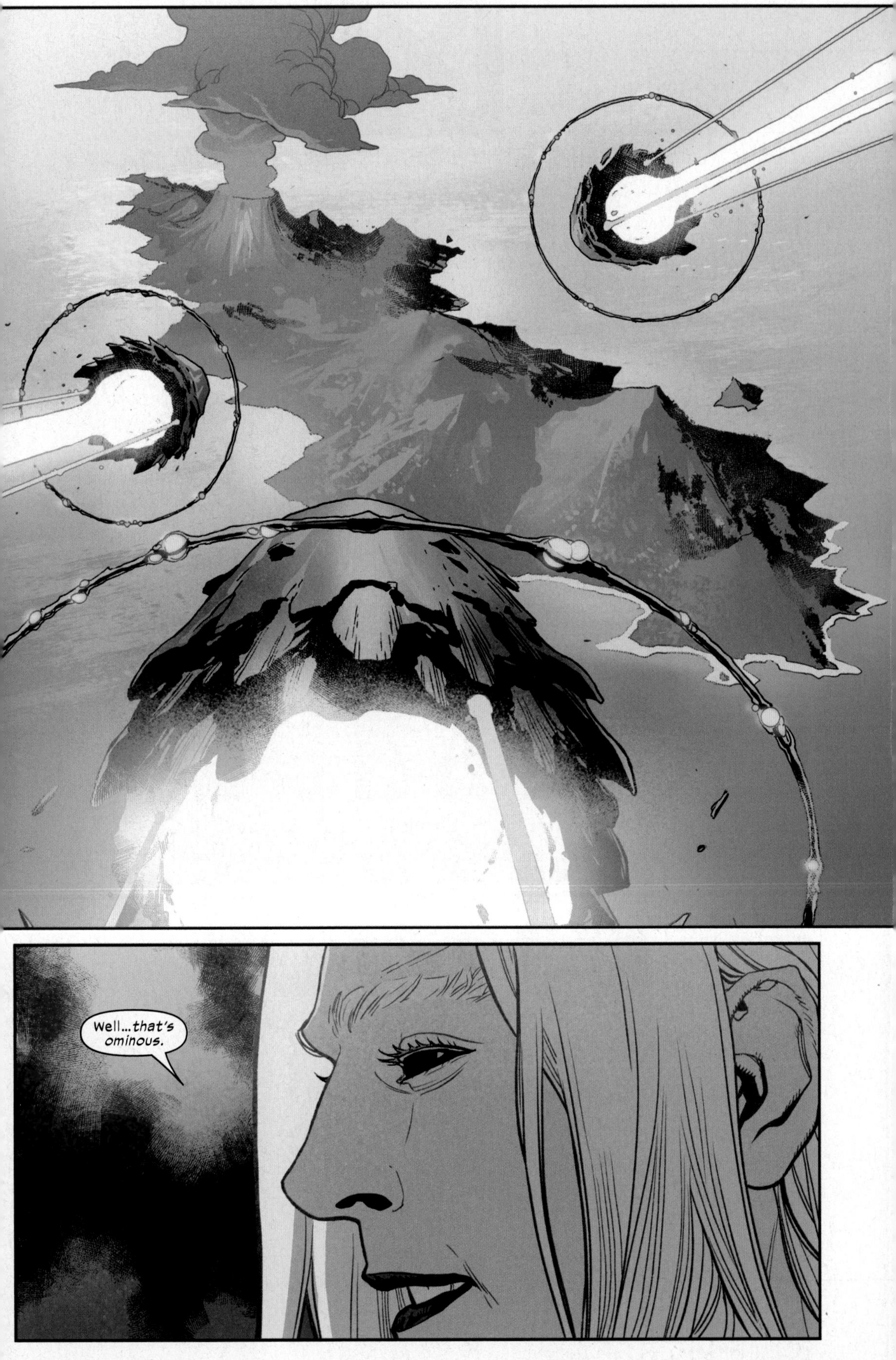
Well...that's ominous.

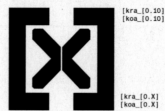

EMPYRE

The Kree and Skrull Empires have united under Emperor Hulkling to fight a common enemy: the Celestial Messiah, Quoi, and his plant-like Cotati, who have claimed Earth's Moon as their own!

The X-MEN began to fight back on the moon, but in doing so drew the attention of the Cotati to a much bigger target: Earth...and Krakoa.

Rockslide   Loa   Anole

Summoner   Exodus   Magneto

Magik   Magma   Iceman

A REPORT TO THE QUIET COUNCIL FROM THE CAPTAIN COMMANDER

RE: ASYMMETRICAL WARFARE

For the eyes of the council only.

This a brief overview of our recent captains' quorum, but what should be of particular interest to you are our recommendations regarding enhanced techniques in combat scenarios for mutants with combat experience.

These proposals come with zero reservations and have the full support of the quorum. Research and expansion in this area has our highest recommendation.

QUORUM NOTES

Island readiness:

Following the multiple recent incursions of Krakoan space, the quorum's position is that our existing dome of protected space should be expanded through a series of encircling chain islands. We can construct these ourselves and moor them to Krakoa at selected intervals, but we first want to check with Cypher to see if the island can -- and is willing to -- do this itself.

—

Mutant training:

We know that we're trying to create an atmosphere that is serene and non-militaristic, but Bishop has been cataloging the amount of actual training being done on Danger island in the Atlantic archipelago, and the numbers are much lower than expected. The Krakoan population is clocking in at less than two percent.

We are not suggesting that everyone be required to become proficient at hand-to-hand combat and using their powers in an aggressive fashion, but the consensus here is that we could do a little more.

—

Archipelago access:

Following the suggestion of the council, we created an escape plan based on tiered evacuations and have had the island telepaths request to seed this information into the minds of all Krakoans. We consulted with Monet regarding extra-island X-Corp employee procedures, and she also recommended packaging this into the language dump for any new mutants arriving to the island and into all resurrection protocols.

[redacted]

Omega Level mutants:

[redacted] See below regarding enhanced techniques.

[redacted]

—

Enhanced combat techniques:

The quorum had a prolonged and rather interesting conversation about the Five and possibilities of conjoined power sets in both offensive and defensive situations.

We workshopped a single mutant's powers [using Magneto as our point of reference*] and how that mutant's power could integrate with others and -- limiting ourselves to three or fewer complementary mutants -- we came up with roughly 40 useful combinations in military scenarios [28 offensive, 12 defensive]. This, we all agree, is worth further study, and I've created a list of necessary resources to move forward. Additionally, Bishop has volunteered to preside over our first mutant war college.

As stated above, this plan has our highest recommendation.

**I've also attached the Magneto combinations to this file for the council to review.*

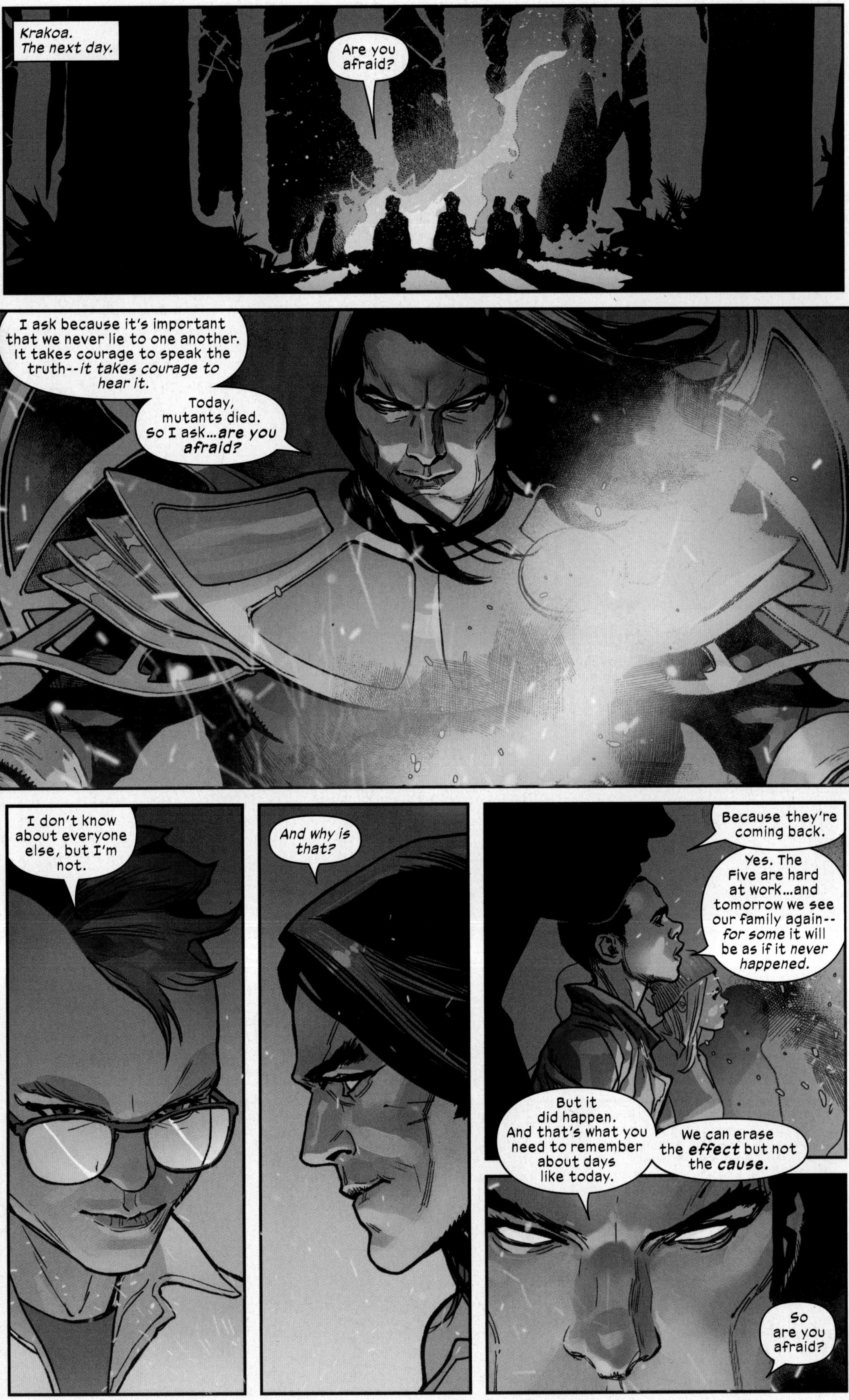
Krakoa.
The next day.
Are you afraid?
I ask because it's important that we never lie to one another. It takes courage to speak the truth--*it takes courage to hear it.*
Today, mutants died. So I ask...*are you afraid?*
I don't know about everyone else, but I'm not.
And why is that?
Because they're coming back.
Yes. The Five are hard at work...and tomorrow we see our family again-- *for some* it will be as if it *never happened.*
But it did happen. And that's what you need to remember about days like today.
We can erase the ***effect*** but not the ***cause.***
So are you afraid?

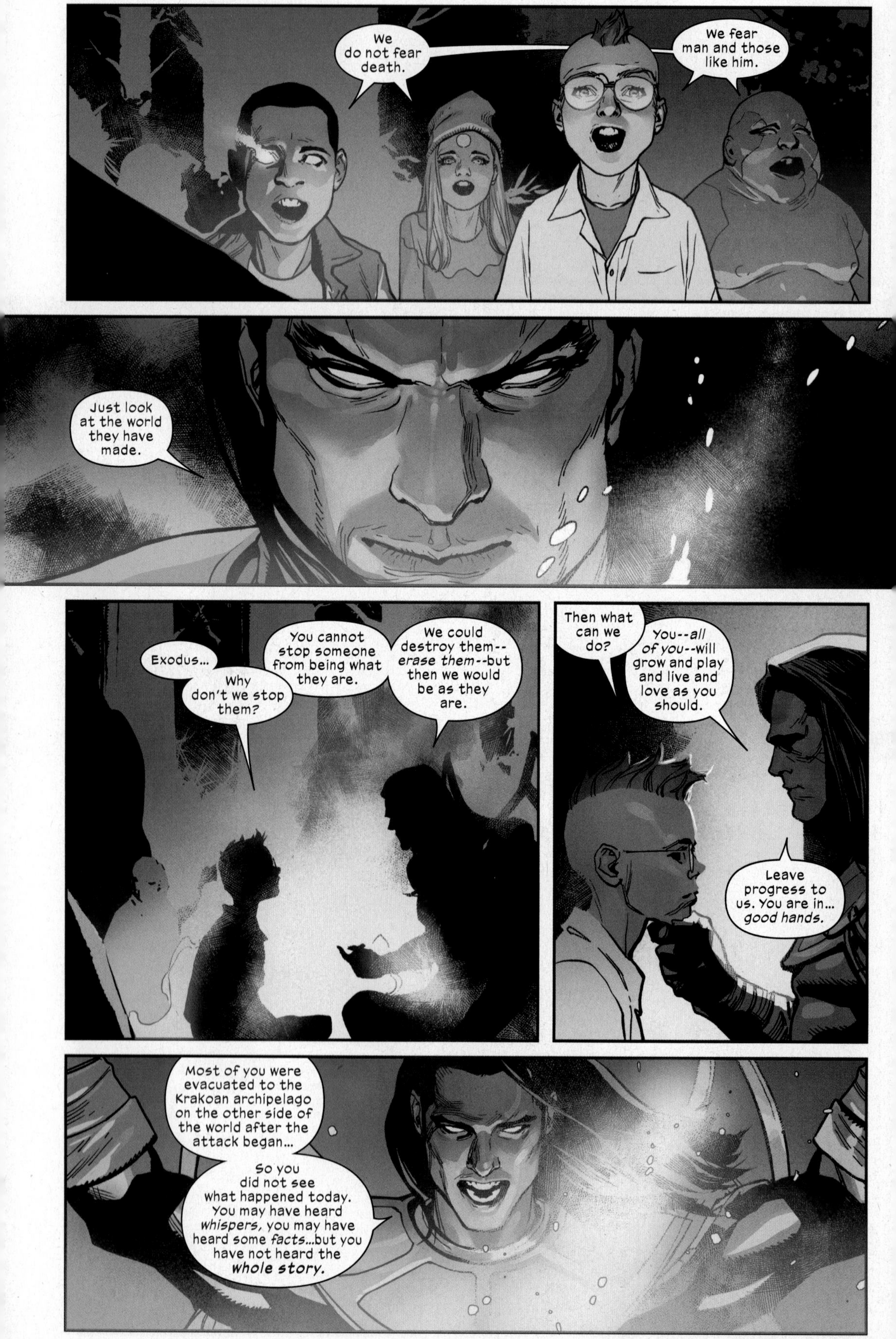
We do not fear death.
We fear man and those like him.
Just look at the world they have made.
Exodus...
Why don't we stop them?
You cannot stop someone from being what they are.
We could destroy them--*erase them*--but then we would be as they are.
Then what can we do?
You--*all of you*--will grow and play and live and love as you should.
Leave progress to us. You are in... *good hands.*
Most of you were evacuated to the Krakoan archipelago on the other side of the world after the attack began...
So you did not see what happened today. You may have heard *whispers,* you may have heard some *facts*...but you have not heard the **whole story.**

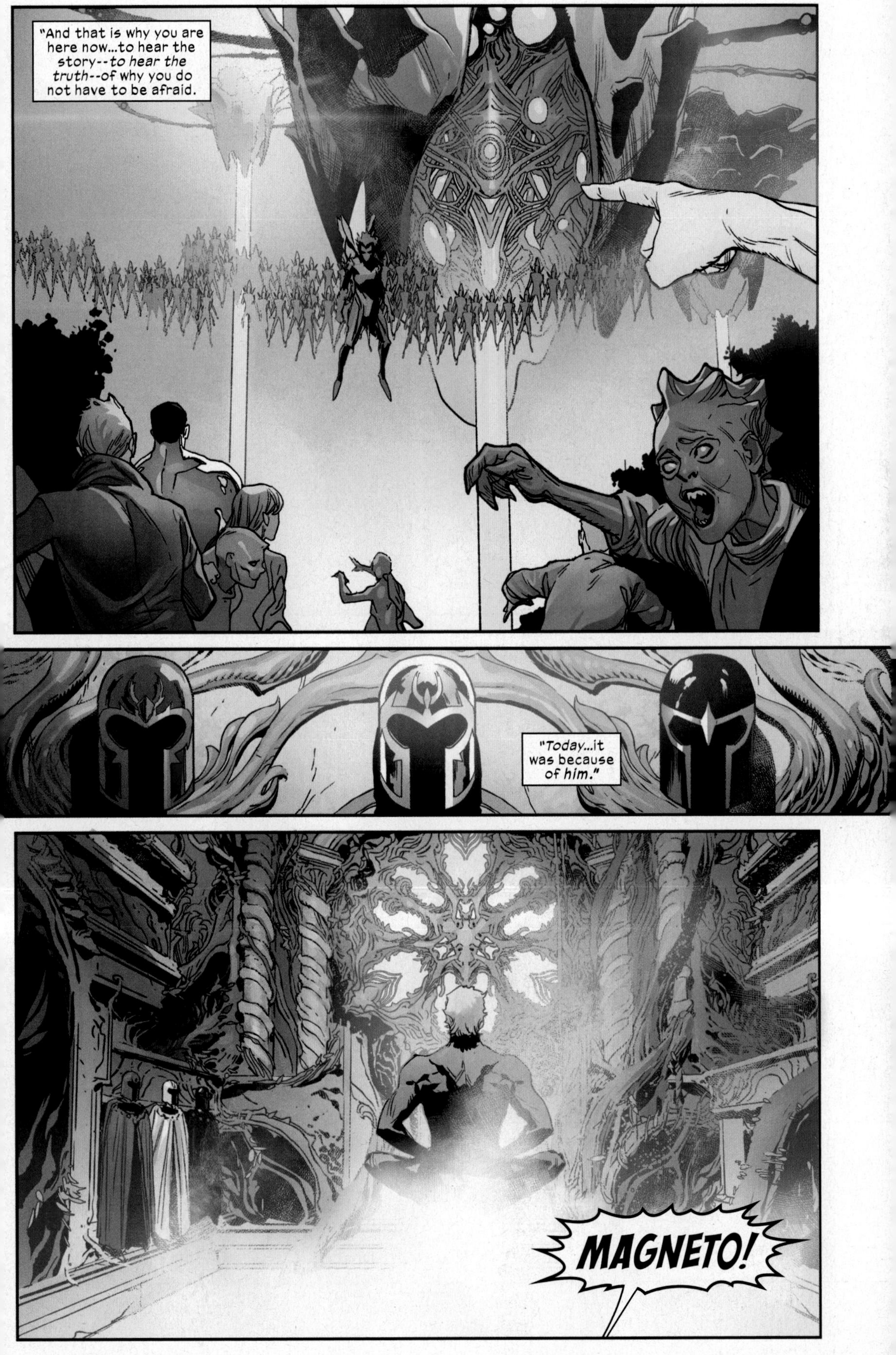
"And that is why you are here now...to hear the story--*to hear the truth*--of why you do not have to be afraid.
"*Today*...it was because of *him*."
MAGNETO!

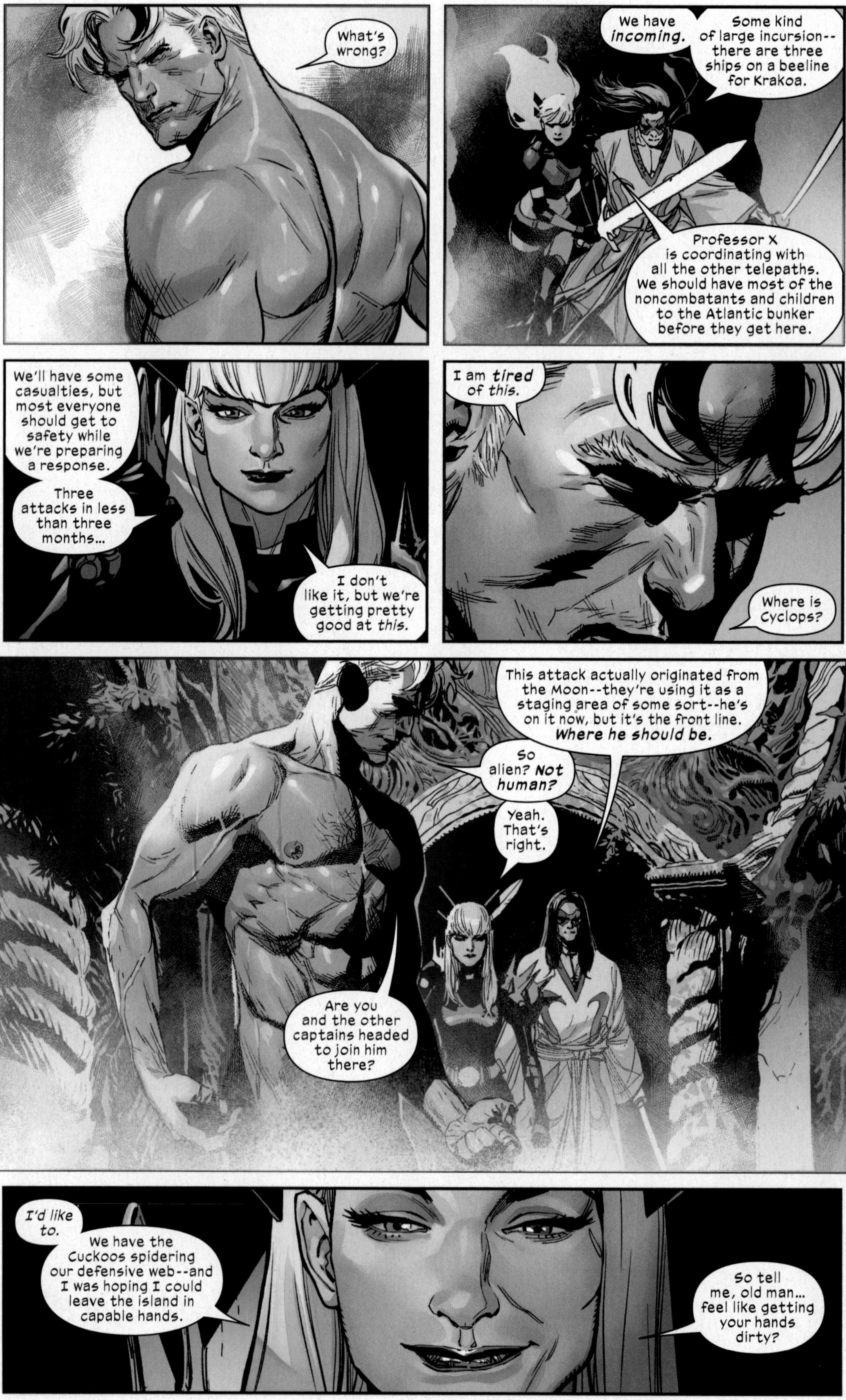

What's wrong?
We have *incoming.*
Some kind of large incursion--there are three ships on a beeline for Krakoa.
Professor X is coordinating with all the other telepaths. We should have most of the noncombatants and children to the Atlantic bunker before they get here.
We'll have some casualties, but most everyone should get to safety while we're preparing a response.
Three attacks in less than three months...
I don't like it, but we're getting pretty good at *this.*
I am *tired* of *this.*
Where is Cyclops?
This attack actually originated from the Moon--they're using it as a staging area of some sort--he's on it now, but it's the front line. ***Where he should be.***
So alien? ***Not human?***
Yeah. That's right.
Are you and the other captains headed to join him there?
I'd like to.
We have the Cuckoos spidering our defensive web--and I was hoping I could leave the island in capable hands.
So tell me, old man... feel like getting your hands dirty?

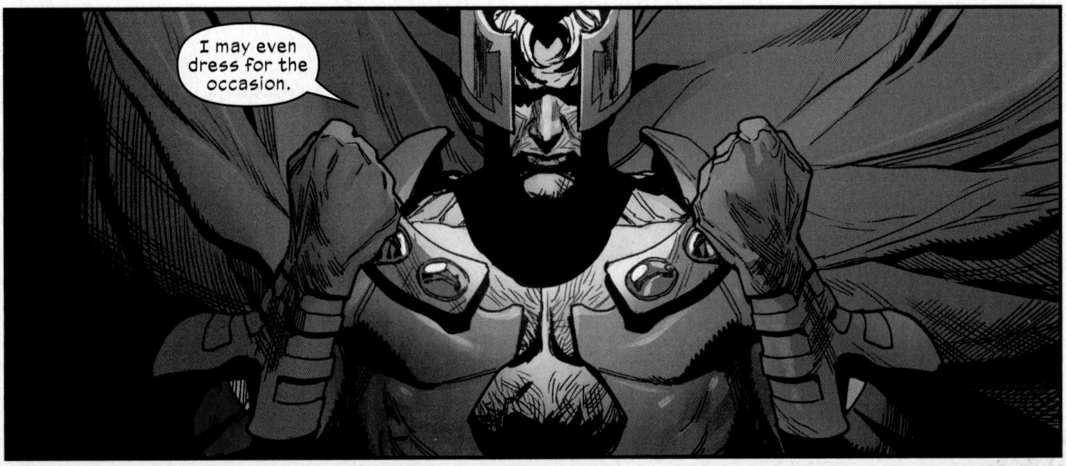
I may even dress for the occasion.

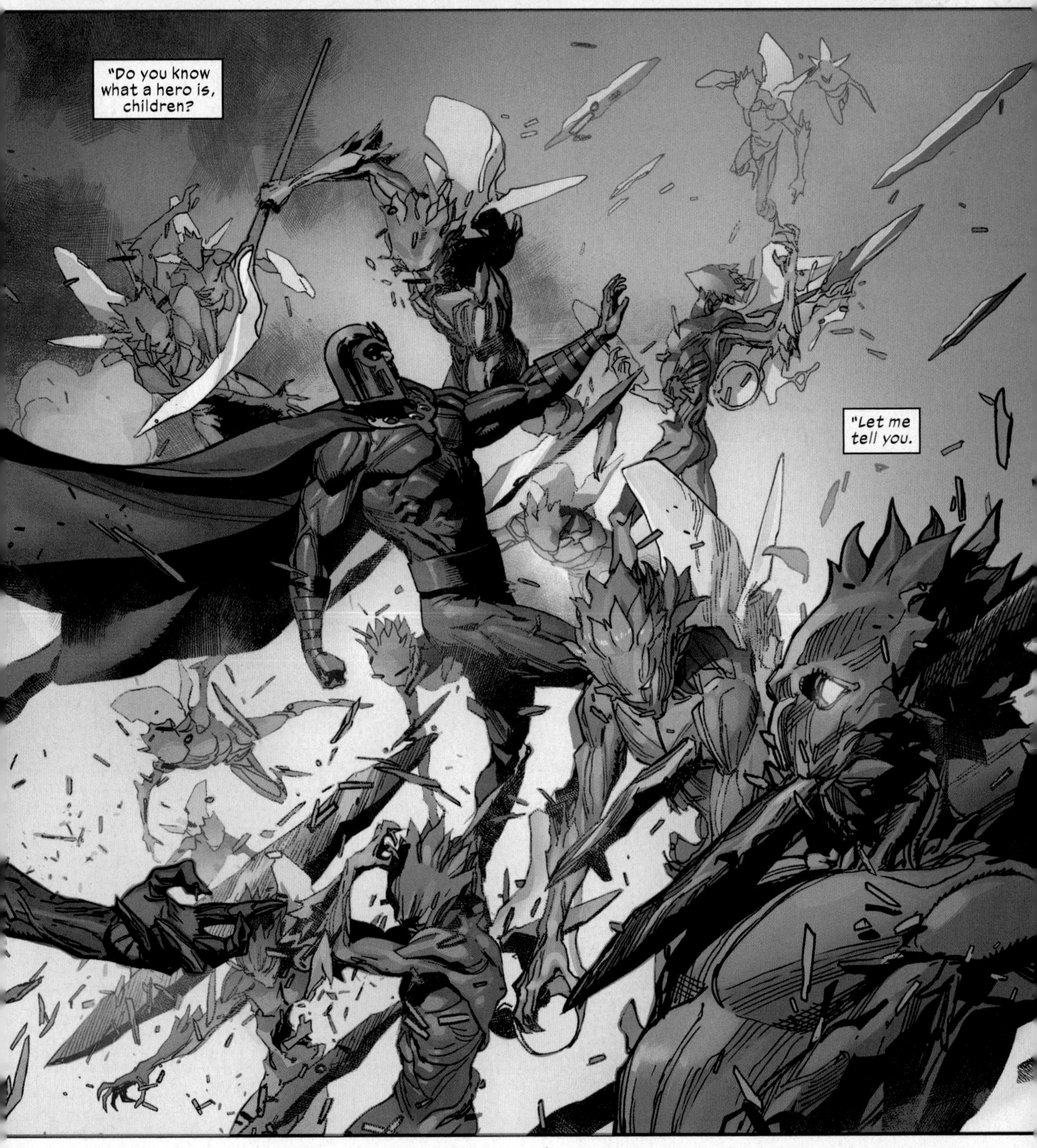
"Do you know what a hero is, children?
"Let me tell you.

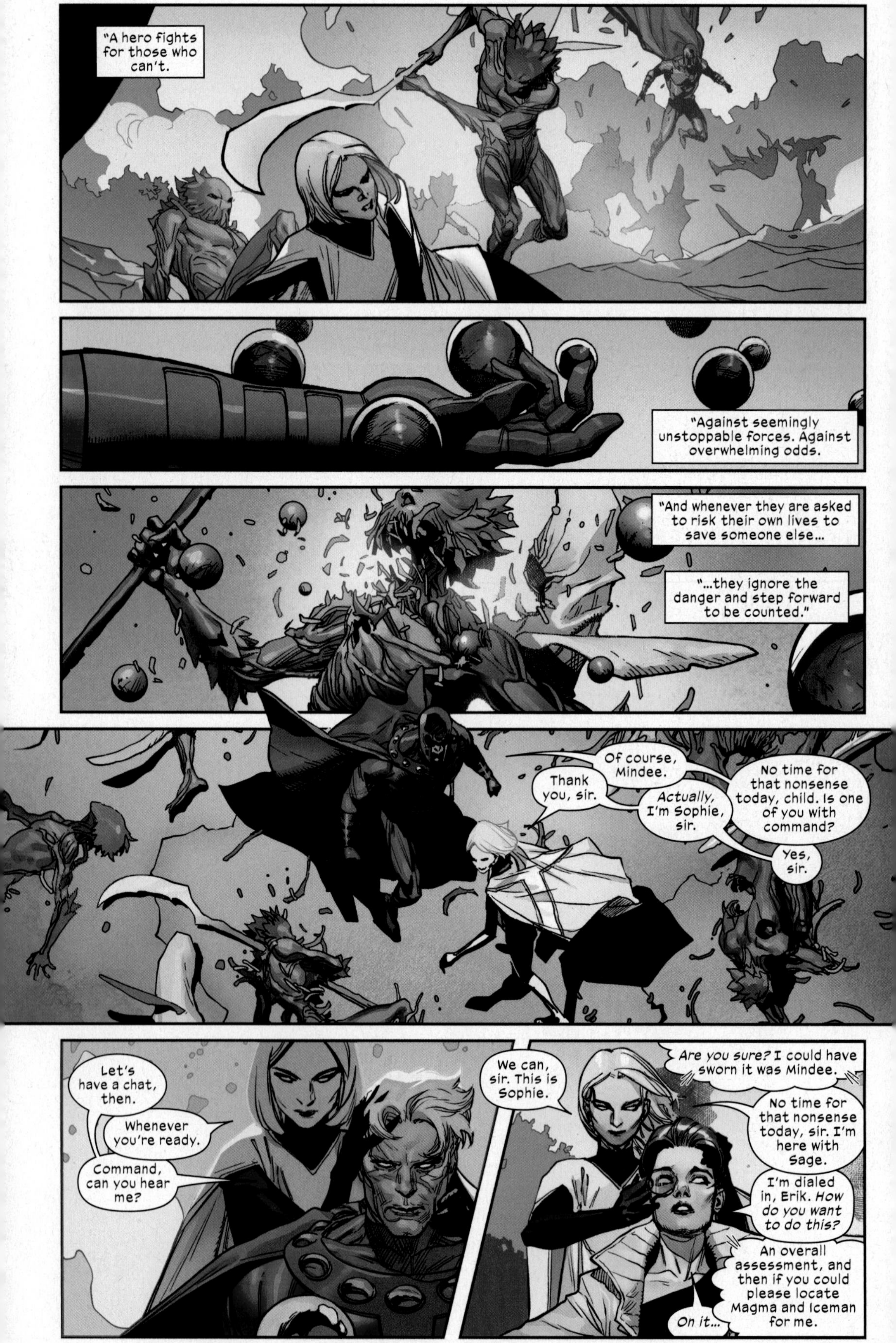
"A hero fights for those who can't.
"Against seemingly unstoppable forces. Against overwhelming odds.
"And whenever they are asked to risk their own lives to save someone else...
"...they ignore the danger and step forward to be counted."
Thank you, sir.
Of course, Mindee.
Actually, I'm Sophie, sir.
No time for that nonsense today, child. Is one of you with command?
Yes, sir.
Let's have a chat, then.
Whenever you're ready.
Command, can you hear me?
We can, sir. This is Sophie.
Are you sure? I could have sworn it was Mindee.
No time for that nonsense today, sir. I'm here with Sage.
I'm dialed in, Erik. *How do you want to do this?*
An overall assessment, and then if you could please locate Magma and Iceman for me.
On it...

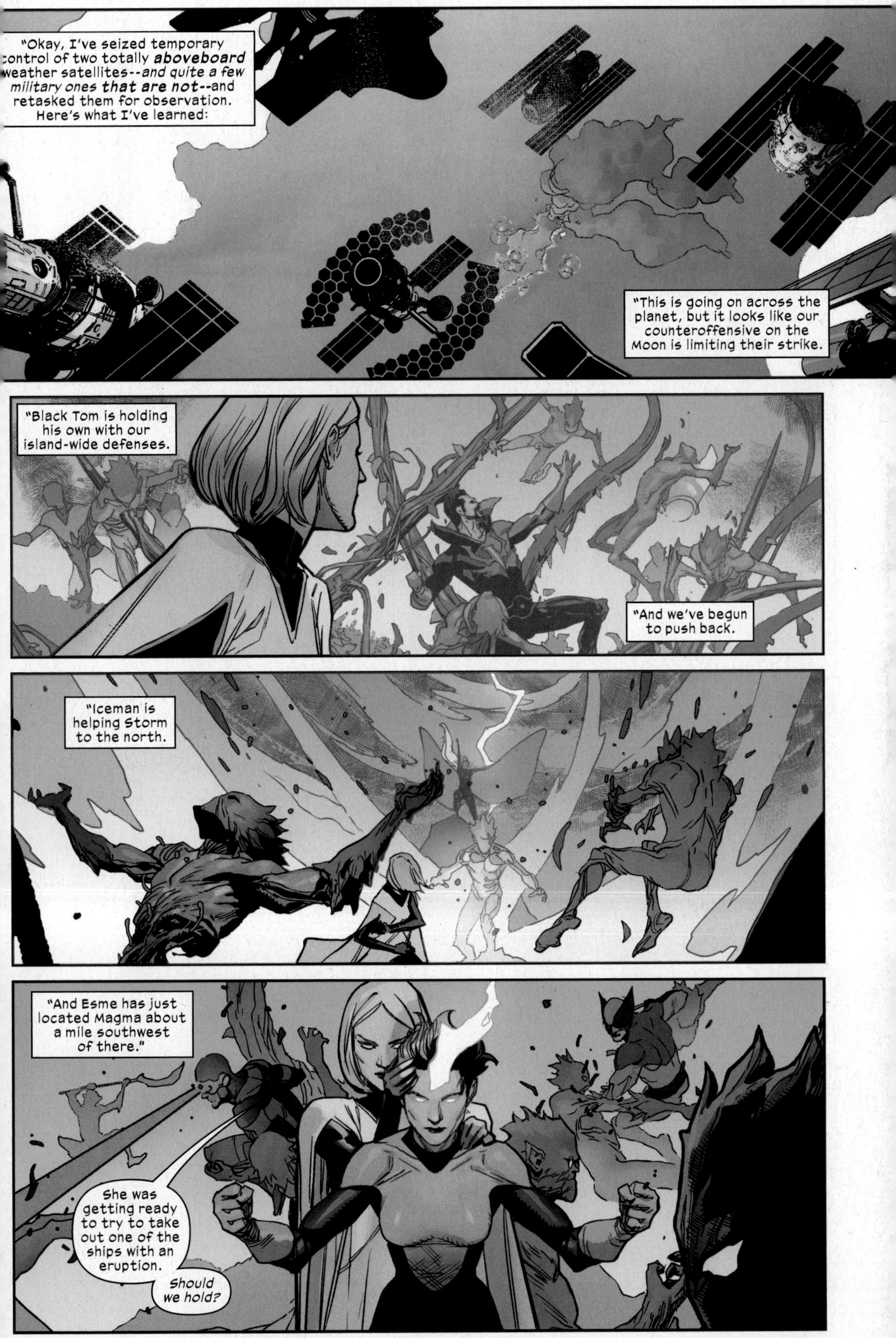
"Okay, I've seized temporary control of two totally **aboveboard** weather satellites--*and quite a few military ones* **that are not**--and retasked them for observation. Here's what I've learned:
"This is going on across the planet, but it looks like our counteroffensive on the Moon is limiting their strike.
"Black Tom is holding his own with our island-wide defenses.
"And we've begun to push back.
"Iceman is helping Storm to the north.
"And Esme has just located Magma about a mile southwest of there."
She was getting ready to try to take out one of the ships with an eruption.
Should we hold?

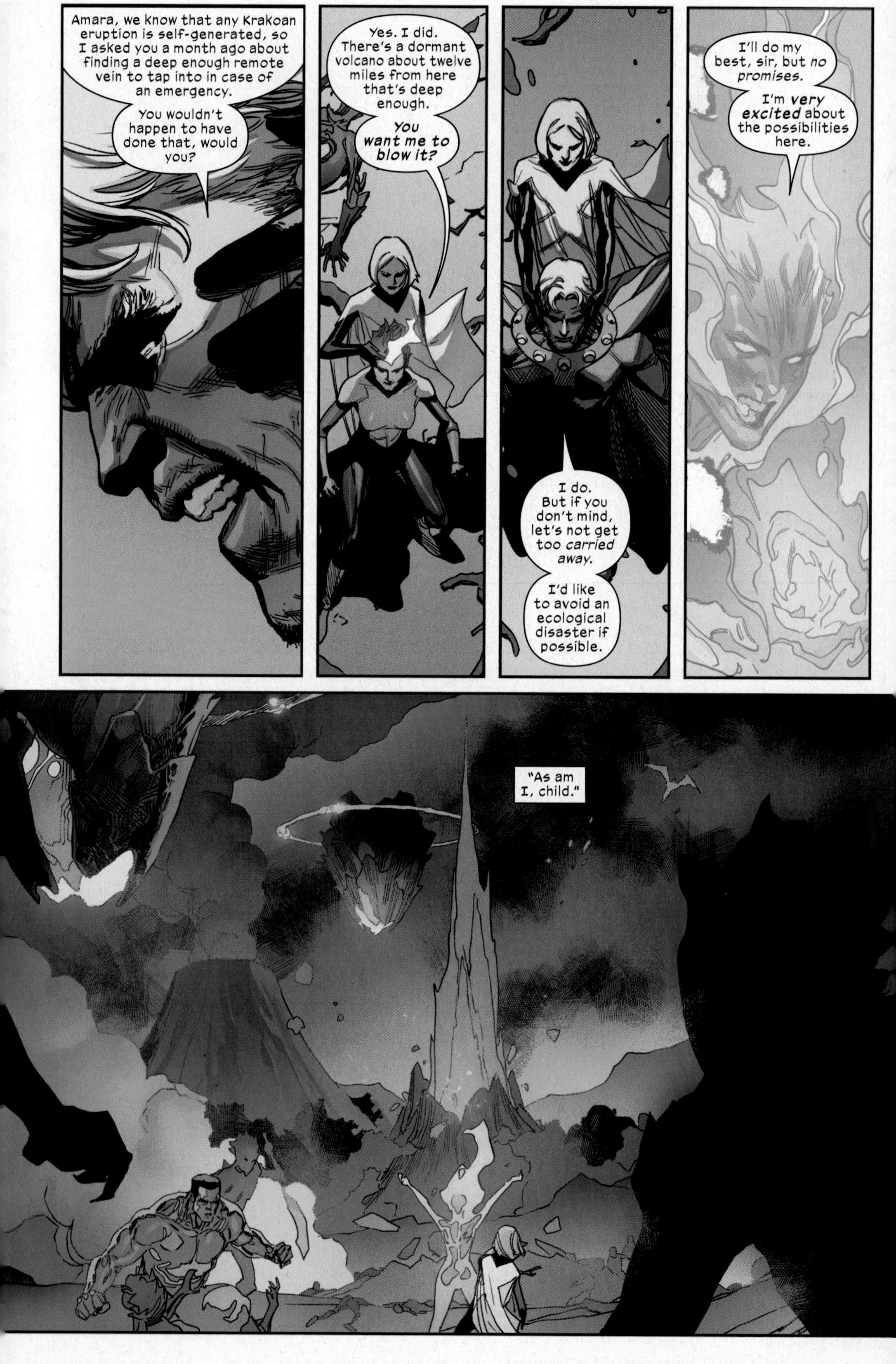
Amara, we know that any Krakoan eruption is self-generated, so I asked you a month ago about finding a deep enough remote vein to tap into in case of an emergency.
You wouldn't happen to have done that, would you?
Yes. I did. There's a dormant volcano about twelve miles from here that's deep enough.
You want me to blow it?
I do. But if you don't mind, let's not get too carried away.
I'd like to avoid an ecological disaster if possible.
I'll do my best, sir, but no promises.
I'm very excited about the possibilities here.
"As am I, child."

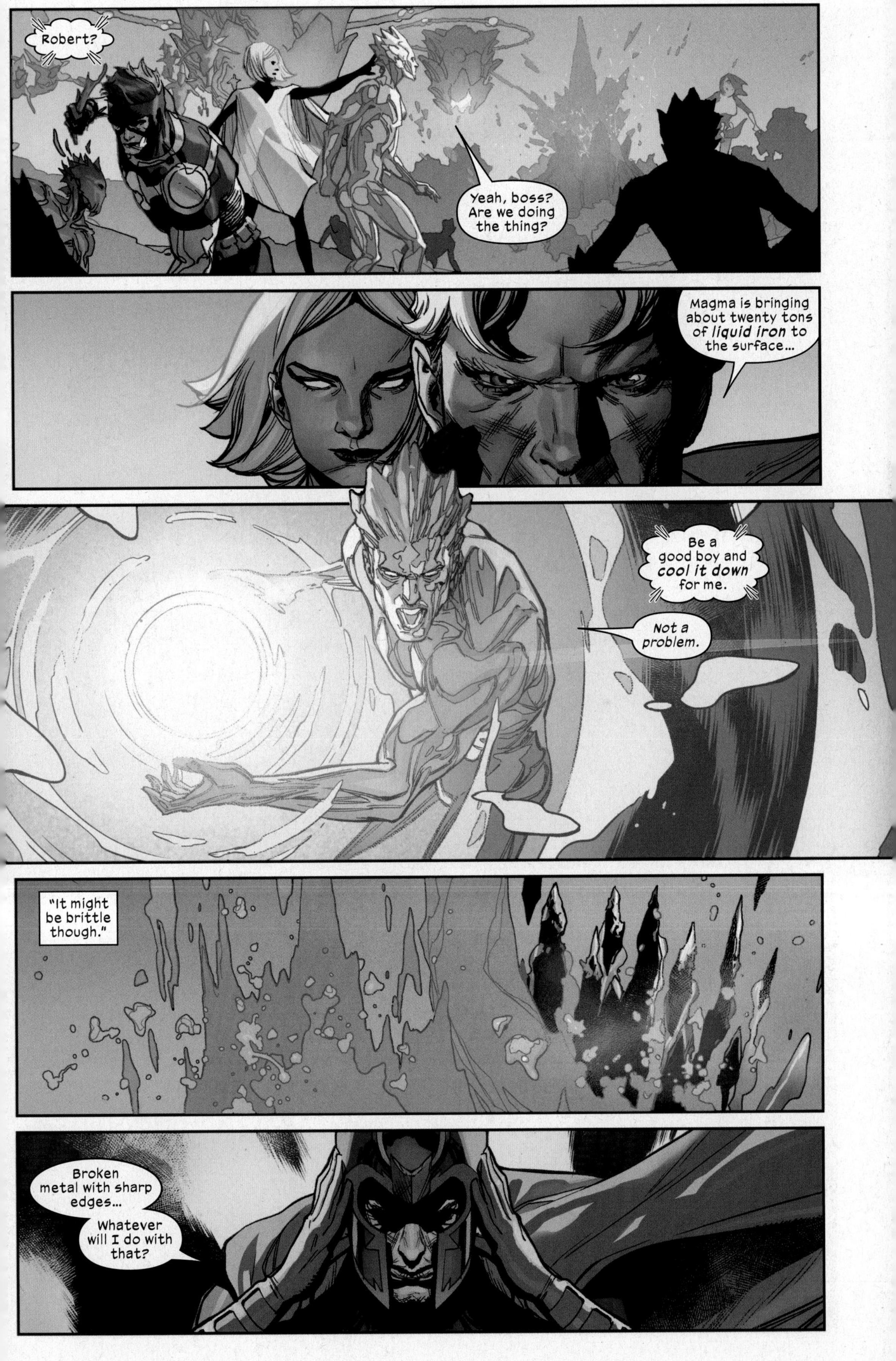
Robert?
Yeah, boss? Are we doing the thing?
Magma is bringing about twenty tons of *liquid iron* to the surface...
Be a good boy and *cool it down* for me.
Not a problem.
"It might be brittle though."
Broken metal with sharp edges...
Whatever will I do with that?

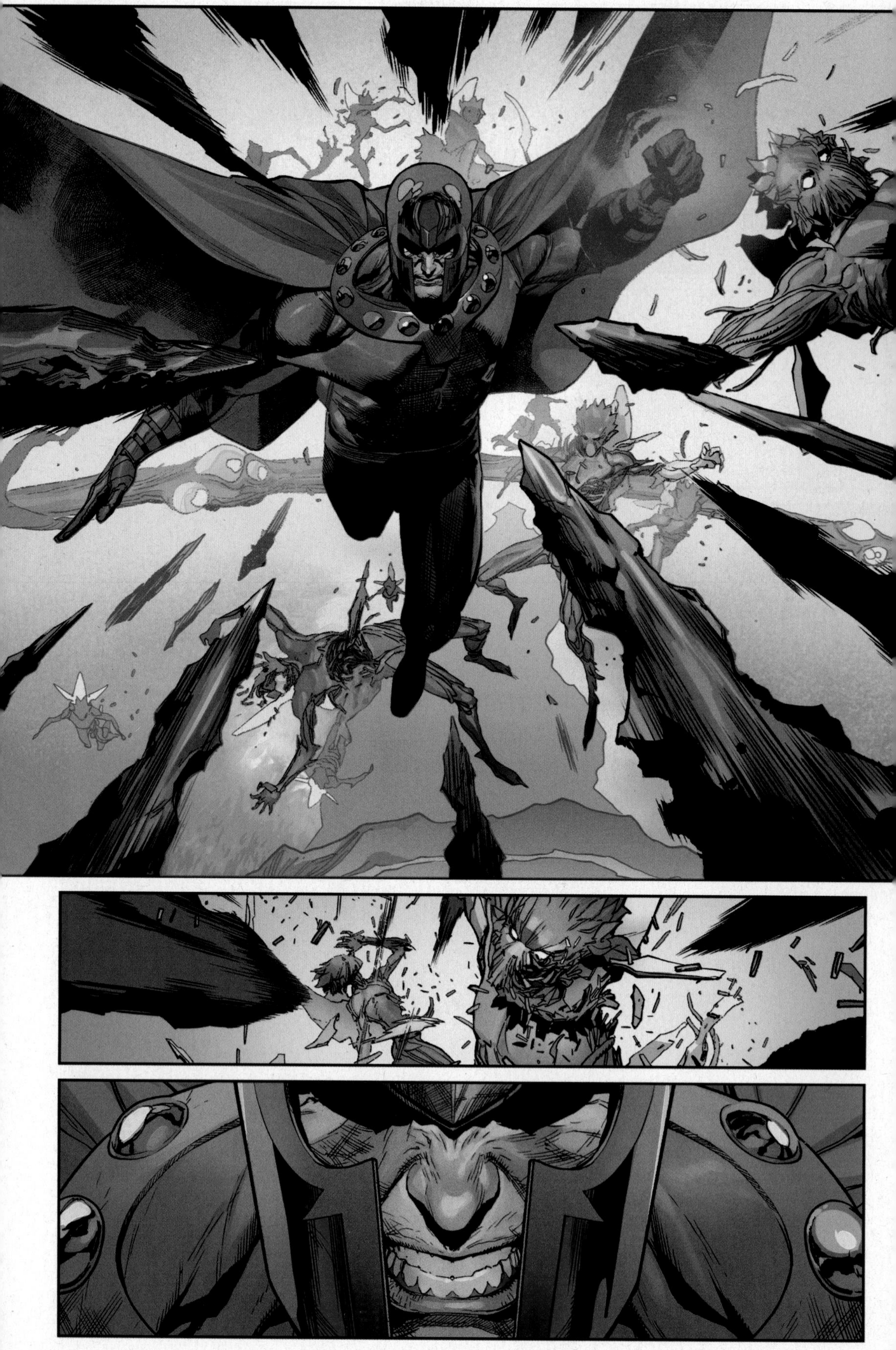

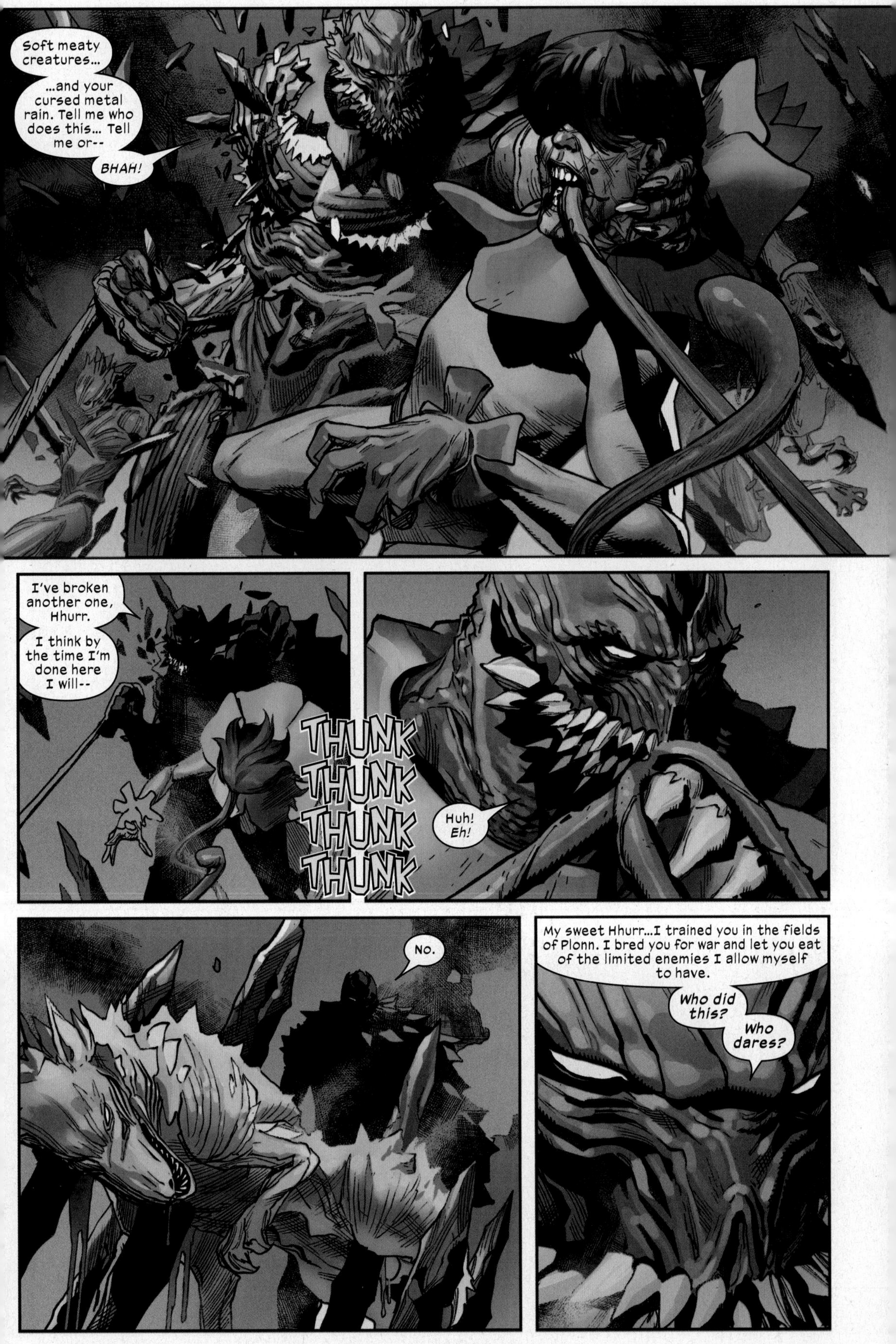
Soft meaty creatures...
...and your cursed metal rain. Tell me who does this... Tell me or--
BHAH!
I've broken another one, Hhurr.
I think by the time I'm done here I will--
THUNK THUNK THUNK THUNK
Huh! Eh!
No.
My sweet Hhurr...I trained you in the fields of Plonn. I bred you for war and let you eat of the limited enemies I allow myself to have.
Who did this?
Who dares?

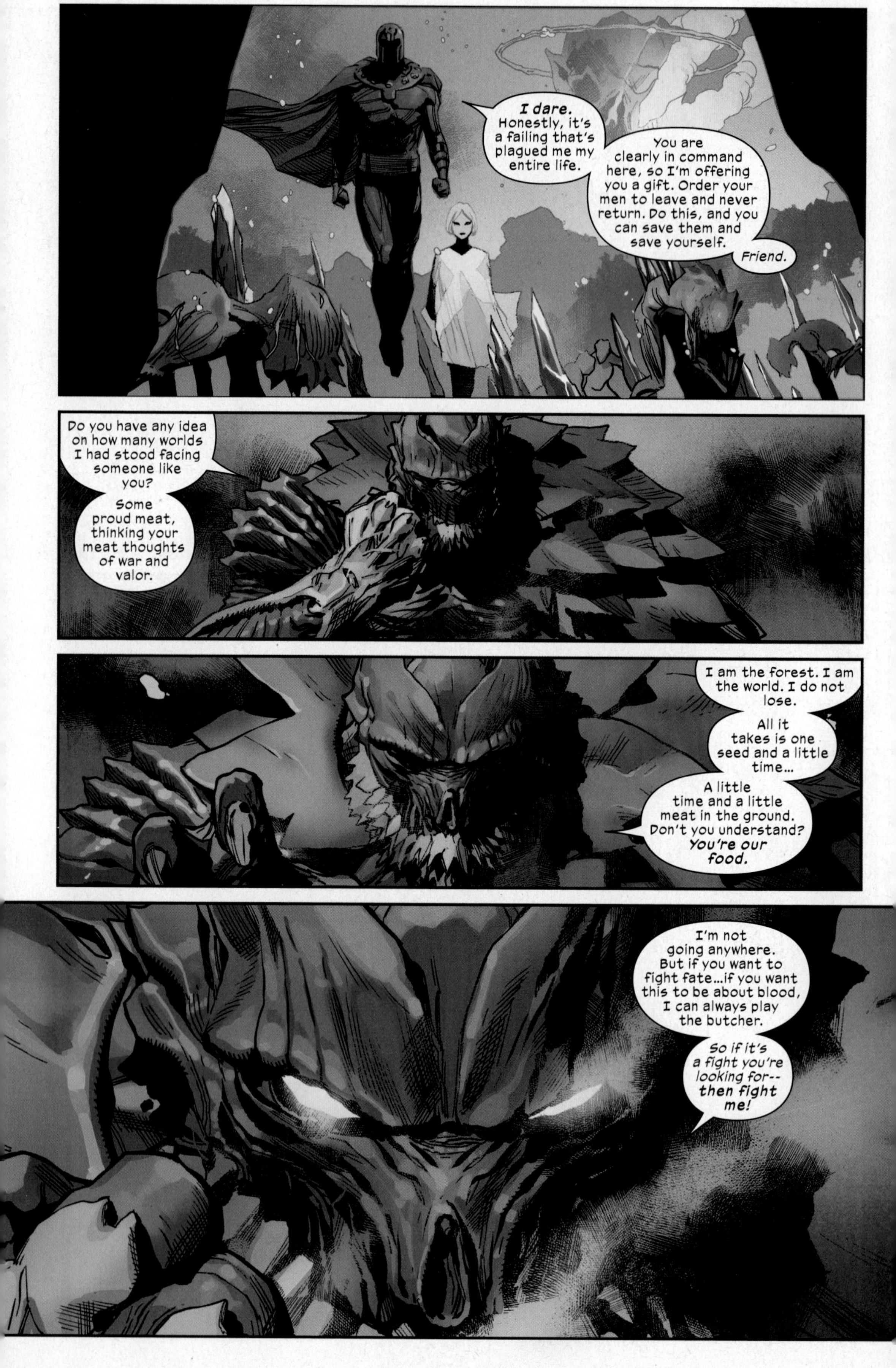
I dare. Honestly, it's a failing that's plagued me my entire life.
You are clearly in command here, so I'm offering you a gift. Order your men to leave and never return. Do this, and you can save them and save yourself.
Friend.
Do you have any idea on how many worlds I had stood facing someone like you?
Some proud meat, thinking your meat thoughts of war and valor.
I am the forest. I am the world. I do not lose.
All it takes is one seed and a little time...
A little time and a little meat in the ground. Don't you understand? You're our food.
I'm not going anywhere. But if you want to fight fate...if you want this to be about blood, I can always play the butcher.
So if it's a fight you're looking for-- then fight me!

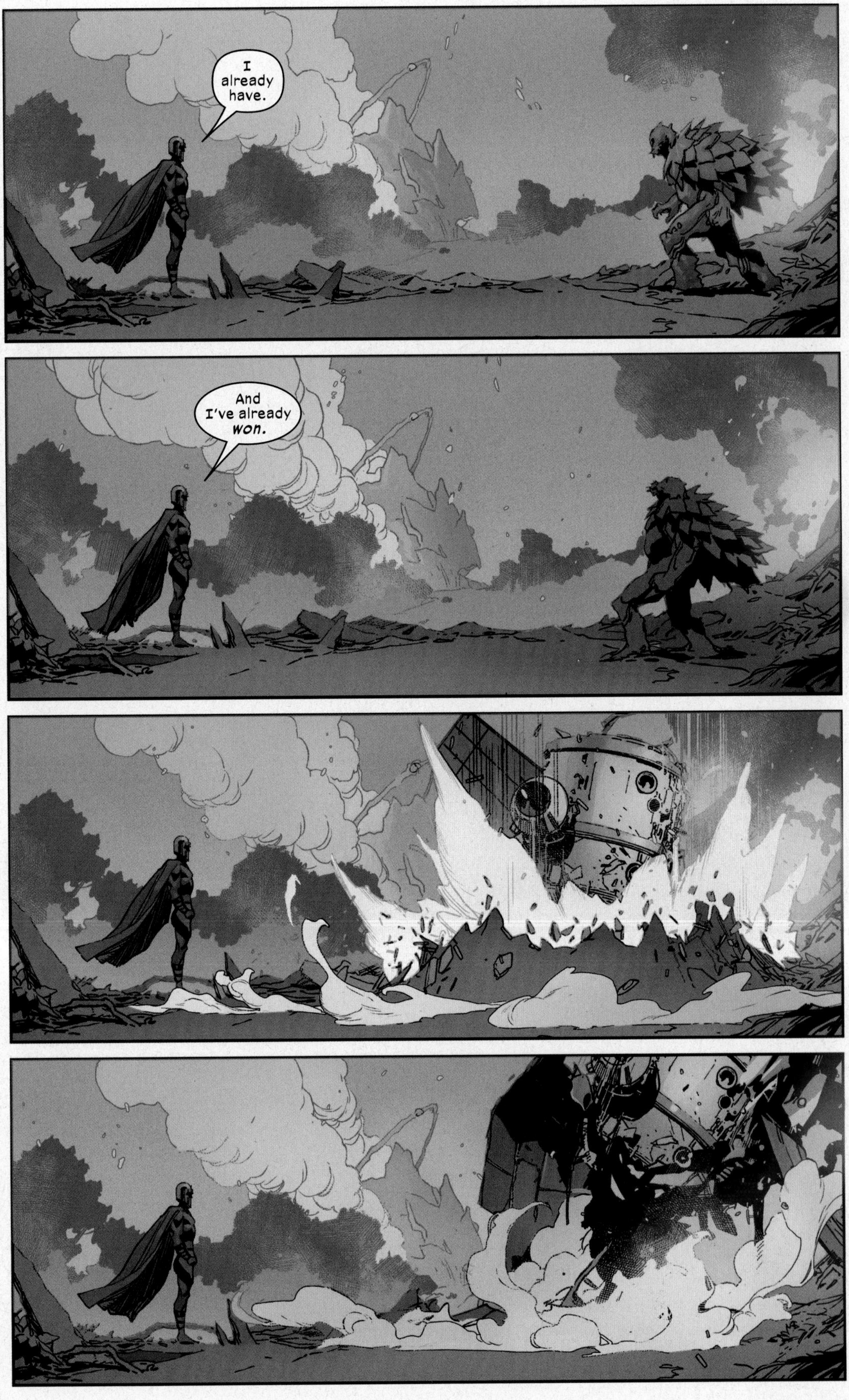
I already have.
And I've already *won.*

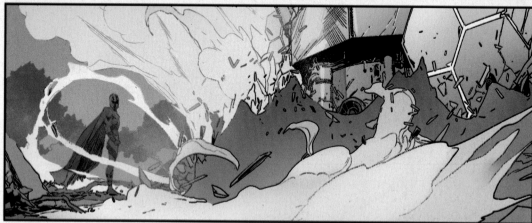

Mindee.

Yes, sir.

Please apologize to Sage for stealing her satellites.

Also, tell her to go ahead and forward payment for the weather satellites to their respective governments.

What about the military ones?

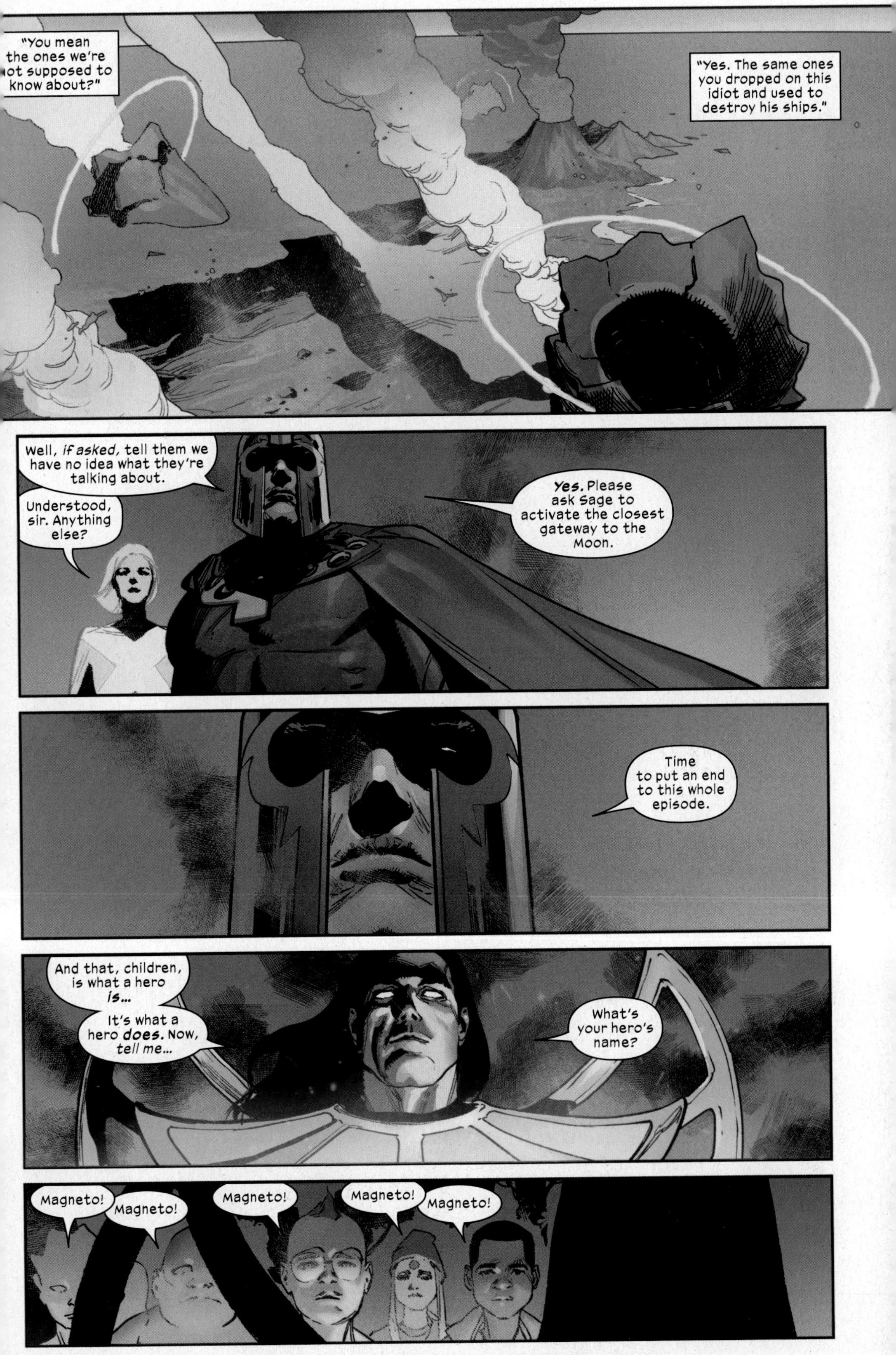
"You mean the ones we're ot supposed to know about?"
"Yes. The same ones you dropped on this idiot and used to destroy his ships."
Well, *if asked*, tell them we have no idea what they're talking about.
Understood, sir. Anything else?
Yes. Please ask Sage to activate the closest gateway to the Moon.
Time to put an end to this whole episode.
And that, children, is what a hero *is*...
It's what a hero *does*. Now, *tell me*...
What's your hero's name?
Magneto!
Magneto!
Magneto!
Magneto!
Magneto!

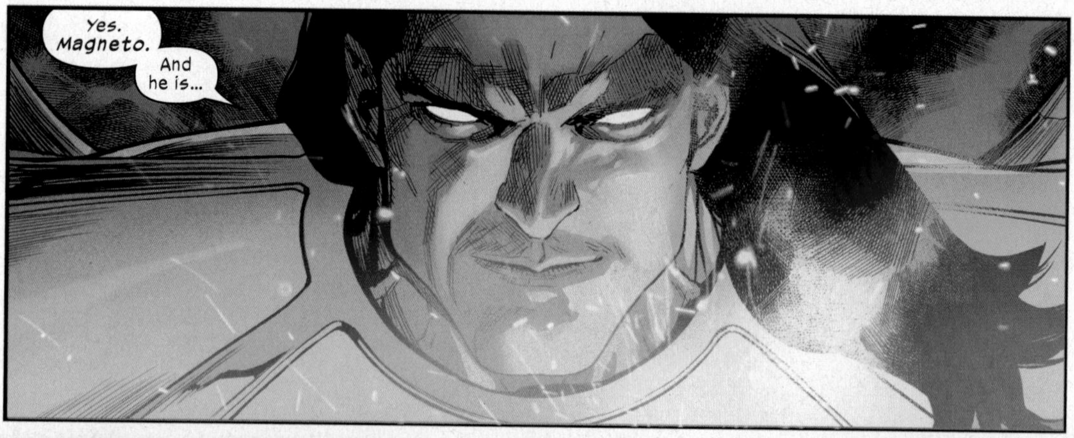
Yes. Magneto.
And he is...

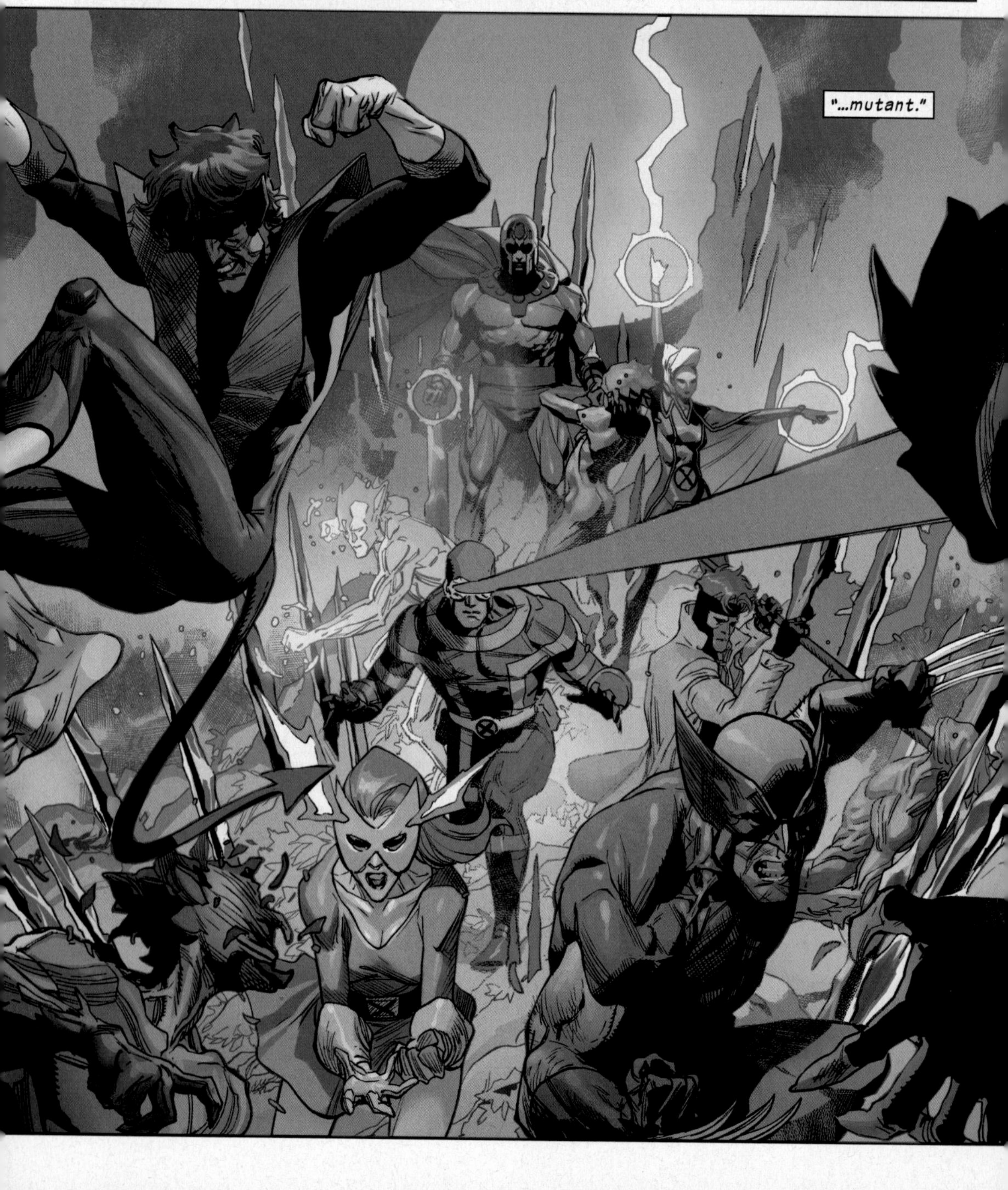
"...mutant."

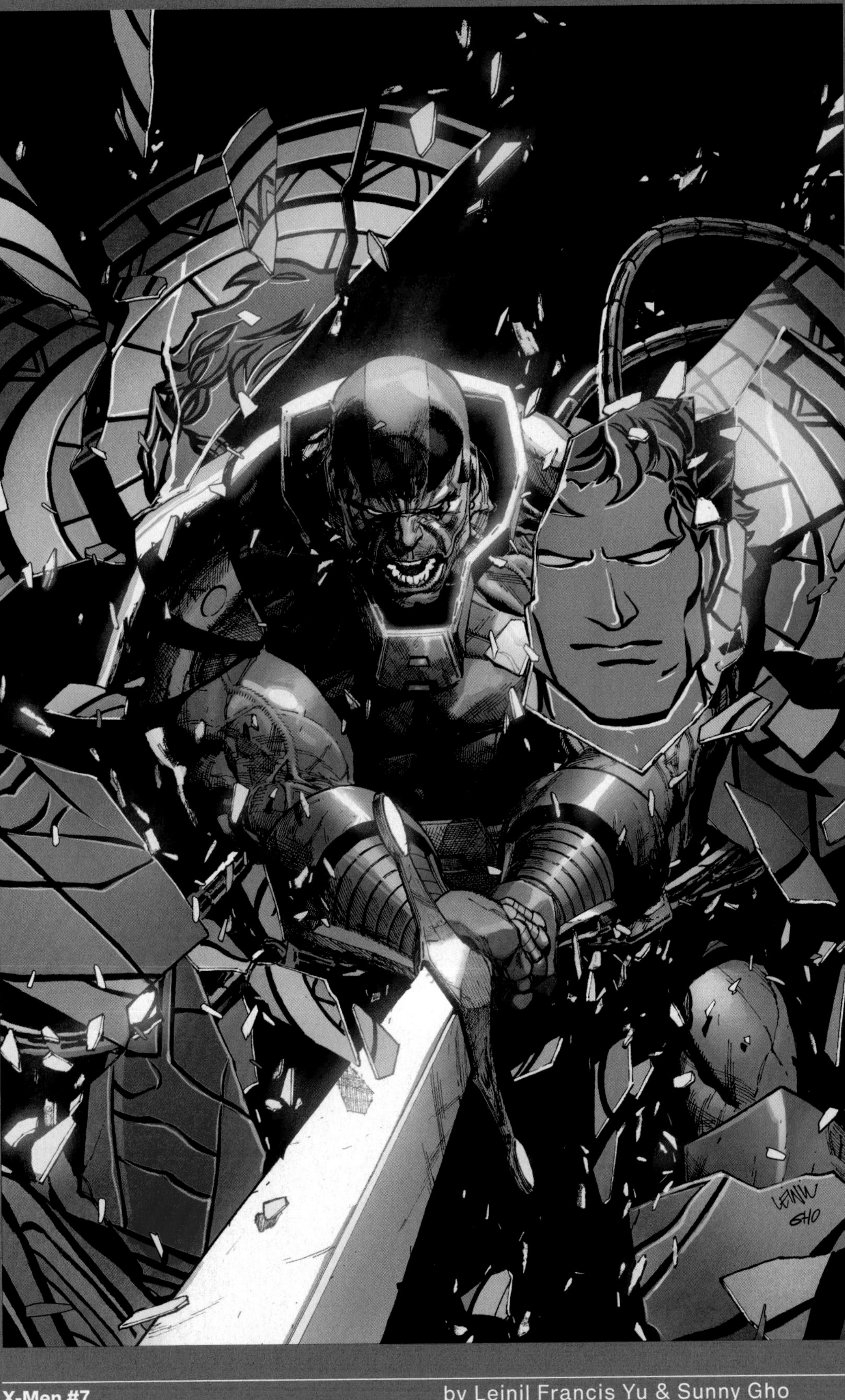

X-Men #7 by Leinil Francis Yu & Sunny Gho

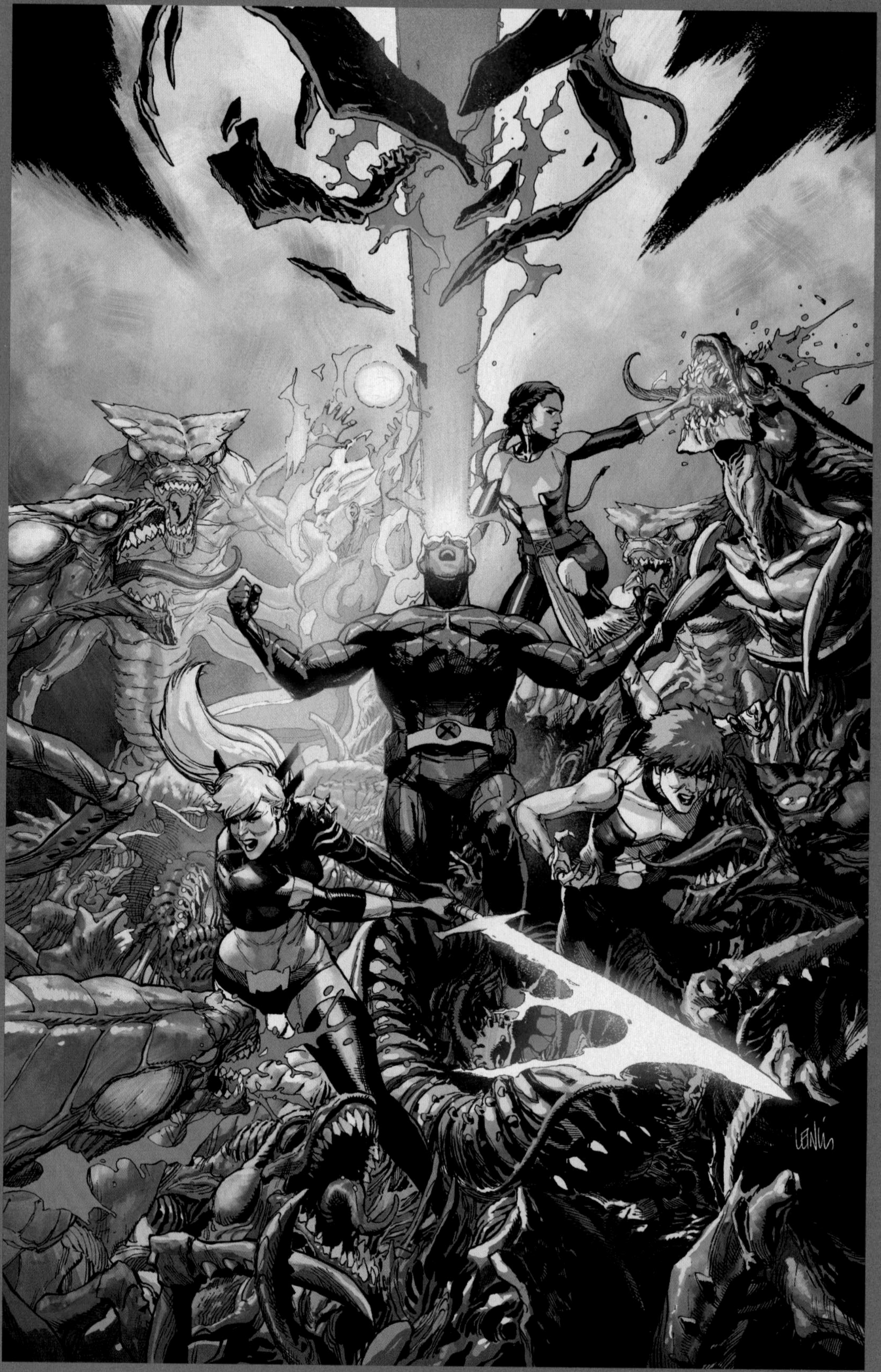

X-Men #8 by Leinil Francis Yu & Sunny Gho

X-Men #9   by Leinil Francis Yu & Sunny Gho

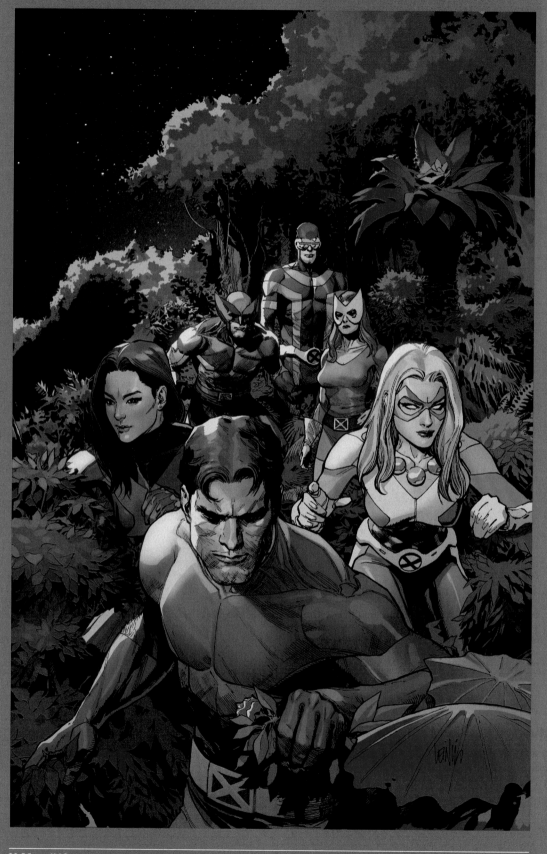

by Leinil Francis Yu & Sunny Gho

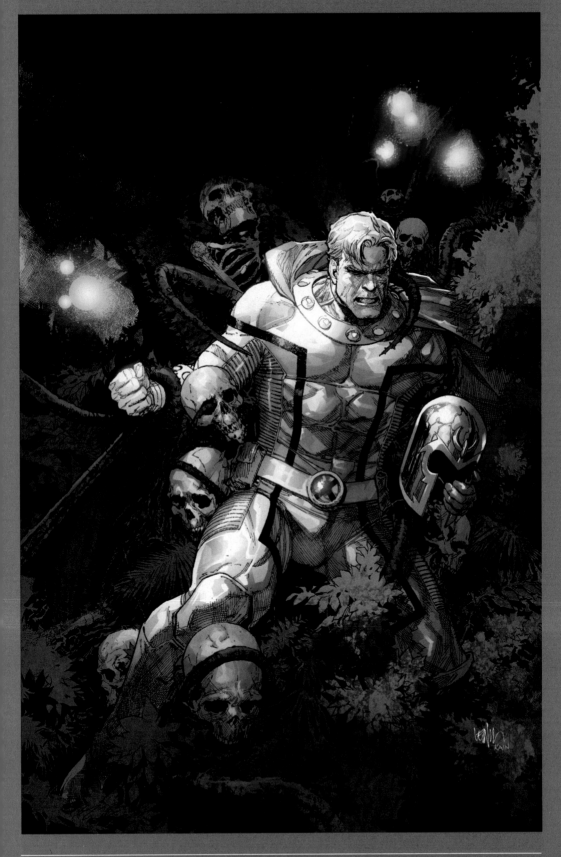

X-Men #11

by Leinil Francis Yu & Sunny Gho

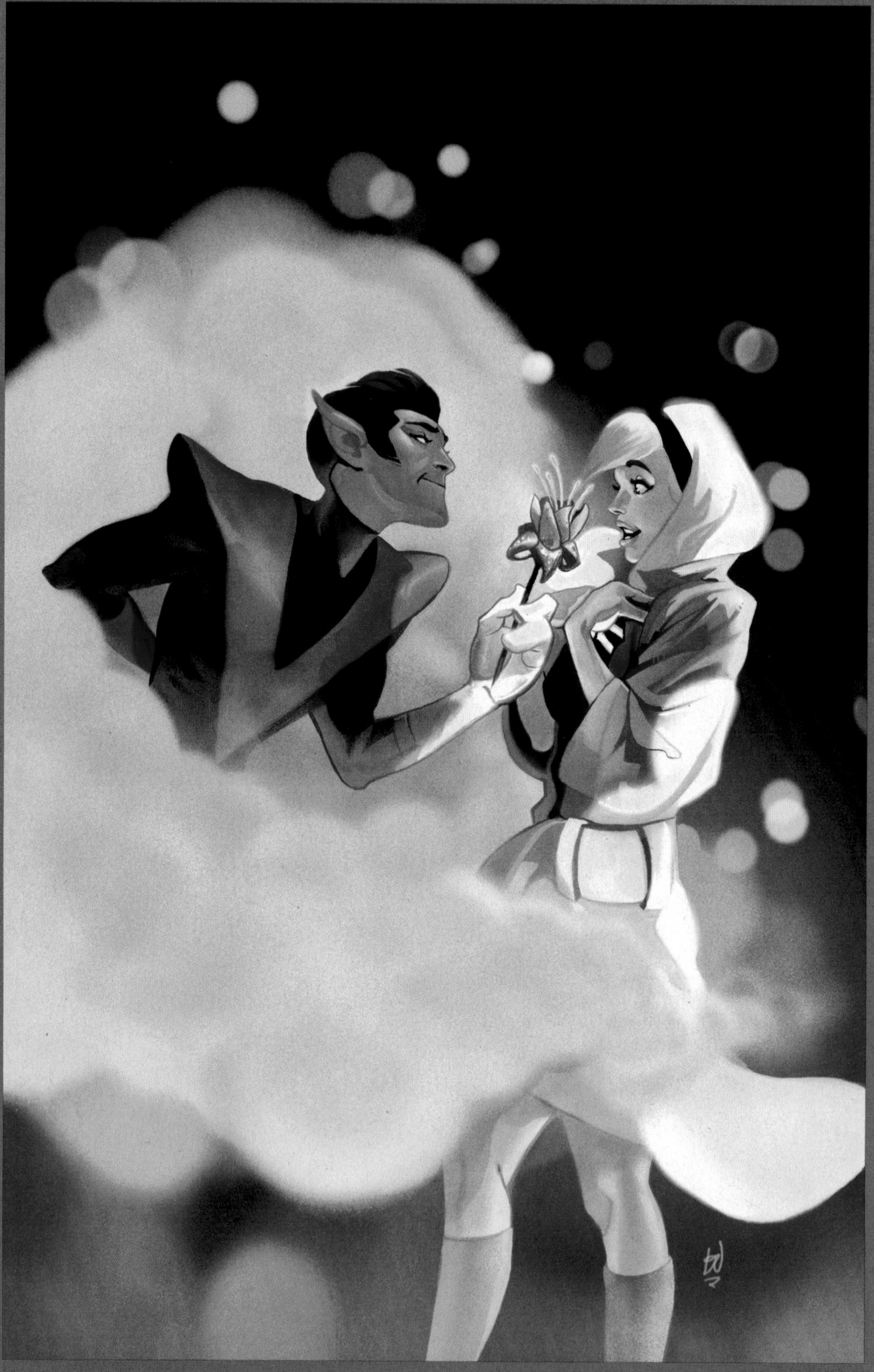

X-Men #7 Variant by Mike del Mundo

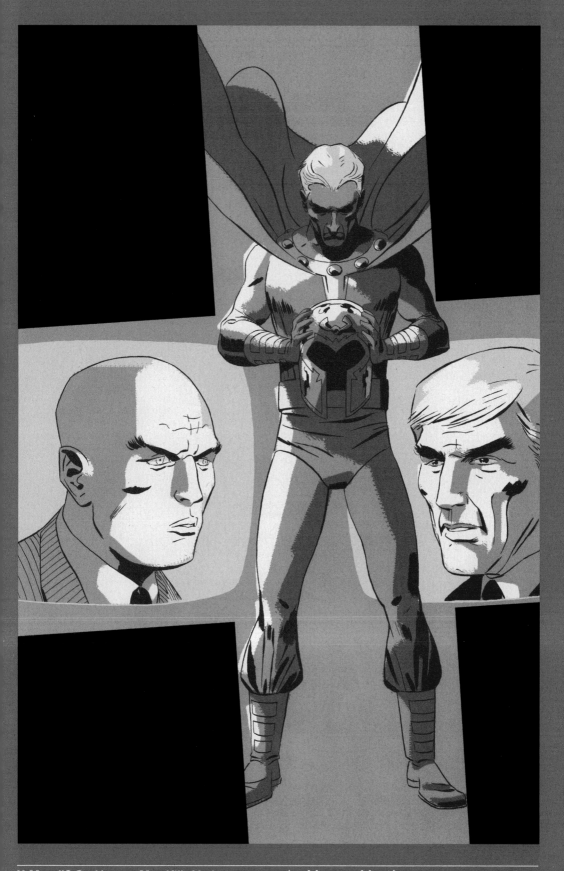

X-Men #8 God Loves, Man Kills Variant   by Marcos Martin

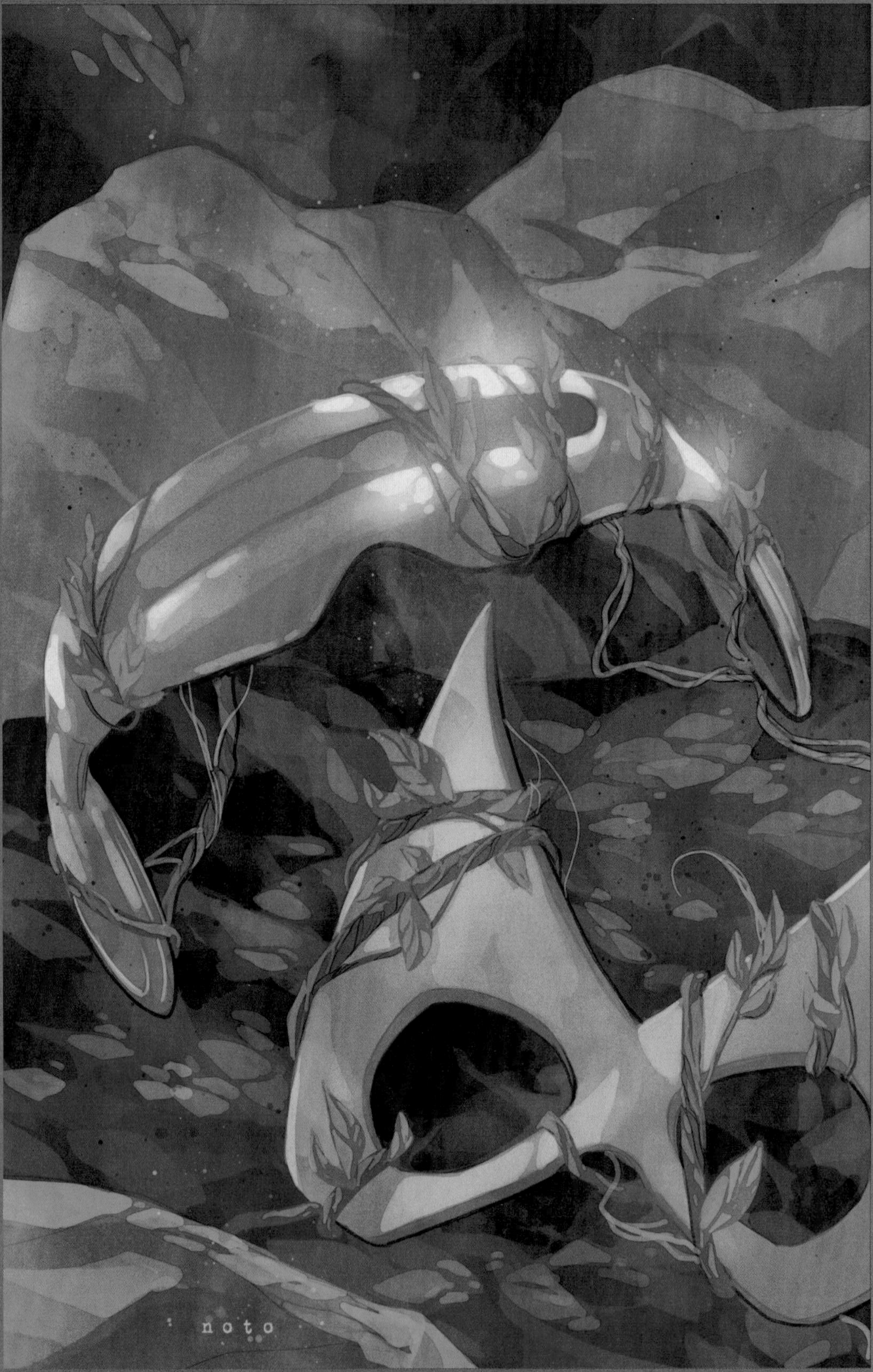
noto

X-Men #10 Variant by Phil Noto

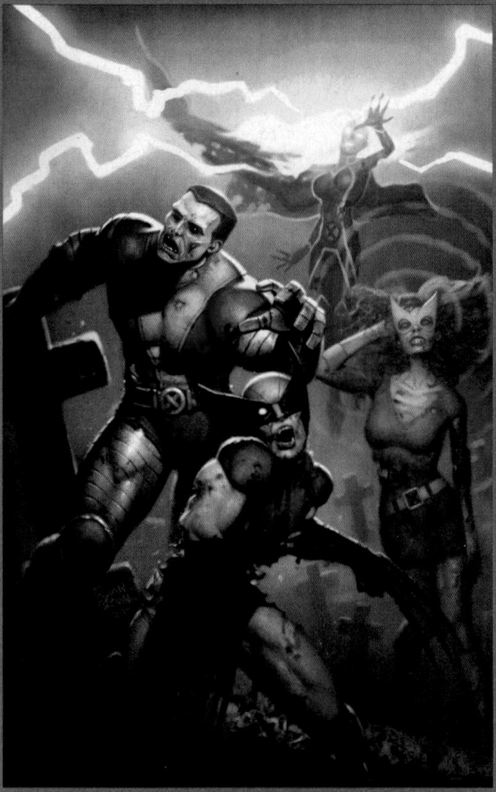

X-Men #10 Zombies Variant
by Ryan Brown

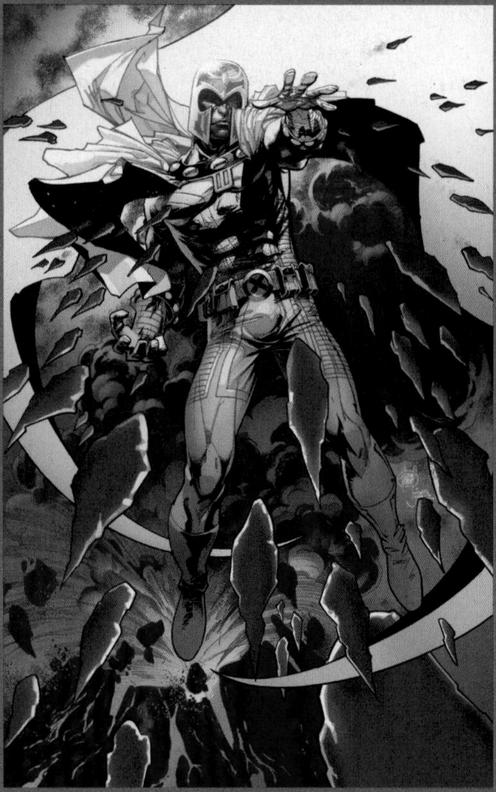

X-Men #11 Empyre Variant
by Adam Kubert

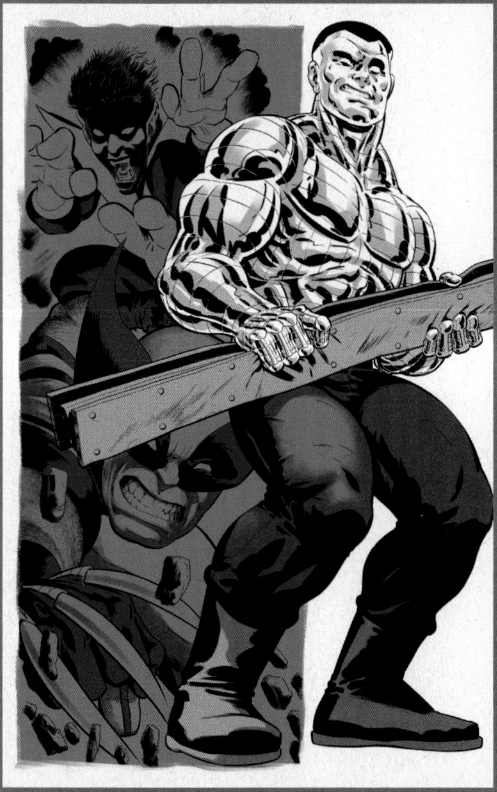

X-Men #11 Days of Future Past Variant
by Javier Rodríguez